negotiate

ne • go • ti • ate (verb)

*Two Definitions

1. To confer, bargain or discuss with a view to reaching agreement.

2. To succeed in crossing, surmounting, or moving through, etc. (to negotiate a deep river, a hazardous terrain, or a complex, ever-changing workplace environment).

This book is about both definitions. It deals with the crucial skills necessary to achieve success in navigating through the difficulties encountered daily in today's demanding workplace.

*These definitions are from Webster's New World Dictionary, with slight amendment by the author.

NEGOTIATING EFFECTIVELY WITHIN YOUR OWN ORGANIZATION

Other Books by Chester L. Karrass

Give and Take

The Negotiating Game

In Business As In Life – You Don't Get
What You Deserve, You Get What You Negotiate

Reality Performance Management*

*Coauthored with William Glasser, M.D.

NEGOTIATING EFFECTIVELY WITHIN YOUR OWN ORGANIZATION

Gain Acceptance for Your Ideas, Connect With Others and Resolve Differences Creatively

CHESTER L. KARRASS

"Negotiating Effectively Within Your Own Organization"

Printed in the United States of America.

ISBN 978-0-615-52041-4

This book could not have been written without the patience,
encouragement, wise counsel and love of my wife Erika.
So many separated hours, so many talks and walks in the woods,
so many ideas tried and tossed, so many impediments negotiated.
Thank you, Erika. I'm lucky to have had your help.

Acknowledgments

Writing a book on a subject as comprehensive as negotiating in your own organization cannot be accomplished without the help of many people. Such help was graciously provided by Frank Mobus, Keith Money, Mel Klayman, Gary Karrass and Rose Greenman with whom I exchanged viewpoints and ideas.

For the assistance it takes to change a manuscript into a book I owe a great deal to Ashley Byock, Pauline Houston, Jennifer Prag and Roy Gechter who patiently and competently carried the ever-changing manuscript through draft after draft.

And finally I wish to acknowledge the research support provided years earlier by the Hughes Organization and two of its executives, Theodore Kotsovolus and William A. Van Allen, both friends and mentors.

Introduction

The purpose of this book is to demonstrate a new approach to working with people in today's fast-changing, increasingly complex economy—an economy where, no matter how smart or technically competent you are, you need good relationships with others to get the job done successfully. To achieve this purpose we will focus on three crucial skills: the collaborative negotiation of differences and disagreements, the exchange of viewpoints and ideas and the building of relationships.

1. The Collaborative Negotiation of Differences and Disagreements

Negotiating behaviors and approaches that help those in organizations resolve differences and problems in ways that promote cooperative, collaborative and creative both-win solutions, as well as stronger working relationships.

2. The Exchange of Viewpoints and Ideas

Behaviors that encourage members of a group or project to exchange viewpoints and ideas candidly, to be heard and listened to in an involved-focused way, and to give respectful consideration to each person's thoughts and concerns.

3. The Building of Positive-Energy Relationships

Behaviors that lead those who work together to interact in positive, energy-building ways, and to get along harmoniously and productively in pursuit of group goals.

I have long been convinced that we at work negotiate every day, though we rarely call it that. We negotiate budgets and scope of work issues with superiors, peers and subordinates. We negotiate matters of service from the technical support and administrative divisions of our organization. On a personal level we negotiate with our boss for compensation, parking privileges and hard-to-get Fourth of July vacation time. We negotiate with difficult people to start or stop what is being done so that we can work more effectively. Negotiations take place every day in every workplace concerning product design configurations, prices and sales and marketing strategies in addition to questions of how best to solve the quality and engineering problems that always arise.

Experience at the bargaining table and elsewhere as a business executive leads me to believe that the negotiating process, when pursued with understanding, leads time and again to collaborative and creative outcomes that neither party thought likely or possible at start of talks. As a result, these new outcomes replace earlier distrust and hostility with positive working relationships and mutual gain.

In this book I wish to show how we at work can deal with one another in a way that moves us step-by-step toward collaboration and creativity until we reach the level of success we need in order to maintain our competitive edge and the standard of living we aspire to.

Contents

PART I

THE ECONOMIC CHALLENGE WE FACE AND THE NEW APPROACH WE NEED

PART I

1

The Economic and Innovative Challenge We Face

THE CHALLENGE

In his best-selling book, The World Is Flat, Thomas J. Friedman describes the challenge facing America this way:

> "Competition in the flat world will be more intense. We Americans will have to work harder, run faster and become smarter to make sure we get our share... The most important attribute we can have is creative imagination... the ability to be first on the block to figure out creative new products and opportunities."

Mr. Friedman's challenge not only applies to every American organization but to each of us now in the workforce. To be the first on the block to create new products and services will require us to work together in more effective ways than in the past. We are all affected by this global challenge. If we do not adapt we will fall behind as institutions and individuals.

Success will depend on our ability and willingness to collaborate more closely with those we work with because innovation today rests not so much on how smart we are, but on our propensity to share and build on each other's ideas. How we in the workplace foster creativity will determine whether our standard of living will rise; and, on a personal level, whether our careers will prosper or fail.

To meet this formidable challenge we need a new approach to dealing with three workplace problems: making choices and constructive decisions, reconciling differences that arise and working together harmoniously. "Running faster, working harder and becoming smarter," as Friedman suggests, will help but not be enough to contend with the onslaught of global competition we confront.

For over two centuries we in the Western world have relied on top-down management to make choices at every working level. If we are to be creative, this way of making decisions can no longer be effective. "[W]e face an Age of Discontinuity in world economy and technology," as Peter Drucker wrote in *The Age of Discontinuity*. In such an age, those lower on the organization pyramid are closer to the global marketplace and its daily demand and supply changes than those higher up. Those closer to the marketplace must do more than merely participate in the group or team decision process. They must also experience the ownership that comes from open negotiation of the terms and details of the agreement reached. Only then will the decision, along with its expected and unintended consequences and work, be accepted and owned by them. Those who merely participate rather than own the final team decision after negotiating will serve it less passionately, especially when later problems surface as they often do.

Innovation in the world we now live in is not what it was. Creativity and inventiveness are no longer only associated with the lone innovator working tirelessly in his garage to come up with the new product everyone will buy. That story began to come to an end a half-century or more ago and is now almost a fable. Inventiveness today depends on groups and teams of talented people collaborating with one another to reach objectives through an open exchange of viewpoints and ideas. Today, large sums of funding are required, development time frames are very long and serious disagreements between talented team members are likely to erupt.

Collaboration itself needs a safe place to nest and grow. It is best fostered where positive relationships and trust are strong. When people feel they are in competition they hesitate to share ideas or get close to one another. Working together effectively as a team depends on nurturing relationships, allowing each person to be heard, helping others to express themselves, and resolving differences through collaboration and negotiation rather than dictums from above.

Maintaining our standard of living in the emerging century will not be easy. We already see the strains. The workplace will put growing emphasis on innovation. The need for collaboration and team involvement will be felt at every level of the organization, not just at the top. People who in earlier times remained silent will demand to be heard. Disagreements will surface as ideas and preferences are opened for consideration. Top-down control will not work well in such a setting. We need a new approach to working together creatively.

This book focuses on explaining how to amicably resolve the rising tide of conflicting differences while simultaneously building a creative workplace environment. The keys to management and personal success in this rapidly changing new century are Both-Win® negotiating principles and relationship-based communication and give and take.

LIKE IT OR NOT, WE ARE ALL NEGOTIATORS

Negotiation has been called "The Game of Life." Not a day passes that fails to confirm its presence in almost everything we do with others. Today the Los Angeles Times headlined negotiations occurring in Congress concerning matters of immigration and military preparedness. In California, the legislature dealt once again with a massive budget deficit. In business, a telephone giant bought a cable company for billions while an oil company closed a huge drilling deal. Negotiations took place in the Middle East, Europe and Asia concerning territory, tariffs and the environment. In basketball, a star who signed a forty-million-dollar one-year pay, performance and publicity contract felt he deserved more. A typical day.

Yet, for every negotiation we read or hear about, hundreds more take place daily inside our organizations between those who work together to get their tasks done. Differences and disagreements arise that have to be put to rest through negotiation. Problems emerge that demand resolution where one party prefers one solution and another prefers the next. Means, goals, viewpoints and ideas are exchanged and often compromised through tradeoffs every hour of the day.

Like it or not, good at it or not, we are all negotiators. Every interaction at work is a matter of give and take, an exchange of benefits and contributions from person-to-person or from group-to-group.

Even the personal relationships we have with others at work are themselves a product of negotiation. Those who desire better relationships must do something to warrant it. At a minimum, they must open themselves to being friendly and reasonably accessible. Men or women who walk around with "Do Not Disturb" sandwich signs on their shoulders or make a habit of closing their office door to others are not likely to win good rapport. Being heard and listened to by members of your team or group is not a birthright; it is the outcome of a negotiated exchange for attention. If you want to be heard you must have something worth saying and relevant to express.

Working with others on a daily basis is one negotiation after another, even though we rarely call it that. Exhibit 1 lists but a few of the issues we deal with regularly even in the smallest of organizations. That's why it's so important to understand the negotiating process. Only then can we settle disputes and reach agreements that satisfy both parties and meet group goals.

TYPICAL NEGOTIATING ISSUES IN THE WORKPLACE

Resource Allocation Issues

- Budgetary distribution
- Space distribution
- Facilities distribution
- Support distribution
- Shop / lab equipment distribution
- Computer resources distribution
- Workload distribution
- Staff talent distribution

Compensation, Privileges, Perks

- Salary and other compensation
- Privileges and perks distribution
- Promotion and growth opportunity
- Training and development
- Termination, transfer, severance

Time and Schedule Issues

- Schedules
- Deadlines
- Time to complete issues
- Time-shape issues (milestones, progress expenditures, resources)
- Time distribution of costs
- Support services over time

Internal Department Distribution Issues

- Sales pricing, discounts, quotas
- Engineering specs, standards, statement of work
- Project goals, targets, staffing
- Purchasing negotiation, targets, strategies
- Finance and accounting control standards, processes, reports
- Systems and procedures
- Human resources issues
- Administrative control issues
- Advertising media tradeoffs
- Cost-benefit choices
- Strategy choices

Workplace Performance-Related Issues

- Quality of work standards
- Quantity, pace of work standards
- Performance review issues
- Authority, responsibility boundaries issues
- Time-shape of performance issues
- Special vacation, absence needs
- Special work hours, dress needs

Exhibit 1

We often assume that the bulk of negotiations take place at top levels of the organization. Not in today's work world. In the listing of internal issues in Exhibit 1 we see that every level of the firm is involved in the process of exchanging contributions for benefits. For example, superiors negotiate with subordinates, not only on issues such as budgets, compensation and schedules, but on personal matters like parking places or favored vacation time periods. Peers negotiate with peers. Managers who handle support functions like internal transportation or information technology deal with their peers in manufacturing to maintain the flow of efficient production lines. These interactions involve important negotiations though few participants accord them the forethought and preparation they deserve.

Engineers have to negotiate with their associates before establishing design specifications or standards on the products they develop. Other functions such as manufacturing, sales and purchasing are always affected by a proposed design. Within the engineering department itself, one engineer prefers this design or specification while another favors something else. In that sense, all engineered products and designs are themselves outcomes of a negotiation process.

Salespeople bargain with their managers and peers about sales commissions and return allowances for favored customers. They deal with peers in the accounting department every time their expense accounts are challenged. They bargain with pricing for lower prices or higher discounts and for special customer privileges or looser terms of payment. It's one negotiation after another for salespeople, both inside the organization and when dealing with customers.

We are all negotiators. Knowing how to do it well is important.

Good negotiators, those able to settle difficult problems and differences amiably, are recognized and respected. They are better able to cut through discord by finding a path to shared benefits. Ben Franklin remarks in his autobiography that those who avoid being confrontational will be received with a "readier reception and less contradiction" to their views.

ARE WORKPLACE NEGOTIATIONS MORE DIFFICULT THAN EXTERNAL ONES?

Negotiating within your own organization is, in my opinion, more difficult than dealing with outside suppliers or customers. In the workplace you have to get along with others in your department or group, whatever your differences. Reasonably cordial and cooperative relationships must be maintained on a daily basis even when both parties in a dispute dislike one another. This degree of close association, while beneficial, is not essential in external dealings.

Indeed, I am convinced that, for most of us, our growth trajectory within the organization depends more on our ability to negotiate with associates than on our technical proficiency or educational level. Many competent engineers, scientists and computer specialists never rise in the corporation because they never learn to work well with others in group settings.

Negotiating with others in your organization is stressful. Aside from having to think quickly, we always feel the pressure to express ourselves carefully. Mistakes take place. Sharp words are sometimes uttered inadvertently in the heat of discussion. Benign statements are too often interpreted by the other as demeaning or derogatory. In crucible of heated negotiations, exaggerations tend to proliferate and promises are made that may later prove difficult to fulfill. These problems tend to leave longer-lasting fractures in internal relationships than they do in external bargaining with customers or vendors.

Internal dealings and agreements are brittle because they are rarely put into writing. They fail to outline detailed quality or performance guidelines by which to measure progress. Later, as organizations change and time passes, memories of what was settled fade. Even those who worked hard to reach agreement are promoted or go elsewhere. Internal agreements break easily unless tended well and often.

Negotiations at work are more difficult than those we have externally. The negotiation I will now describe took place a while ago, but remains vivid in my mind primarily because I know the individuals involved quite well and respect both of them. What happened in the end could have turned out differently.

AN INTERNAL NEGOTIATION THAT SHOULD HAVE TURNED OUT DIFFERENTLY

Some years ago I was interviewing David, a well-groomed professional man of fifty, for the position of sales manager and lead presenter of our training company. It was an important position in our firm and well worth taking extra time with. David, after twenty years with his company, was now anxious to leave. His current employer specialized in presenting professional programs for businesspeople who were considering selling their firms and wished to learn how best to go about it. Those presenting the seminar were expected to conduct dynamic presentations and also sell consulting services. David's experience as a dynamic seminar leader who could teach others appeared to fit our needs.

As the leading company presenter and salesperson David had for some years been assigned to train all new leaders in how to present the programs, and to teach them how to best solicit consulting prospects. He earned a substantial salary and commission in this three-part role as presenter, trainer and salesperson. His financial incentive in training new leaders well lay in a considerable override he received from their subsequent sales. For David, the greater satisfaction was personal and deep.

Each trainee was like a member of David's family. He found it fun to party with them at holiday times and celebrations. Working to improve their skills was a joyful experience. Busy enough with making presentations and training others, he did not mind that once trained they were assigned to work under Charles, the marketing and sales manager. David felt that he had no time for such administrative work and was happy to leave it with Charles.

From an organizational standpoint Charles and David were peers. Neither had direct authority over the other and both reported directly to the president of the company. The president, often away on business trips, expected his subordinates to settle their problems and disputes without involving him.

Being interested in the cost of training, I asked David what it cost them to train a professional presenter. "About $70,000 including the many prospects who were interviewed and later failed to do well or dropped out," he said. The high cost surprised me somewhat because we had never really calculated our own full cost of training.

He added that the payoff for the $70,000 investment lay in the

80-20 rule. Among the successful leaders were that special 20% who made 80% of all consulting sales. He felt that was the key to the company's success.

Everything went well at his company until the economy slipped into recession. Suddenly the number of seminar attendees dropped precipitously. Soon there was not enough work for all leaders. None were earning nearly what they had grown accustomed to. As the recession progressed, some chose to retire while others moved elsewhere or were terminated by Charles for budgetary reasons.

As marketing manager, Charles favored a sharp layoff policy to weather the bad times. David disagreed. He favored a policy that would equitably distribute the reduced workload and limit the layoff to a few marginal producers. Not only did David believe that the well-trained presenters should be kept, he also felt that one or two new ones should be hired and developed. He felt that the economic storm would soon pass and their competitive position would be stronger than ever.

David proposed that the company could recruit better candidates when jobs were scarce. People, he felt, were motivated to work harder and learn more quickly. He estimated that the training cost per successful person could be reduced from $70,000 to as low as $50,000 in such times. He reasoned that he could accomplish this cost reduction by finding better prospects, accelerating the learning process and having trainees do more for themselves on their own time.

Although David and Charles were peers from an organizational standpoint, both reporting to the president, it was Charles who was the key decision-maker as to whether marketing personnel were to be hired, laid off or re-assigned to other duties. David's views, by virtue of his long tenure with the company and his successful role as a presenter and trainer, were respected but not controlling in this allocation of resources discussion.

From Charles's viewpoint, the choice was clear. He saw little point in developing new leaders when there was not enough work for those still employed. He viewed David as a dreamer whose strategy made little economic sense in a recession. David, on the other hand, was able to demonstrate that the most successful leaders produced almost eight times the consulting revenue of less proficient leaders. The trick was to leverage the unemployment level at that time into a cadre of super-successful presenters who would pay off as the economy recovered. Both views were honestly felt by each to be in the best interests of the company.

Both failed to negotiate in a collaborative Both-Win® way. Their prior relationship never helped. In fact it hindered their need to find a better way. Despite working together for so many years, they enjoyed only a casual, "Hello, how are you" rapport with one another. While there was no hostility between them there was little reserve in their "relationship account" to bridge the viewpoint gap they faced.

Every time they talked, voices were raised. Accounting figures were bandied about by both sides but all too quickly dismissed by the other as inaccurate or irrelevant. Neither listened to the other or came up with alternate ideas. They lost respect for one another and soon avoided contact unless absolutely necessary.

A good settlement was beyond their reach. Both suffered in the process. David, a competent and loyal employee, decided to leave. The company lost one of its best people. The training level of Charles's remaining staff will soon slip. People like David with passion for their work are rare.

Yes, I hired David at a good salary. He turned out to be one of our best presenters. But I still think there is something missing in David's demeanor. I believe that if he were asked in private, "What's the best job you ever had," he would say: "One where I was surrounded by those many close friends I trained and helped grow. What fun it was." That's what David lost through that poorly conducted negotiation. I believe there was plenty of room for creative compromise and a better deal for both sides in this difficult situation. Had they handled the negotiation in a relationship-centered collaborative way, both would have gained.

In Chapter Two we will propose an entirely new approach to dealing with others based on a collaborative negotiating process that builds pathways to stronger relationships, fosters an open exchange of viewpoints and sets the stage for creative Both-Win® outcomes whenever differences occur at work. We will learn how to win agreement and negotiate anything with anybody, be they your counterparts from other departments or your peers, subordinates or superiors. You will see that the behaviors and techniques that lead to better relationships at work are applicable to dealing with those you live with and love at home.

2

The Effective Negotiating® Virtuous Cycle
A New Approach to Dealing with Others at Work

How you collaborate horizontally and manage horizontally requires a totally different set of skills from traditional top-down approaches.
– Carly Fiorina, CEO, Hewlett-Packard Corp.

It seems to me that the factors that lead to a productive goal-directed organization and a harmonious workplace environment are much the same as those that guide happy families at home. In both settings people work together not only cooperatively but also collaboratively on a daily basis. In both, arguments, disruptions and disagreements do take place but are resolved amicably most of the time. Happy families are happy because they have learned to deal with internal differences by communicating with one another candidly and by negotiating differences between them with mutual gain and relationship building uppermost in their minds.

Happy families maintain their felicitous relationships because they have learned to negotiate internal discord in a collaborative way: a way that supports good relationships and mutual gain. Those in charge, the elders or parents in this case, use their strength to encourage an open exchange of viewpoints rather than paper-over or bury discord to make peace.

The same appears true in successful teams and work groups. Where people work together collaboratively and cooperatively to meet goals, and where they show respect for one another by listening to diverse views, work becomes fun and gets done more effectively. When individuals in organizations fail to communicate or fail to work out disputes through civil give and take, the organization wastes its collective energy and resources in bickering and discord. Production and the capacity to meet challenges innovatively diminish. Satisfaction is lost. Unhappy families suffer the same fate for similar reasons.

With that in mind, I would like to propose a new relationship-based approach or model for working together that sets the stage for encouraging the creative imagination and productivity we need to meet the global and workplace challenge facing us. This new model, as you will see, rests on a mix of four factors that together produce a successful working environment. That model, "The Effective Negotiating® Virtuous Cycle," is illustrated in Figure 1 below.

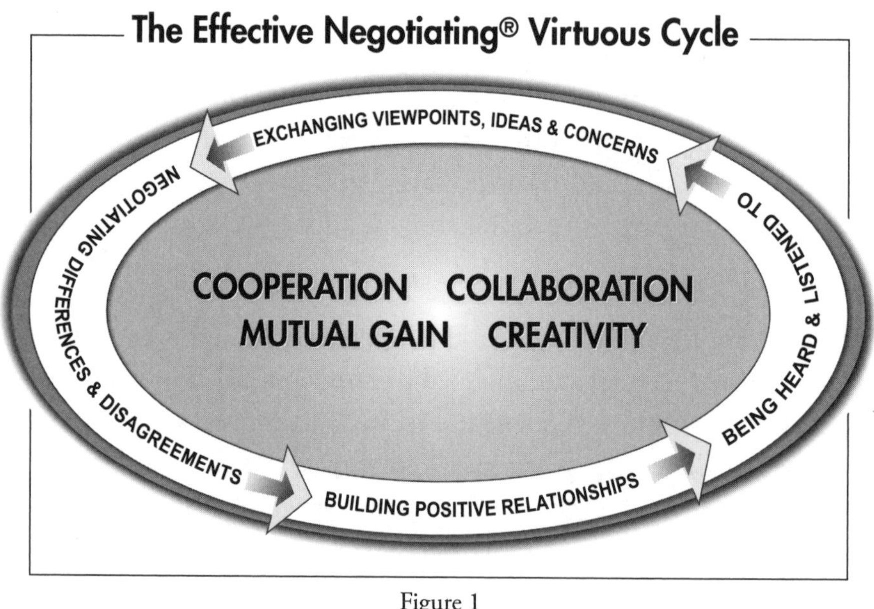

Figure 1

The Virtuous Cycle, whose motion is shown by the arrows flowing from one factor to the other, is designed to illustrate that each factor influences the next in a direct way. Where people enjoy a good relationship they find it easier to be heard and exchange opinions even when they disagree. This, in turn, helps them to reconcile their differences through negotiation. From that success comes a flow of growing rapport, trust and increased togetherness or belonging.

Three of these virtuous factors—being heard and listened to, exchanging viewpoints and building relationships—have been with us as long as people have been thinking about how to work together in a better way. The fourth factor of this cocktail mix, "Collaborative Both-Win® Negotiating," represents a new approach to amicably handling differences and getting along in any team or organization, especially one that strives to be creative.

Not only does the Virtuous Cycle illustrate how each factor influences the other, it also points out how a positive action or behavior in one area of the cycle leads to improvement in another. In this respect a virtuous cycle is the opposite of a vicious cycle that operates in an increasingly negative way. We have all seen people who are unable to resolve their conflicts and grow more distant because they cannot communicate with one another. Things always get worse where talks and relationships fail.

The Virtuous Cycle shows that even when relationships between parties are fragile they can be improved somewhat if one party listens to the other. That alone helps, but more is possible than even that success. If they are then willing to exchange ideas and concerns openly, they will be in a better position to work out a compromise or innovative agreement that benefits all concerned. Success breeds success. From such an agreement, their relationship will grow and with it their ability to communicate more effectively in the future. Each disagreement, well resolved, makes the next easier to settle. Wherever a person enters the process and does so in a positive way, the bond between participants becomes stronger.

The model is like a bank in which you have four different insured savings accounts to protect you from a bad disagreement day. The more time and energy you invest in building relationships with others before trouble arises, the easier it will be to handle it. The better you've learned to listen to the other when they speak, the more they will be willing to communicate. The more you have previously strived to exchange ideas and concerns in a candid way, the more they will dare to share with you. As for the negotiating account, the more effective you become in bargaining with others in a collaborative relationship-based way rather than in a self-centered approach, the easier it will be to reach Both-Win® settlements now and in the future when new problems arise.

Returning for a moment to the disagreement between David and Charles, the marketing executives described in Chapter One, we can see how much better that negotiation might have gone had they made use of the Virtuous Cycle with its cocktail-like mix of four factors.

Instead, neither had invested the relatively little time necessary to build a stronger working relationship earlier when things between them were going reasonably well. Neither had bothered to communicate at more than a minimal level. Each knew almost nothing about the other's personal life. Both were too busy or didn't think it mattered much. They were both so busy and proficient at doing their work that building positive relationships and bridges for the future escaped them. That is often the case with those who are technically competent and focused only on their tasks.

Creative people like David do not get great joy from administrative matters and "bean-counting." Managers like Charles, harassed by a myriad of daily personnel and operational problems, are glad to be left alone by people like David. The trouble was that later, when a serious issue divided them, they were not familiar enough with each other to resolve it.

The Effective Negotiating® Virtuous Cycle, with its emphasis on collaboration, Both-Win® negotiation, communication and relationship building, is a guide to positive behavior in a creative, self-starting workplace. It is designed to help people work together effectively not only on a day-to-day basis, but also when differences divide them. Its principles apply as well to personal and family interactions.

THE PROBLEM OF DEALING WITH OTHERS WHEN MORE AND MORE HAVE MINDS OF THEIR OWN

A little more than a century ago Thomas Edison was still tinkering around in his small laboratory. There, working with little help and relatively limited funds, he advanced and developed three great inventions: the electric light bulb, the phonograph and significant improvements to the motion picture projector. By the time he died in 1931 these products were common in millions of homes worldwide. This was an incredible achievement of invention and creativity by one man in such a short time.

When I was young, partly owing to the success of people like Thomas Edison, parents used to tell their children, "If you want the world to build a path to your door invent a better mousetrap." That is still true, but the path to entrepreneurial success is far more complicated today.

What brought the "better mousetrap" idea to mind the other day was the fact that I needed a mousetrap. To my surprise, I found one at the hardware store almost identical to those we used a hundred years ago. Also unexpected in this age of technology and change was the fact that the manufacturer of this old-fashioned spring-loaded trap was located in the American Midwest, not China. I believe that even as I write this, some entrepreneur in Asia or elsewhere is working on a better mousetrap and dreaming of people beating a pathway to his or her door. "Why has it not been done," I wondered.

A century ago, all it took to improve or invent a mousetrap was a clever mechanic working in his garage. All he needed was spare time, a few tools, spring wire, some experience with mice and a little money. If he built a good mousetrap he could start by marketing it locally and wait for word to spread.

Let's say you want to build the trap in today's world. You will need a lot of money and a team of diverse specialists, each with an advanced degree in some field of science. You'll need at least a chemist or toxicologist, an environmental engineer to guarantee that handling the trap is user-friendly and environmentally safe, an anthropologist to evaluate cultural attitudes toward mice and their destruction, and finally a mouse psychologist who understands what mice like to eat and how they move from place to place to get it. Of course you'll also want the usual array of computer specialists, accountants, marketing executives, an MIT graduate to lead the technical team and a Harvard MBA to head the business. As for the team itself, each member will surely have a mind of their own, not only about their specialty but about others on the team and the soundness of their ideas. Every decision and position taken on any issue will be subject to someone else's counterposition. Every problem the group encounters will be further complicated by the personality, background and opinions of those on the team.

Many of the team of experts will come from different cultures and hold different values. Some will speak English with heavy accents. Some will eat strange foods that exude odors others are not accustomed to. Many will never really join the main group and will prefer to break bread only with others like themselves. Some of their families will be thousands of miles away while others will be sharing a single room locally with five others. Listening, exchanging ideas, winning rapport and working with them will not be easy. Building a better mousetrap with so diverse a team will require a new way to get along and a new way to handle the many differences sure to arise.

Dealing with associates in the emerging century is going to be more difficult than in the past. The pyramidal organization structure we relied on to get work done for more than two hundred years is changing under our feet. The "top-down" authority organization we are so familiar with is far less dominant than it was. There are reasons for this management evolution.

Institutions and business firms are like living organisms. When their survival is threatened they adapt. Figures 2-4 illustrate how the pyramid is changing in response to technology and pressure from abroad. The need to handle exceedingly large and complex projects in efficient and creative ways has brought about decision structures and information channels not welcomed earlier.

ORGANIZATIONAL CHANGES

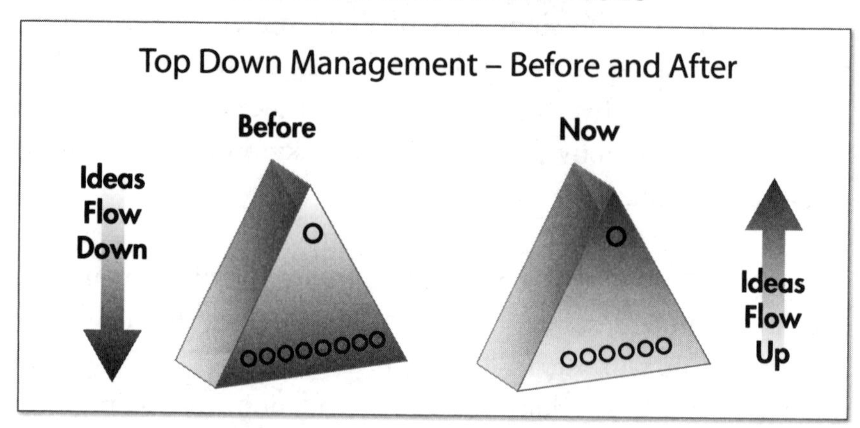

Figure 2

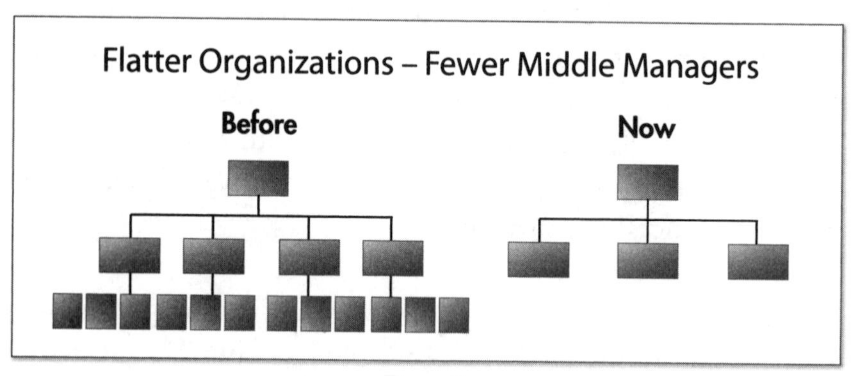

Figure 3

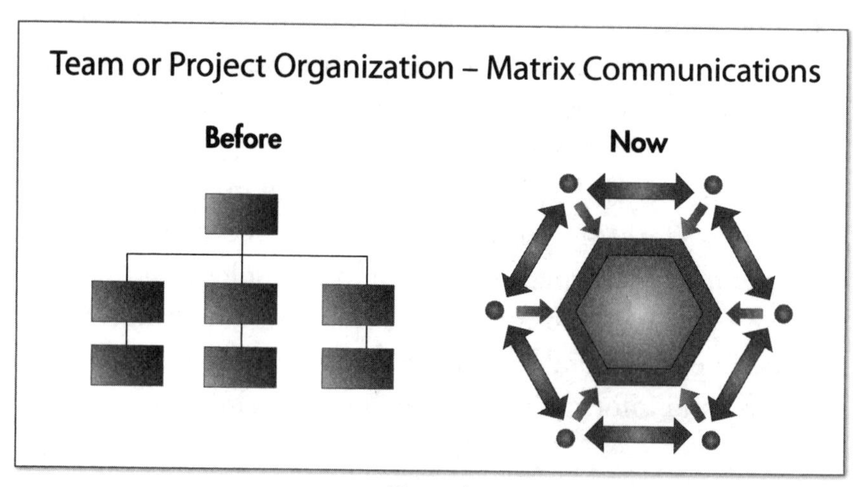

Figure 4

Top Down Management – Before and After

Information and ideas are now feeding up to management rather than flowing "top-down."
(Figure 2)

Not long ago, "top-down" authoritative management ruled; now, the importance of real-time knowledge in making sound decisions has moved the flow of information in the opposite direction. Executives in charge know that they cannot make prudent strategic or operational decisions without current information and ideas from below. They need input from those who interact daily with other groups or departments and with the world outside.

Those in charge are now less able to put together a picture of reality from a desk on a higher floor or a knowledge base that provides limited visibility. Their best source of information comes from those closest to the changing marketplace or technical environment. When organizational wisdom came from the top down, there was little need to negotiate differences. Mavericks with other views were not welcome. The top was heard and listened to. The middle and bottom were expected to do as they were told.

Now few, if any, top managers have the broad knowledge necessary to cope with the pressures imposed by today's major economic and technical trends. An organization is likely to do poorly if it fails to allow those below to be heard and express themselves without fear of censure. Differences will surely come up. The way to resolve them is not by assigning fault or inducing fear, but through collaboration and negotiation.

Flatter Organizations – Fewer Middle Managers

Organizations are flatter than they were and the number of middle managers is far smaller (Figure 3)

Until late in the previous century, most large and medium-sized organizations had layer upon layer of mid-level managers and employees, each processing and analyzing the data generated by the one below. Now, with the growth of the digital age, there are fewer middle managers and their work is now done with the help of sophisticated computer systems, access to databases and knowledge sources, and the internet.

The digital age also introduced a change in the span of authority. Earlier senior executives managed five or six lower-level managers all doing related departmental work. Each lower-level manager supervised about six employees all doing roughly the same work. The senior manager in charge understood what those below were doing because they themselves had done the work for years before being promoted to a higher position. Very little negotiation between them was necessary. Each did what was prescribed by procedure or supervisory order.

Today the many layers are gone and with it most of the middle managers. A new and flatter span of authority has taken their place. Middle managers are now in charge of numerous specialists, each from diverse disciplines and educational backgrounds, some of which have small staffs and laboratories of their own. The new middle manager has broader authority than before, when they took full direction from those above, but exerts less control over those experts reporting to him. The specialists themselves are often assigned to various project teams where they are authorized to make important decisions almost completely on their own.

Amazingly, as much as 20 to 25 percent of America's knowledge and analysis workforce now work in such flatter organization structures, and their numbers are growing. On the one hand, they are more satisfied by their broader authority and independence. On the other hand, they are discomforted by having to get along with ever-changing teammates and their isolation from technical peers and higher authority. It is no surprise that this is one reason they move from company to company every three or four years when economic times are good.

Team or Project Organization – Matrix Communications

Team and project organizations facilitate collaboration and streamlined communication between specialized members.

(Figure 4)

Important projects, especially those that are large in scope, complex or on the frontier of knowledge, require teams to get them achieved successfully. "Top-down" management, with its bureaucratic "stove-top" information structure, in-fighting and diminished communication flow, will not do. The circular structure and flow of ideas shown in this diagram provide the best model suited to assuring that difficult and complex projects end well.

The Effective Negotiating® Virtuous Cycle, with its cocktail-like mix of factors, is the way groups and teams can best work together to achieve difficult goals and creative challenges. With its four-part focus on building positive relationships, its assurance that each member is heard, its encouragement of a candid exchange of viewpoints, and its implementation of collaborative Both-Win® negotiating to settle differences, the Virtuous Cycle and its behavioral approach in the workplace will help us be "first on the block and to get our share" of the "flat world's" economic well-being.

3

Separating the Other Person from the Opposing Position or Viewpoint They Express

Good negotiators learn in their careers to separate the person opposing them from the contrary position or viewpoint they express. They recognize that what they differ with are the ideas proposed by the other, not the person delivering them. To personalize, stereotype or otherwise demonize the person delivering the unwelcome message assures that an amicable and reasonable agreement will only be harder to reach.

In Chapter One, we visited a workplace negotiation between David, the seminar leader and chief sales training executive, and Charles, the marketing manager. Both were sincerely concerned with the firm's success in surviving a severe recession. Both were also convinced that their position was best for the company. David advocated for the hiring and training of new salespeople despite the current bad times. Charles was in favor of not hiring anybody at a time when other company salespersons were being laid off or suffering severe declines in earnings.

Each presented reasonable arguments to the other in support of their position. Each was aware of the potential gains and risks of hiring new recruits at such a time. What caused the talks to break down into deadlock was not, in my opinion, the difference in their viewpoints but their tendency to support their positions by personifying the issue separating them.

In the course of the argument, David was called "foolish" for suggesting that new people be hired. "Only a poor businessman would do such a thing when customers are scarce," said Charles. Charles, in response, was termed a "short-sighted bean counter" by David. "Penny wise and dollar foolish," were the words David threw at Charles. "You don't even really understand our business," David shouted loud enough for others in adjoining offices to hear. The talks broke down soon after. Both lost. David left the job he loved. Charles and the company never found anyone as good at training salespeople as David.

When negotiators fail to separate the person opposing them from their position, the likelihood of deadlock increases. Even a small gap grows when one describes the other overtly or silently in pejorative terms such as "foolish," "stupid," "illogical," "untruthful," or "dishonest." You would be surprised at how often I've heard these words bandied about by one person or another in the heat of negotiation. Once said, they cannot be taken back, nor are they easily forgotten. Hard feelings are inflamed. The gap grows larger. Their ability to work creatively to forge an agreement diminishes.

Most of us recognize from experience at work and elsewhere the corrosive effect of stigmatizing or attaching personal labels on differences between us. Yet we continue to do so whenever such differences occur. It's as though we are plagued by a harmful habit that we must rid ourselves of, but which we find it difficult to let go. In the balance of this chapter we will suggest how to better understand this habit and wrest ourselves from its debilitating effects on getting along and negotiating. We will start by understanding the sources of disagreement and the factors that influence our perception of these discords.

SOURCES OF WORKPLACE DIFFERENCES AND DISAGREEMENTS

DIFFERENCES ARE BASED ON

- Assumptions
- Facts
- Means
- Goals
- Values

OUR PERCEPTIONS ARE INFLUENCED BY

- Where we sit and our experience
- Our emotions
- Our motivations, concerns, hopes and ambitions
- Our expectations
- Our information
- Our communication channels
- Our resources or assets
- Our alternatives
- Our beliefs, attitudes and relationships to those who make the presentation of facts, etc.
- Our cultural background
- Our forecasts and estimates

Exhibit 2

As we scan through these sources of workplace differences and factors that influence perceptions, it becomes easy to see why so many disputes arise. One person argues that, based on the facts, this course of action is warranted. The other disagrees not with the course of action but with facts themselves. He or she challenges how the facts were gathered, what they include or fail to include or whether the facts are relevant having been aggregated years past. Facts and figures are always negotiable.

Ways and means are often subject to dispute. An engineering problem arises that demands prompt resolution. The spin mechanism of the drone camera that took three months to design and fabricate has just failed the stress test. One engineer suggests that all will be well if the base of the mechanism is made an inch thicker. An associate calculates that this change will exceed the weight and space specifications of the Boeing drone and is impractical for production purposes. Another member of the design team is certain that the Boeing-stipulated spin speed is unnecessarily high and that the problem lies not with them but with Boeing. Each approach to resolving the problem is complex, time consuming and costly. Which way the team should move is the issue under contention.

While most differences at work concern facts or ways and means, many also involve group goals and values. For example, a purchasing team, including an engineer, is set up to reduce the cost of an anticipated project overrun. The team, anxious to meet the goal, wants to negotiate a very low price with the supplier of a key component. The engineer assigned to the team vehemently disagrees with so low a price. He reminds his associates that a more important goal, project quality, will be placed in jeopardy by pursuing such a low price on so high a component quality specification. A complex goal negotiation with lots of crucial tradeoffs is sure to follow.

More difficult than negotiating diverse objectives is the negotiation of different values. A management team of executives is organized to develop corporate personnel policies. Each member has a mind of their own and the confidence to express their preferences. What kind of people should or should not be recruited? Ivy League or not? Should a group be laid off every year to clear out those less capable? General Electric chose to replace ten percent of their executive staff each year. Is that percent suitable for people who have been with our company for 20 years or more? In the event of a recession who should be laid off? Should tenure and competence be factors? Is our choice an ethical one? Should we do business in another country as they do or stand by our standards and possibly lose the business? Is so much information secrecy on this team necessary when many believe they have a need to know and resent restrictions? Negotiations between team-members that involve values make for emotional give and take and heated sessions.

Differences between people are influenced by their perceptions. If they saw things the same way, then they would find it easy to agree. The job of a good negotiator is to help the parties see the major factors influencing the agreement in reasonable, comparable terms.

One of the most important factors influencing the perspective of both parties in negotiation is where they sit; that is, what their area of responsibility is. If I am responsible for cutting costs on a project and your idea, good as it is, increases costs, then I am likely to resist your idea. Our feelings about the issues in dispute affect how we perceive the opposer's proposal or idea. If I have seen an idea like the one you are favoring fail in the past, then I will be skeptical that yours could succeed. If, however, I perceive you to be a highly competent engineer, I might give your approach the benefit of the doubt.

Our personal motivations, concerns and ambitions also condition our responses to and acceptance of whatever is offered or set forth. If I believe that what you say will help my career I lean toward it. If it jeopardizes my job I want no part of it. If we both enjoy the same communication and information channels, we are likely to hold similar viewpoints. The same is true if we share a common cultural background and beliefs.

It is obvious that these factors play a role in exacerbating or narrowing differences at work. The best way to reach agreement is to give thought to these driving forces when differences arise and to speculate on how they may be affecting the issues under consideration. The worst approach is to stigmatize the other party and close your mind to their point of view and driving forces. Yet that is exactly what so many of us do when differences with others happen.

To better understand this "Downward Spiral" to the personification of differences and its harmful progression we will now return to the "better mousetrap team" we met in Chapter Two. We rejoin them in a disagreement that is growing increasingly heated.

Step 1 in this "Downward Spiral" occurred two days ago when our distinguished team chemist quietly proposed a low-level, low-cost poison to kill mice soon after they enter the trap. He cites experiments that assure that the poison will not be harmful to people at such low levels. He presents further research showing that, even if ingested accidentally by humans, it will make them only slightly ill at worst.

Only one member of the team expresses any discomfort with the chemist's proposal. The environment engineer, an Indian Ph.D. from Mumbai, mumbles half-aloud, "I'm not sure of that," but says no more. He is a quiet person who expresses himself hesitatingly in English and speaks rarely; that is, only when he has to or has command of the subject matter. A second meeting is scheduled tomorrow to reach accord on the poison decision. The team will have a day to think about it.

The second meeting opens dramatically. Soon after some cordial remarks the chemist presents new reasons for choosing the selected poison and opens the floor for further discussion. This time the environmental engineer from India reacts heatedly. He shouts, "I believe that the degree of toxicity you have selected is far too high." He adds:

> "Having worked as a sorter on Mumbai trash dumps as a youth, I was required to handle many mousetraps every day. These toxic traps you are proposing will leave garbage sorters in danger of small but cumulative toxicity effects. Sorters often cut themselves while working. Handling these toxic traps with open wounds is cruel and needlessly dangerous. What you are proposing will also lead to many future lawsuits as these sorters become increasingly infected over time."

Finally, he screams, "Yours is a very bad choice!"

It becomes obvious that some members agree with the chemist, others with the environmentalist. Coalitions form in favor of each view. A buzz grows as team members whisper to one another. The negotiation between the chemist and the environmentalist continues more loudly. Each side presents its position with energy and conviction not seen before. An air of hostility is palpable.

What we now have is Stage Two of the "Downward Spiral." A

rational discussion of issues is marred by ill-considered remarks and personal charges. Both sides are threatened by possible loss of face in front of peers.

When people speak in the heat of argument they do not choose words carefully. What they sometimes do is experiment with how they express themselves. To make matters worse, those listening may interpret what is said in ways not intended by the other. That's why we would all gain if, before responding, we gave the other in any discussion or negotiation the benefit of the doubt when we hear something untoward. We know from experience how easily things get out of control when personal remarks are mixed with issues that we feel strongly about.

In Stage 2 of the "Downward Spiral," it takes but a few poorly chosen words to move the talks from a peaceful discussion to a full-blown argument. The contestants, if I can now call them that, are no longer negotiators. Their egos are at stake as well as their status and reputation on the team. Unless defused by the team leader or the group, reasoning degenerates into a flood of pejorative characterizations involving such matters as the other person's competence, bad habits and questionable motivations.

Returning to our mousetrap team, we find that the environmentalist describes the chemist who advocated the low-cost mildly toxic agent as cold and insensitive. The chemist then depicts the environmentalist as a naïve, impractical person lacking in business sense. The team, after all its work, is no closer to a decision than before.

Each side has now compounded the problem of getting together by personifying the gap between them. They say or imply evil or pejorative attributes about the other thereby separating them further. Things can get worse and do.

Step 3 of the "Downward Spiral" takes place when each side stops listening and makes little attempt to understand the opposing viewpoint. They talk past one another primarily to those who agree with their views. The process of negotiation is, for practical purposes, over.

Instead of seeking collaboration or compromise by allowing the other to be heard and understood, they frame their arguments in self-centered ways. They give no credence to the other, nor do they leave room for "saving face." Power and politics then dominate the debate and subsequent decision rather than the negotiating process. The opportunity for collaboration and mutual creativity has been lost by personifying the issues. The opportunity for reconsideration and compromise has been lessened or lost by hardening differences.

Perhaps worse as a consequence of this now out of control argument is the likelihood that others on the team, who are less assertive or articulate, will in the future choose to stay quiet in expressing their ideas. Those with the best ideas are rarely the most gifted in expressing their thoughts. They, the quiet ones, may not wish to risk their reputations or careers on matters so potentially threatening. The "Downward Spiral" creates an environment in which the best views will probably remain unspoken.

As for the entire mouse team, this important negotiation about toxicity and chemical choices will not be the last. As the project progresses each member will also find himself or herself favoring one design approach over another, or one production method over an alternative. Each will defend their views with passion and documentation. Hardly a day will pass on our mouse project without the need for collaboration, compromise, creativity and negotiation.

The team will succeed only if its members work together to avoid the "Downward Spiral" and its three steps. The all too human tendency to personify differences as we strive to move others to our position stands in the way of rational debate and argument. The subject of the next section is how best to avoid the dysfunction of personification and separate the person opposite you from the disturbing message they bring.

EIGHT APPROACHES THAT HELP SEPARATE THE PERSON FROM THEIR OPPOSING POSITION

Avoiding the pitfalls of characterizing those who oppose us can be accomplished if we pay attention to some common-sense rules. The eight approaches that follow will help us to recognize that personalizing differences only make them more difficult to reconcile.

SEPARATING THE PERSON FROM THE OPPOSING POSITION THEY EXPRESS

1. Workplace negotiations, to be effective, must be relationship-based.
2. When disputes arise, move quickly to joint involvement in finding Both-Win®, mutual gain solutions.
3. Search for common interests, goals and values. Open the talks by articulating commonalities.
4. Speak up promptly against any personification by anyone on either side at all team meetings or negotiations.
5. Know the work they do. Understand the picture in their head. Focus on their needs and problems, not just your own.
6. Never throw "garbage on their lawn."
7. Separate the search for new ideas from how their benefits or costs are to be distributed or shared.
8. Practice and more practice.

Exhibit 3

1. Workplace negotiations, to be effective, must be relationship-based.

Nurturing good relationships early inhibits the personalizing of differences later. The stronger the relationship between the parties, the easier it will be to avoid demonizing or demeaning the other as negotiations heat up. An experience I had with a close associate shows how important strong bonds can be in softening a difficult disagreement.

Frank and I have worked side by side for a decade. We write and develop training programs for business executives. We not only get along well at work, but also spend time with each other's family. A year ago there was a difficult difference of opinion between us. We were assigned to work on a major customized training project with good marketing potential. Three disagreements soon surfaced: the scope of the training program, how long it would take to complete and the estimated total cost including development and production. He believed that writing an extended analysis and detailed script related to the subject matter was essential. I thought a rough script and modest workbook would be sufficient. We recognized that these critical decisions had to be made early on with so large and costly a project and so tight a timeline.

Negotiations on a course of action began almost immediately and continued sporadically over a four-week period. I was surprised at how contentious and uncomfortable it was to disagree so sharply with someone I had so enjoyed working with in the past. My guess is that he felt much the same.

What helped most during these difficult sessions was that neither of us uttered a word of disparagement or criticism at the other.

Past errors on other projects over the years, some by him and others by me, were not brought up. At one time in the talks, to make a point, I was tempted to bring up a huge overrun Frank had created on an old project. Knowing from experience that finding fault over past problems always complicates matters, I resisted doing so. All it would have done was entrap us in a "Your fault, my fault" quagmire of problems from the past. Nothing good could have emerged from that.

The fact that we had worked together collaboratively for so long facilitated an amicable and sound agreement on a course of action. It helped us explore conflicting ideas and handle opposing viewpoints in a good-natured way. We gave each other the benefit of the doubt. Neither had to be perfect in proving our claims. Words misspoken were overlooked. Contingencies were freely discussed and jointly evaluated as to their probability of taking place. Rough notes of these discussions were taken.

An agreement was reached and sketched out for both to review. The important thing was the spirit of the deal, not the exact words. This was not a legal contract but a workplace agreement. He agreed to specific actions. I said I would supply the necessary support, the personal help and the funds required. We both recognized that unknown things would be learned later and renegotiations necessary. Later, when things went wrong, as they usually do from time to time on so large a project, we renegotiated based on reality and our notes from earlier talks.

Today, I can say that the project worked out well. The video Frank created and produced was funny and successful. It also encompassed a larger overrun than we anticipated. All things considered, that was pretty good for such a relatively ill-defined but important company undertaking. Above all, on a personal level, I now remember it as a creative, fun-filled experience. I know he feels the same way. I do not believe it could have been done had our relationship been less sound.

2. When disputes arise, move quickly to joint involvement in finding Both-Win®, mutual gain solutions.

Some workplace disagreements explode almost immediately into open hostility. This occurs most often when people dislike each other for a long period of time or harbor hidden anger at habits or behaviors highly distasteful to them.

Such was the case in an office I worked at. One person wanted the other to stop speaking so loudly over the phone because it inhibited his ability to think. The other, a salesperson, when asked to lower his voice responded by saying that he spoke as he did on the phone because most of his clients were older and somewhat hard of hearing. Each had taken what I thought was an opposing but reasonable position that seemed open to fair agreement.

Unfortunately, even as simple a problem as this can get out of control. One day, in front of everyone in the office these two went at it. The person complaining, we soon learned, had been disturbed by the loud talk from the day he started work six months earlier. A shy person, he chose to say nothing but seethed in anger every time the other spoke on the phone. Nobody else in the office seemed to care about the noise because they sat slightly further away and were buffered by an upright wall section.

Today, it turned out, he had had enough. He made his complaint clear for all to hear. "Please stop speaking so loudly. When you do I can't think," he yelled. The other person, totally surprised at the demand and the tone it was delivered in, responded by saying,

"What kind of nut are you? I talk this way because my clients are old. If you don't like it, go somewhere else or get another job. Nobody but you has complained since I started here five years ago." As far as he was concerned the discussion was over. They never spoke again. The other person, after being moved behind another partition, quit two months later.

When long-buried differences are exposed to negotiation and reconciliation, they all too often reveal a trail of hostility and recrimination close to the surface. The discussion can quickly turn into a full-blown fight with each describing the other in explosive terms. These are the "hot potatoes" of internal negotiations.

When I was young and lived in New York City, in the winter boys used to build small fires on the street to warm themselves as they roasted potatoes in the embers. They were, it seemed at the time, especially delicious when cooked this way. Most times we waited patiently for the blackened potatoes to cool but occasionally one boy or another couldn't wait or wanted to prove his courage by picking up the biggest hot potato and taking a bite of it. What followed was always funny to the rest of us but very unpleasant to the one who embraced the "hot potato." I've tried not to forget that when explosive situations arise between me and someone I am dealing with at work or at home.

The best way to handle such a hot potato is to cool it by moving the talks to a private place. The talks should be opened by affirming that you wish to reach agreement on a matter that has troubled you and that the other person or group may not be aware of. Let the other party know that you believe compromise is possible and that a better way for both can surely be found if you all put their heads together.

The sooner the search for a Both-Win® solution begins in such a situation, the more likely that the negotiation will result in friendly compromise and agreement. The longer we wait to explore mutual gain possibilities, the more likely it will be that frustration or hostility will explode in open recrimination and failure, especially if such feelings have been long suppressed.

3. Search for common interests, goals and values.

Open the talks by articulating commonalities. Invite the other side to add other positive values they feel contribute to a common bond between the parties. In every negotiation, be it internal or external, the parties share common interests. These are not always apparent when talks begin or in the heat of negotiation where competition between positions and personalities takes center stage.

Listing these commonalities and putting them on the table softens differences and deters the tendency to personalize them. It sets the stage for fair and reasonable settlement. It also serves as a base for bringing talks that are veering toward dissension or deadlock back on track.

William Van Allen, an outstanding negotiator and Vice President in the Howard Hughes Organization, opened every major negotiation by joining with the highest-level executive of the opposing firm in having each state what their companies had in common and why a fair and reasonable agreement would benefit both. Their joint declarations set the stage for a more rational discussion of issues when so much was at stake and served as a beacon for those at the table responsible for the myriad of give and take necessary to reach agreement.

4. Speak up promptly against any personification of issues by anyone on either side at all team meetings or negotiations.

In the United States we have learned to respond to politically incorrect statements of others by making it clear that such statements offend us and cannot be accepted. Gradually the number of such negative comments has declined. We are all better for the change.

The same approach is warranted in addressing the personalizing or characterization of differences in the workplace. All this does is make it harder to settle disagreements. Demeaning or labeling the person carrying the opposing message serves only to accelerate the "Downward Spiral" and harms our ability to get along. The sooner we rid ourselves of such harmful behavior the better.

Our role as members of a team or workgroup is clear. Those possessing authority or influence by virtue of knowledge or position have a responsibility. Whenever someone utters pejorative words demeaning or disrespecting another at a department meeting or negotiation, an objection must be raised. The person doing it should be told to stop. If the team leader fails to speak up, other members should. Over time, this firm attitude against the personification of differences will diminish and perhaps stop, not only in management affairs, but also in public discourse.

5. Know about the work they do. Understand the picture in their head. Focus on their needs, interests and problems, not just on your own.

This, at first glance, seems counterintuitive but it isn't. There is always good reason why the other side takes the position they do. It may not be a position you like but it is, from their viewpoint, appropriate because it is based on their wants and perceptions. Their wants and perceptions are, in a work setting, largely determined by where they sit, that is, the work they are paid to do and the channels of information and communication they are open to.

One thing I have found useful in understanding others and the setting in which they work is knowing what they really do at work and how. Job titles are of no help in this. All job titles are vague abstractions that tell us almost nothing but fool us into thinking we understand.

Why is it important to know what those you work with daily really do? It not only helps us build a better relationship with our colleagues, but also sets the stage for resolution when problems or discord come up later. Where people stand in a disagreement depends much on what they are responsible for. If we understand their point of view and how the problem between us fits into their work picture, we stand a better chance of reaching a more stable agreement.

The time to get the picture in their head is not when disagreement occurs, but long before that point, perhaps when you share a casual lunch. You'll be surprised at how much you may learn about their day, as long as you don't pry like an attorney. Most people like to talk about their work with those who are genuinely interested and willing to share their thoughts.

6. Never throw garbage on their lawn.

There is a tactic of negotiating that buyers use to soften a salesperson's resolve to hold their asking price. We call that tactic "Throwing garbage on their lawn."

The buyer goes into the bargaining session with a long list of seller mistakes: problems or inadequacies created in the past by the opposing selling organization. As each of these negative factors is thrown on the seller's lawn, the seller's determination to hold their position lessens. Their expectations fall and, with them, their prices.

This negotiating tactic has worked on salespeople for centuries but has no place in workplace give and take. There, positive relationships between the parties must dominate every strategy or approach. Reminding others of their past inadequacies rarely if ever leads to better performance or relationships. There is also another problem associated with throwing garbage on their lawn: the other side can always throw some back. And they usually do.

7. Separate the search for new ideas from how the benefits or costs are to be distributed or shared.

For example, let's say that I, as a long-time resident of Palos Verdes, an upscale mountain community overlooking the Pacific Ocean, am disturbed by the huge tree on your property blocking my view. I meet with you in hope of doing something that will help. Cutting it down, from my now angry standpoint, would be the perfect solution.

Shortly after we meet, my neighbor, as an environmentalist, makes it clear that no tree should be cut down for cosmetic reasons. In response, I suggest that we search together for a better way to solve the problem. A reasonable person, he agrees to explore alternatives with me. Nevertheless, he reminds me, the problem is mine, not his.

In the process of collaboration I learned that he is not as fond of the tree as I thought. Apparently the tree has a down side. Twice a year it sheds a torrent of leaves and sticky avocado-like drops of muck on his manicured lawn and expensive garden furniture. Both require lots of time and work to remove.

Three alternatives emerged from our discussion. The first, and best from my viewpoint, he rejected. My suggestion was to cut his tree and replace it with a slow growing shorter tree that would retain its leaves all year.

The second approach was to radically trim the big tree twice a year. This would of course restore my view shortly after the trimming but would then reinstate the blocking problem three or four months after the leaves grew again. From his standpoint, this approach would create a needless tree-trimmer annoyance twice yearly even if I paid the recurring costs, something I did not want to do.

The third idea he rejected after some thought and talk with his wife. In that approach we felt that it might be nice if the big tree was cut down and replaced by a new garden of beautiful blooming bushes and planting. The trouble with that idea, he said, after talking to his wife, was that the family enjoyed sitting under the shade of a tree on warm California days as they looked at the ocean.

The negotiation closed with my paying for cutting down the big tree and half the cost of planting a shade tree chosen by my neighbor. He chose whatever plants he wished for the new garden and planted them himself. I volunteered to spend a weekend helping him do so.

Had we earlier discussed who was going to do what, and who

was going to pay, we would have created an impediment to collaboration and inventiveness that could have brought talks to an end. It was far better to separate the collaborative phase of searching for Both-Win® ideas from the competitive process of deciding who pays what share and who does the extra work. These divisive issues can wait while the process of working together creatively through collaboration grows.

8. Practice and more practice.

In our earlier discussion of the "Downward Spiral" we indicated that people, in the midst of a disagreement, tend to blend the person opposing them with the positions they take. Separating one from the other is essential if we wish to reach long-lasting agreement. But it takes practice to do so.

For most of us, separating the messenger from the messages does not come naturally. Practicing almost every day will help. You'll have more opportunities to do so than you think. Every disagreement or difference experienced at home or at work, or even when watching television can provide a good opportunity to do so.

A talk show like "Meet the Press" will allow you to measure how well you handle viewpoints with which you strongly disagree. Instead of clicking off or fast-forwarding the television person expressing the view you so dislike, force yourself to listen intently through their arguments and reasoning. I know from personal experience how difficult this can be.

Your tendency, like mine, will be to disparage the ideas you don't agree with. You may find yourself making negative remarks to others in the room or surfing for a new channel. You may even find yourself calling the person speaking an idiot or worse and seek revenge by moving to a good basketball game.

Once the tendency to dismiss or disparage opposing views is recognized you will be in a better position to change this habit. The reality is that opposing negotiators will rarely advance arguments you like or find easy to listen to. Learn to listen intently to television pundits expressing opposing ideas. It will help you become more open-minded in dealing with others. If you hear them out without building personal barriers, they will give you clues that lead to creative collaboration and reasonable compromise.

Another good place to practice is at the dinner table at home. Try it when dealing with your spouse, loved one, children or mother-in-law. If you can separate the person from their position in contentious home disputes, you will be better able to do it anywhere.

PART II

RESOLVING WORKPLACE DIFFERENCES AMICABLY AND PRODUCTIVELY

Reducing Friction When Viewpoints Clash

PART II

4

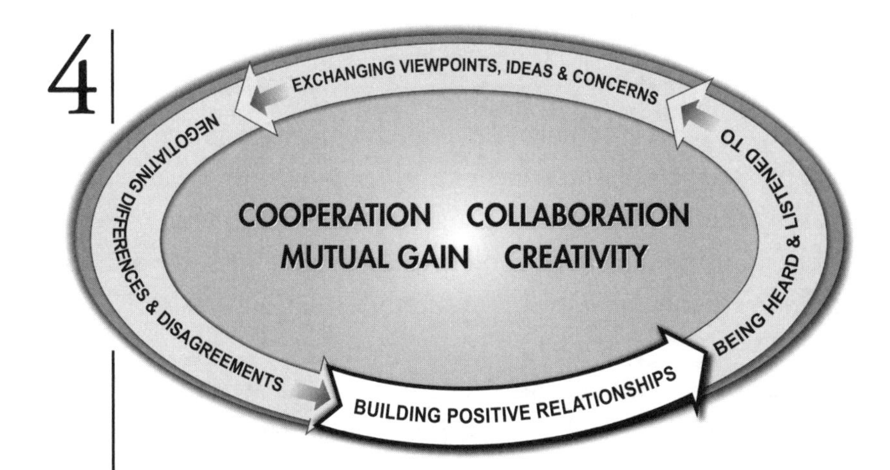

Building Relationships that Lead to Cooperation, Collaboration and Sound Agreements

BUILDING CONNECTIONS THAT WORK

Positive energy relationships are the WD-40* of successful internal negotiations. They are the lubricating oil, the catalyst that allows you to be heard and settle differences without rancor. Harmony in working together follows directly from good relationships. The chapter will focus on the behaviors that lead to building this vital career skill.

Positive energy relationships are vastly different from passive or negative ones in shaping the interactions of people at work.

*WD-40 is the brand name of a well-known fine lubricating machine oil often used to reduce friction between metal parts or to loosen machine or metal parts that are bound together in motion.

When two persons have developed a positive relationship they are pleased to see one another and show it with a warm smile or handshake. When the meeting ends they leave with a feeling of well-being even if the problem they sought to solve still eludes them. Their energy level grows rather than diminishes.

Interactions with negative-energy people work the opposite way. One leaves such encounters feeling depleted and dejected, and sorry to have been there. Each of us knows from personal experience that we look forward to dealing with those who exude positive energy. We avoid those who do not. Working with positive people is a joy.

The ability to build positive relationships may be more important to your success at work than being highly intelligent or well-skilled. At work we often make the mistake of overvaluing intelligence at the expense of appreciating how well they get along and deal with associates. Intelligence and talent are important. One cannot be a competent manager, engineer, scientist or employee without a reasonably high level of intelligence. However, in today's complex economic and social world, with its interconnecting spheres of knowledge, another measure of competence has become increasingly necessary: the ability to build connections with those you interact with on a regular basis, whatever their role in the organization.

The capacity and willingness of every employee to build relationships should, in my opinion, be made part of each person's job description and evaluation at performance review time. It matters not if the individual is Chief Executive Officer, a physicist involved in launching a spacecraft, a scientist or someone responsible for cleaning the office. Each employee should recognize that relationship building is part of their job and an important factor in determining their career trajectory.

When people are aware of its importance in their work they will pay more attention to it. They will strive to strengthen their day-to-day connections and will benefit from the reduction in friction that flows from improved relations. People who trust and like each other may differ at times, but they are less likely to personalize their differences or bicker constantly. When the need for collaboration is anticipated, they will willingly join hands.

What led me to think more about this matter was a rather distressing conversation I had with a man who for several days sat next to me on a bus tour in Spain. He was an upper-level computer programmer from Microsoft, about 40, who had worked for the company since graduating from college eighteen years earlier. We had time to chat between tour stops.

After some time talking together about small things he surprised me by revealing how angry he was about his work at Microsoft. Apparently others, younger and less experienced than he, were being promoted. They were, in his opinion, far less competent and creative than he. He was distraught. Microsoft was an important part of his life, more than just a job. It wasn't fair.

Angered about the disappointing trajectory of his career, he asked his boss why. He was told that, while his work was always outstanding, his relationship with others in the department left much to be desired. Many of his peers considered him aloof and arrogant; he was smart with computers but had little regard for much else. One associate described him as always outside the team tent, looking on, but never really involved in what was going on inside.

When he asked why he had not been told this before, the answer only half surprised him. He was advised that it was assumed from his behavior that this was the way he wanted it – to be left alone. I asked, "Were they interpreting your views correctly?" He replied that he had never really tried to mingle with associates. He had never felt comfortable making small talk with them or with anyone. He did however have one acquaintance in another department with whom he occasionally had lunch. Other than that he preferred eating lunch in the office while reading current computer publications.

As for being recognized for his work, he had always felt that his outstanding work would speak for itself to those in charge. And for years it did. They gave him good reviews and above average raises every time. Now things were different in his life. Being recently married, he now wanted to get ahead.

We lost touch after the tour so I don't know what happened afterward. His prognosis for a successful upward mobile career at Microsoft doesn't look good to me. His growing anger and disdain for associates was evident and probably too hard to hide or change. Perhaps there is a chance. I also met his new wife on the tour. Unlike him she is outgoing, charming and a spirited mixer. She may help him change if he chooses to.

Looking back at this situation, I am convinced that if Microsoft had discussed the man's dismal relationship history in performance reviews over the previous eighteen years, he would have strived to improve along the way. Had they shown the same interest in relationship- and network-building as they did in computer programming skills, he would have responded.

Each of us is capable of improving relationships at work. It's a matter of devoting the time and effort necessary to do so and then acting accordingly. That's what this chapter is about: highlighting the behaviors and approaches we can pursue in order to negotiate positive relations in our everyday workplace lives.

GOOD RELATIONSHIPS ARE NEGOTIATED – NOT INBORN

Relationships, both good and bad, are products of negotiation. One way to look at the status of our relationship with someone is to see it as an account at the bank. Our daily actions contribute to the goodwill we put into the relationship account. Everything we say or do at work builds or reduces the account and affects the other person's attitude toward us. It is an ongoing negotiation, though rarely called that.

The issues we exchange and negotiate are shown in Exhibit 4. These sensitive issues are rarely discussed openly with associates at work; and yet, they are the building blocks on which good relationships and harmony are founded. They are called intangible issues; these are issues people feel strongly about but find difficult to discuss. Our relationship to another person may be viewed as the sum or calculus of attitudes and beliefs each has about the other.

Most commercial contract negotiations are conducted in a quiet room with two or more persons sitting on opposite sides of a desk or table discussing their positions or matters on which they disagree. This is not the case in relationship negotiations. There, intangible issues are negotiated in an informal way as the parties interact on a daily basis. They negotiate relationships through indirect communication, overt behavior and body language clues.

Relationship issues are rarely, if ever, addressed in open forums.

Yet there are definite similarities between commercial and relationship negotiations. To achieve their objectives, both parties must decide what they want from the other person and what they are willing to give up to win it. They must strive to understand the motivations of the other side and to determine how to persuade them to perceive the matter as they want them to. In both types of negotiations, a compromise is reached through mutual and reciprocal give and take as well as some collaborative communication and exchange.

THE RELATIONSHIP ISSUES WE NEGOTIATE DAILY

1. Respect
2. Negotiating an Open Mind
3. Caring: Giving Something Personal of Yourself
4. Positive Attitudes Toward Cooperation and Collaboration
5. A Willingness to Give Others the Benefit of the Doubt
6. Reasonable Access to Your Time and Attention
7. Trust and Acceptance
8. Reliability and Credibility

Exhibit 4

We will next discuss each of the relationship issues shown above and will explore the behaviors that lead to stronger bonds between associates, a reduction of bickering and better organizational functioning.

1. Respect

Guards at Corcoran Prison, one of America's most dangerous penal institutions, are taught that even the most violent inmates calm down and cooperate when treated with dignity and respect. If showing respect helps with difficult people like that, it will surely help in dealing with anyone.

Even those whose accomplishments are well-recognized are hungry to be heard and respected. During the presidential election campaign of 2008, a distinguished New York Times editorial columnist interviewed several experienced United States senators about their interactions with then-candidate Barack Obama. The columnist reported that the senators expressed keen pleasure in how candidate Obama intently listened to their opinions and understood what they had to say. They added that it showed how much respect he had for their views. You would not think that senators who have risen to so high a place in society would be concerned with a demonstration of respect from so new a member of the Senate, but that's the way good listening works. It signals respect like few concessions one person can give another.

Respect is something we must negotiate for. It does not come solely from holding high position, having great wealth or being skilled or learned. Gaining respect from others has to be earned. Indeed, we have all worked for people whom we did not respect because, after working side by side with them for long periods, they failed to acknowledge our existence as human beings or associates. This is a small thing you might say, the failure to emit a warm smile or hello in our direction as they pass us in the office. Others lose our respect for failing to say "Thank you" for tasks completed well on difficult assignments. In dealing with others at work we sometimes discount how important courtesy and consistent friendliness are in conveying and cementing mutual respect. Small things and actions contribute much to the give and take of relationships.

Respect can grow even when people sit at opposite sides of the negotiating table. It has been my experience that when opponents present their positions truthfully, listen courteously, seek to understand and strive to reach fair agreement, they almost invariably leave the table liking and respecting one another. When problems of administration or execution arise later, the respect they have accrued at the negotiating table stands them well in fostering smoother resolution.

A similar result occurs when associates in a department or team work together to meet a difficult goal or time target. Their joy in jointly achieving a mutually valued objective is shared by all who contribute to the outcome. Salespeople putting together a tough proposal or accountants assembling an annual budget gain respect and rapport for one another. Organizations would do well to encourage respect-building joint endeavors. The benefits accruing from such endeavors can last a lifetime.

2. Negotiating an Open Mind.

In the global marketplace it is difficult to enjoy long-term relationships with those who are closed-minded about viewpoints and opinions not their own.

There are far too many executives in every organization who have a bad habit. They've learned to say "NO" to every new idea presented to them. In a sense, they wear hats that bear the word "NO" in bright letters and thereby serve to shut off discourse before it starts. To be at the same meeting with people like that is dismaying. Their very presence guarantees that your viewpoint will meet with closed-minded resistance and not be heard.

Everybody benefits when associates open their minds to opinions they do not agree with. There is no way to exchange ideas or negotiate a reasonable compromise with a close-minded person. The best we can do with people like that is to maintain as good a relationship as possible and hope for a better time.

Good relationships are built on open-mindedness on the part of both parties. Only then can they reconcile differences. It is far better to work with people who value and welcome dissent without squelching or personalizing it. Only through the give and take of argument and persuasion can better, more creative solutions be found and relationships enhanced.

3. Caring: Giving Something Personal of Yourself.

One of the most unexpected and nicest things you can do for someone you are dealing with at work is to give something personal of yourself. People appreciate when you expend some personal talent, work or skill on their behalf without being asked to do so. They rarely forget the experience.

For many years, five friends and I would meet on Sunday morning at Murray's tennis court in Beverly Hills to play a slow game of what we called tennis. None of us were very good so it didn't bother us that the net sagged a few inches at the center. Over the years the sagging got worse but all we ever said to each other was, "The net is sagging." We then went on to play our mixed foursomes. After a while, one of our regulars moved away and was replaced by Phil, a man of sixty who owned a small business.

On the first day Phil played with us, he, like us, said, "The net is sagging." On the following Sunday, to our surprise, Phil brought along his bag of tools and a heavy duty sewing kit, one he used for mending sails on his boat. The next thing we knew, without a word said, Phil was fixing the net, snipping a bit here and there and sewing the rest as straight as Wimbledon. It took him less than an hour to do the job. With that gesture, Phil, the newcomer, won the acceptance and respect of our group. He didn't do it for that reason. He recognized that something needed doing and did it.

There will be occasions when you work alongside associates who are overloaded or have to meet tight deadlines such as annual budgets or urgent sales proposals. If at that time you have some slack in your department, give your associate a hand in getting the job done.

I worked for years under Bill Coombs, a superb supervisor. We developed a close friendship along the way, each visiting the other's home every month or so. One day Bill saw that my newly purchased stucco house needed painting. I did not at that time have enough money to hire a painter, having used almost all of my funds in buying the house. Bill suggested I whitewash the house rather than paint it. Enough whitewash to do so cost only about $35 at that time, not a small sum then, but doable. On New Year's weekend Bill came over with sacks of whitewash and two used brushes. He not only taught me how to whitewash, but worked with me to finish the job. The whitewash stood up reasonably well for almost three years. My friendship with Bill lasted a lifetime.

4. Positive Attitudes Toward Cooperation and Collaboration

Nothing promotes strong relationships more than working closely and successfully with others on a joint task. The joy of such an experience stays with us for a very long time and warms us to the opportunity to do so again.

The need to work collaboratively with others on teams and tightly knit project groups will increase as this century progresses. Those averse to doing so or to the idea of sharing ideas will find themselves outside the relationship tent. Almost everything we do already requires close cooperation with co-workers who must help when computer systems fail or stoppages occur. As for creative and complex endeavors, the age has long passed in which a lone inventor like Thomas Edison could produce such world-changing work without close collaboration with many multi-disciplined associates.

A positive attitude to cooperation and sharing is essential when a problem or dispute arises about a project team's engineering design choice or how a difficult production problem ought be corrected. When team members are open to working closely with one another they are more apt to find not only possible compromise, but also the opportunity to discover a better way neither had thought of earlier. Those without a positive attitude toward working closely with peers, subordinates and service personnel will impose limits on themselves and alienate others.

5. A Willingness to Give Others the Benefit of the Doubt

Every architectural design, television commercial, management system or computer program, no matter how good, can be made better by further thought and effort. Such improvements usually come with negotiated compromise and concessions on the part of those involved. Costs and benefits are always assessed in the decision process. The trouble is that one can never be certain that the system proposed will work as designed or at the estimated cost. Future benefits are hard to predict with accuracy. Assumptions are often wrong. Skeptics are always ready to express their doubts.

Managers and supervisors who search for flaws or differences will find them. They will also antagonize and alienate those assigned to do the work. Mr. Draper was such a manager; the worst I ever worked for. He was, for the most part, intelligent and well-organized, but had one bad habit I found hard to live with. He never gave anyone the benefit of the doubt.

Mr. Draper questioned everything he heard. If someone said it was 2:00, he would look at his watch and say it was 2:05. If a subordinate submitted a report he would assume there was a grammatical or spelling error in it and search for it. If someone said, "These are the facts, Mr. Draper checked them out." He was sure to challenge it in some way. When a production control specialist estimated that a machine part would take 30 minutes to produce, he would check the estimate by testing the assumptions it was based on. He made every visit to his office difficult. Most who worked for him were professionals, unaccustomed to being treated that way. Later, when there was a management shakeup, not one peer or subordinate stood up for him to higher management. Joy reigned when he was replaced.

The new manager assumed that we were well-trained professionals who knew the difference between quality and inadequate work.

Unlike Mr. Draper, who intimidated us and expended our creative energies on small stuff, his replacement gave us a greater "benefit of the doubt." If the matter under consideration was important, we had to defend our position strongly. If not, he didn't waste our time.

As a result, job satisfaction went up, as did productivity. By giving us the benefit of the doubt and the freedom to meet our own professional standards, the new manager benefited from superior performance and a better relationship than Mr. Draper could have dreamed possible.

6. Reasonable Access to Your Time and Attention

You cannot build relationships if you wear a "Do Not Disturb" sign on your back. If you give peers and subordinates reasonable access to your time and attention, they will reciprocate by being more open to your needs and ideas.

People who keep their office doors closed most of the day or eat lunch by themselves pay a price. They fail to utilize the power of breaking bread to facilitate exchanging ideas and establishing stronger network associations. Disassociated from the group, these loners find it more difficult to find support for their ideas or viewpoints when differences of opinion occur. Whatever the quality of their work, their influence diminishes as does their chance for promotion.

Of course, an open door policy has its problems. There are some who may take advantage of your accessibility by taking up more time than you can spare. In that case, negotiate an arrangement that suits both of your needs without hurting the other person's feelings or dismissing their concerns. Most who want your attention will understand your needs if they are reasonable and made clear.

7. Trust and Acceptance

While not long ago we worked in the same office or production group for years at a time, now it's all changed. Almost everyone is now a member of a team, a project, a matrix organization or a work group whose members change as often as every few months or once a year. Where once we were employed at only four or five companies in a lifetime, now we change jobs every four or five years. People with long tenure in any company are rare, whatever their position or skill level.

Building trust and acceptance between associates in such fast-changing groups is difficult, especially when the members themselves represent such diverse disciplines and cultures. Yet, we can only hope for success if we learn to work together harmoniously in an environment that encourages trust and acceptance.

People, no matter how bright they are, cannot perform at their best if they do not feel accepted by the group. The impediments to acceptance and trust are formidable for new arrivals. There are usually team-elders, close-knit with one another for months or longer, who form an elite inner circle of their own. These insiders are often wary of newcomers as a threat to their well-being or security, whatever their credentials.

Every member of the team has an important role in genuinely welcoming newcomers in a warm and accepting way. Each member of the existing or original group should personally go out of their way to avoid the "We" versus "They," small group clusters that serve to separate those who have been on the team for some time from those just joining. They should discipline themselves to listen and hear out new members. Unless all are under the same umbrella, mutual trust and acceptance between all team members will not be fostered. Creativity will suffer. Whatever project the team was organized to accomplish will not be done.

8. Reliability and Credibility

It is difficult to maintain a good working relationship with those who are unreliable or whose words we cannot depend upon. That's only common sense. What surprises me is how many people I've worked with who remain undependable without recognizing the harm they do themselves.

Mitchell was such a person. I inherited him as part of a cost-estimating group when I was promoted section supervisor. Almost everything Mitchell said or promised to do was open to doubt without further verification.

When he said he would have the estimating report done on Tuesday, he had it ready one or two Tuesdays later. When he said it would be done, sometimes the word "done" meant a rough draft, sometimes it meant an outline and only occasionally was it done reasonably well. When his production estimate for a machined part was two hours I was never sure whether it would include setup time as well as machining time. He was unreliable unless I pinned everything down in advance in writing. How or why his prior supervisor tolerated him I don't know. I could not.

A person's lack of credibility makes it impossible to work with them. When someone says, "This is what happened," or "These are the facts," one must have reasonable faith in what they say.

Reliability and credibility are essential in the workplace. Without them, positive relationships cannot exist.

What we say or do in daily interactions with associates affects how they feel about their relationships to us. It's a negotiation that takes place virtually from moment to moment on the job. In this section we explored some of the key negotiating issues that make for a positive working relationship. Without such relationship avenues, communication, collaboration and personal growth will dry up and fail.

In the section that follows we will discuss behaviors and approaches for dealing with others that influence their psychological well-being and the direction their relationship to us will take.

WHY SOME PEOPLE FORM STRONG AND EFFECTIVE RELATIONSHIPS: THE FLYWHEEL EFFECT

One way to explain why some relationships are strong and energy-building while others are not is by understanding the "Flywheel Effect." Imagine a wheel upside down, suspended on its base as shown in figure 5. The flywheel shows relationship strength and weakness as a moving object, spinning sometimes rapidly, sometimes slowly, and sometimes turning hardly at all. In a sense, the rate of the flywheel spin is a barometer of a person's ability to build and maintain positive relationships.

Figure 5

Every time we experience a successful relationship, our flywheel spins faster. A strong, successful relationship has a fast-spinning wheel that will spin for a long time. The longer this relationship's flywheel spins, the more momentum the flywheel has to keep on spinning. A slow or stopped flywheel, however, denotes weakened relationships. It occurs when successful interactions are few and far between. It is a sign that connections are failing.

Between successful interactions, the flywheel of a good relationship continues to spin. This inertial spinning can be looked at as our reserve strength, the strength we use to cope if difficult times occur between us. People who have weak relationships have slowly spinning flywheels and therefore have little or no reserve strength, a fact that is apparent in the way they fail to establish rapport or psychological connection with each other, especially when problems occur. Successfully working together puts a lot of spin on our wheel and can keep us going for a long time. For most of us life consists much more of a series of small but pleasant experiences that work together to keep our wheel spinning smoothly and regularly.

Failure in a relationship, on the other hand, acts like a brake. It can bring the wheel to a screeching halt and make us feel as though we can't relate well to anybody. Even a small failure is felt as a perceptible loss of strength, and each failure slows the wheel down and robs us of needed reserve. A series of failures, or a long period without reasonably close positive energy relations with others, may slow our wheel to the point where we find it very difficult to get together with anyone.

When you see someone survive a massive relationship failure and keep going, you can assume that person's wheel was spinning very rapidly before the failure occurred. That's why those with successful relationships, even those who have had periods of failure themselves, find it so difficult to understand those who cannot maintain reasonably strong and lasting bonds.

As more and more success causes our wheel to spin more and

more rapidly, we become aware that we are developing a reservoir of strength that we can draw on whenever necessary. Too much failure, on the other hand, slows our wheel and drains our energy reserves, undermining our confidence in ourselves. Convinced that there is little we can do, we attempt less and less. When this happens, we become immobilized with our flywheel virtually motionless. If such a person is in charge of others, his or her lack of strength affects everyone being supervised. A manager or team leader whose relationship flywheel has slowed or stopped spinning can slow down or stop a whole organization and with it group cooperation and creativity.

APPLYING THE FLYWHEEL EFFECT TO EVERYDAY AFFAIRS IN THE WORKPLACE AND ELSEWHERE

The flywheel effect applies as much to social and family relationships as it does at work. Everything we say or do in dealing with others has a role in spinning the other person's inner flywheel for better or worse. We have it within our control to have them walk away from us feeling good about themselves and us, or to be so bothered by our actions or words that they distance themselves from us or anyone else they may subsequently interact with. How we use the power we have in the workplace will determine the relationships we enjoy.

In that respect, flywheel spin is a measure of how we feel toward one another. When our relationship is strong and regular we have an "I'm OK, You're OK" feeling. If, on the other hand, one criticizes, finds fault or disagrees sharply or tersely with the other then their spinning strength may slow and leave them with a negative energy flow; that is, with a sense that they haven't enough strength to do what has to be done.

The Relationship Flywheel gives us a graphic picture of what we are doing to the relationship when we treat another in unfriendly ways, make snide remarks, raise our chin, berate them or treat them like children. It would be better if we stopped for a moment to visualize what we are doing to the flywheel deep inside them, its spinning force and their flow of positive energy. Seeing that picture in your head should serve to modify your behavior. Perhaps there ought to be a model of the flywheel in every home and office to remind us of its positive and negative effects on others and ourselves.

GETTING ALONG AND WORKING TOGETHER – BEHAVIORS THAT GET POSITIVE RESULTS

We do not choose those we work with, yet we have to get along with them day by day. Others are obviously different from ourselves in many ways. Is it any wonder that people argue and differ so often at work? The disharmony and bickering that accompanies these disagreements erodes our capacity to focus on useful productivity and inhibits our capacity to develop new ideas in concert with others.

Knowing how to get along and work effectively with others is as important as the skills and knowledge we bring to the work. What follows are eighteen suggestions that will help you deal with superiors, peers and subordinates whatever your administrative, production or technical position in the organization.

1. Previously buried issues erupt later in dysfunctional ways. This occurs because too many people prefer to bury problems or paper over differences in the hope that they will fade away with time. The trouble with hiding the problem is that it will usually return later, more difficult to solve than ever.

Benjamin Disraeli, Prime Minister of Great Britain under Queen Victoria, once said that only from disagreement can new policy and consensus emerge. What we need in this new and competitive global economy is a workplace that favors an open discussion of diverse points of view and ideas without discord, criticism or anger. Only through the give and take of rational argument and persuasion can creative solutions be found that will benefit all involved. The temptation to find peace by papering over differences and problems is strong. The better path in the long run is to face disagreement energetically in order to find a better way.

2. Here is a counter-intuitive suggestion. The harder it is to get along with someone who disagrees with you, the more important it is to interact with them as pleasantly and as often as you can. Breaking bread with them at lunch can break the ice between you, but only if you keep the conversation away from contentious issues during the meal.

3. Don't get in the way of new ideas or approaches that others propose to solve problems or overcome obstacles. Far too many people take joy in being obstructionists when what we really need are facilitators. The word "No" springs out of their mouth even before the person with the idea is done explaining it. It is far better for the organization and for yourself to be known as the person who helps bridge differences and impediments. They are the ones best regarded by peers and associates and most in line for promotion and growth.

4. Emotions are contagious. People who bring anger, frustration and fear to the group infect others. Those who bring warmth, caring and collaboration move the group in their direction.

The workplace is much the same as home in this respect. A father who comes home storming from a bad day in the office leaves everyone in the family on edge. When a team leader or department manager brings their frustration from another meeting to the group, the group quickly senses that all is not well and takes cover in silence or dysfunction. Good ideas and possible remedies remain to be expressed another day.

Recognize as a carrier that emotions, both good and disruptive, are contagious. Indeed, a large-scale experiment recently reported that people who are happy radiate their happiness to family members, neighbors and people they intersect with on the job and elsewhere. Better to postpone a meeting than to have one clouded by team or leader tension. Better to watch a basketball game on television by yourself than ruin a family dinner when angry or disturbed.

5. Working together is not a matter of black and white. The facts are never exactly right or wrong. Every idea or design, no matter how good, can be improved. Giving others the benefit of the doubt helps the negotiation of differences move more smoothly. Another person's contributions, however imperfect by your standards, deserve a hearing and may lead to a better outcome.

Instead of immediately questioning every flaw in reasoning or fact in someone's presentation or proposal, it's wiser to hold your tongue and listen. By refraining from questioning every detail on the spot, you will benefit from not putting them on the defensive.

You will get more out of what they have to say and why. There is usually enough time at meetings to question crucial points after you have fully heard them. Take notes. Your patience in giving others the benefit of the doubt as they speak is a trait that others in the organization appreciate, respect and reciprocate.

6. Trust is gained when we share information and lost when we provide it to some associates and not others. Access to information has to be negotiated. If, for good reason, there must be limits to the distribution of information to some but not others in the group, such reasons and limitations must be known to all. If not, those excluded from the need to know will lose faith in group objectives and with it diminished feelings of acceptance and trust.

7. Members of a group tend to do the opposite of what they should when someone in the group fails. Instead of helping to correct the problem, they make matters worse. When things go well, it's easy to interact in a friendly way with those who did well. When things go wrong, the best hope for correction lies not in erecting distancing barriers between you and the failed person, but in getting closer and helping them. Moving further away only makes it harder for them to learn a better way.

8. Play down competition between team members. When people feel they are in competition, they protect themselves by realigning group relationships and becoming more careful about expressing thoughts and concerns. Group trust and acceptance suffers. "We" versus "They" member clusters form and diminish team cohesion.

9. When you commit to finishing a task by a certain date, do it. If you cannot, let others know as early as possible and be prepared to negotiate a new commitment. When this is not done, credibility and trust erode, especially when such commitments are broken time and time again.

10. Break bread regularly with those you work with. Celebrate Fridays and personal things like birthdays or graduations. Then, when problems turn up or things don't work out as they should, your lunch partners are likely to help, not judge or preach.

11. People like and respect good listeners. When someone at a meeting speaks, those attending who give them their undivided attention are more likely to be listened to and heard when their turn comes. Listening is an art we can all get better at.

Unfortunately there are far fewer good listeners among us than poor ones. Perhaps that is why we recognize a good listener the moment we speak to them. Their skill lies in their ability to focus fully on what we have to say. By their words, gestures and body language we know they are authentically engaged in trying to know what we are expressing and why. Is it any wonder that such behavior conveys their liking and respect for us and quietly demands the same from us?

12. When next you disagree with someone think carefully how to express disagreement as tactfully and diplomatically as possible. Unfortunately this is not easy. In the heat of argument words flow from us in a less-than-controlled way.

The best thing we can do is to slow down, say less rather than more and keep the other person's psychological flywheel in mind. What slows their flywheel is best not said even if you are tempted to say it. If, however, you disagree or express yourself in a wrong or heated manner, a sincere and prompt apology will help.

13. In every group, be it in a department, team or project, there will be some members in the "We" coalition corner and others in the "They" coalition corner. The more you rid yourself of "We" and "They" division, the better the group will function, get along and attract new members with good ideas.

People who feel they are accepted by the group are motivated to contribute more to its welfare. Cliques of insiders and outsiders reduce group cohesiveness and effectiveness. They build invisible walls that separate participants from sharing ideas and helping one another. The trouble with being outside the "in" group in any organization is that it slows your psychological flywheel and your incentive to perform.

14. How people get along with someone at work is related to how well they know that person in their social or family lives. The better you know the person you work with on a personal level, the easier it will be to talk to them and get along. This suggestion may come as a surprise for some, but one way to learn about them is to ask directly. Many people are surprisingly candid about family and personal affairs if they believe you care and will not exploit or take advantage of the personal information gained. As I look back at my career in business, those closest to me at work were also an extension of my family. We regularly partied, went to basketball games and enjoyed holiday dinners together. Collaboration at work was part of the fun we shared.

15. How you negotiate can change your ability to work with another for better or worse. Everything you say or do in moving toward agreement serves to spin their relationship toward you or away.

If they leave the negotiation feeling that they have lost face, been abused, dismissed or manipulated, your chances of dealing with them effectively in the future are lessened.

16. There are two things you can do that will help you get along with associates, even difficult ones. One is to enjoy frequent and pleasant interactions with them, devoid of sensitive or confrontational matters. The second is to maintain a high ratio of pleasant encounters to unpleasant ones. In this way you build a reserve of goodwill that helps when difficulties arise.

Find genuine reasons to praise others for their contributions to the group's welfare whether their input is modest or significant. No contribution, however small, should be taken for granted.

17. Few habits seem to anger others as much as those who fail to take responsibility for their own mistakes and those who adopt the ideas of others as their own without a word of acknowledgement.

18. Physical and psychological proximity to one another helps groups work and get along with fewer personal and communication problems. The project I remember best was one in which our company had mistakenly underbid a fixed price contract by nine hundred million dollars, a huge amount to lose on a single contract.

To cope with this potential disaster, a highly-focused cost-cutting tiger team was formed. Thirty of us were seated together on makeshift tables in a windowless room designed for fifteen at most. Our job as tigers on the team was to aggressively challenge every seller's price, design and service offer to the extent possible. The working environment, oddly enough, was awful but fun. It was boisterous, difficult, crowded and uncomfortable; nobody was sure whose phone was ringing. What happened was miraculous. We reduced the loss by $70,000,000 and loved every minute doing so. I'm still close to two associates on that tiger team. We still laugh about it when we meet. What a joyful experience.

Successful organizations are successful because their members relate in positive, energy-building, cooperative ways. Unsuccessful enterprises flounder because their employees deal with one another in dysfunctional ways that lead to wasted effort, bickering and disharmony.

In this chapter we have suggested an array of behaviors, approaches and habits that encourage positive relationships. In the next chapter, we will consider the next quadrant of the "Effective Negotiating® Virtuous Cycle"; that is, behaviors that lead to "Being Heard and Listened To." Unless we can be heard, even our best, most creative ideas will contribute little or nothing to the success of the group or to ourselves.

5

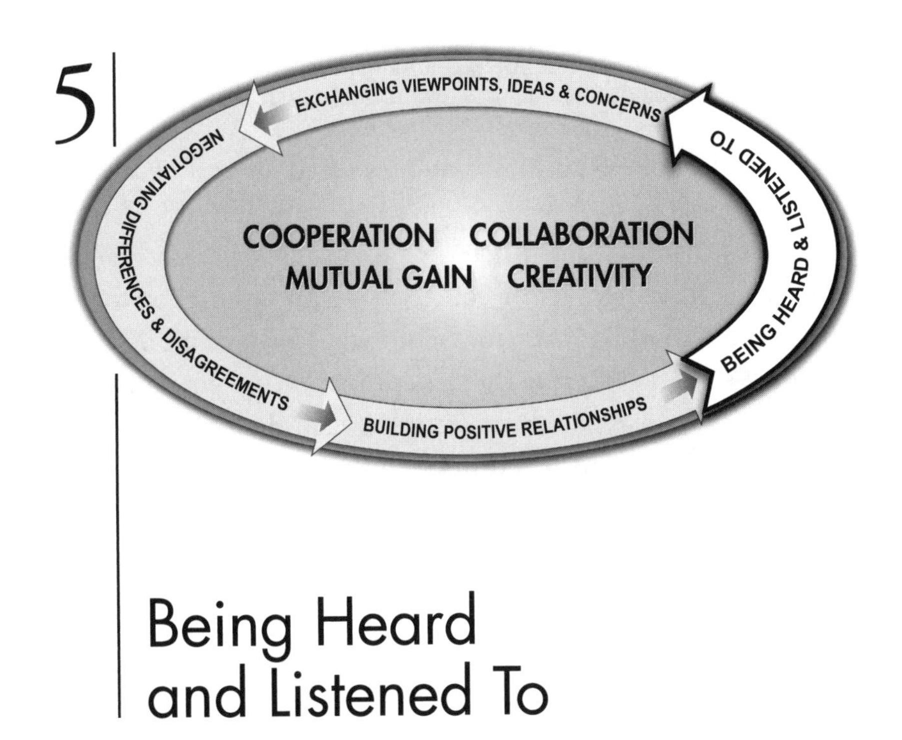

Being Heard and Listened To

Many at work, at every level of the organization, feel that they are not being heard. Often, when I talk to people about their work, I hear these words: "They never listen to me," or, "It's like I'm not there." People are desperate to be heard. Not being heard or listened to can contribute to the frustration and conflict so pervasive at work and, for that matter, at home.

This chapter will center on the "Being Heard and Listened To" quadrant of the "Effective Negotiating® Virtuous Cycle™." The path to improved collaboration and creativity in any organization lies in allowing people to speak their minds openly and listening to what they say. Only then can the best ideas be discovered, sorted out and negotiated for mutual benefit. Yet, as desirable as being heard and listened to is, it is not something we are born or entitled to, but something that rests with ourselves and how we negotiate for it.

Three aspects of Being Heard and Listened To will be discussed. The emphasis in each will be on what we as individuals can do to be heard, not what others in our group or team can do to help us. Other people, of course, have a role in allowing us to speak and respond to our words, but what we say and do to make it worthwhile to interest them is primarily in our hands. This chapter will consist of three sections, each designed to facilitate the art of being heard in a different way. They are:

Section I. The Give and Take of Being Heard and Listened To

Section II. Leveraging Your Being Heard Power

Section III. Behaviors, Habits and Approaches That Lead to Being Heard

I. THE GIVE AND TAKE OF BEING HEARD AND LISTENED TO

To be heard and listened to is a privilege that must be earned. People at work are usually too busy to listen to everyone who wishes to speak to them at length. Being heard and listened to, in my view, has to be negotiated through daily interactions with others.

In the economics of being heard and listened to, there is an exchange process at work. You have to give quite a lot of yourself to gain what you want.

THE GIVE AND TAKE OF BEING HEARD AND LISTENED TO

1. YOU HAVE TO KNOW WHAT YOU ARE TALKING ABOUT.
2. YOU HAVE TO DO A LOT MORE WORK TO GET READY THAN YOU THOUGHT.
3. OTHERS WILL DISAGREE STRONGLY WITH YOUR IDEA AND FORCE YOU TO DEFEND IT.
4. IF OTHERS LIKE YOUR PROPOSAL THEY MAY ASK YOU TO IMPLEMENT IT.
5. THERE ARE OTHER RISKS YOU'LL HAVE TO TAKE IN ORDER TO BE HEARD.
6. AFTER ALL YOUR EFFORT GETTING READY, YOU MAY NOT EVEN GET A CHANCE TO SPEAK.

Exhibit 5

1. You have to know what you are talking about.

To negotiate for their limited attention, your team or group will have to believe that you know what you speak of. It will help if you have a history or reputation proposing sensible ideas that can be presented and implemented effectively.

Your passport for being heard also rests on your relationship with others in the group. If trust and credibility have been established you'll get a chance to express yourself. As in any negotiation, your reputation and relationships sit alongside you at every meeting. They help determine whether you will be listened to and can influence the group.

2. You'll have to do a lot more work to get ready than you thought.

A coherent, readily understood proposal requires considerable preparation. The group you are addressing has little time or inclination to listen, involved as they are in numerous matters perhaps more urgent to their interests. You'll have to get to the heart of the matter quickly and address their needs, not yours. If not, their attention will wilt. To make things more difficult, you'll have to be somewhat entertaining as well. All of this is not easy. A measure of creativity is necessary and lots of work as well.

3. Expect others to disagree with your idea or position. You will be forced to defend it.

Don't hope for the best. Assume others won't be as fond of your ideas as you are. They will demand that you defend whatever is proposed and have at your side the reasoning and proof of its soundness.

They will ask questions you will find difficult to anticipate or answer. Some will do so in unpleasant ways. That's part of the price you have to pay to be heard. Your ego will take some sharp bruises in the process. Some may decide not to love you. Those are risks you have to be willing to take.

4. If others like your proposal they may ask you to implement it.

The paradox of having creative ideas and proposing solutions to difficult problems is that those who hear them may, if they approve, insist that you, not they, do the work necessary to implement them. They will profess to be too busy to do the job as well as you.

Be ready for your new assignment on top of everything else you've got to do. Not only will you likely accept the assignment but subsequently find yourself working twice as hard as anybody else to get it accomplished well. After all, it was you who proposed that it could be done, not them.

5. You'll have to take further risks in order to be heard.

Risk is a factor in every negotiation. Those who vie to be listened to place themselves in jeopardy to some extent. There are people on the team who will resent your speaking up as "showboating" your intelligence. Others may quietly attack the position as self-serving, impractical or shortsighted. Attacking a good idea is easier than formulating or facilitating one.

The Japanese say that the nail that stands its head above the surface is the one that gets hammered first. You may wish, when the negative hammering begins, that you had not been heard at all. Defending ideas is especially complex and is a lot more difficult than presenting them. It demands a great deal of preparation to anticipate the questions and the persuasive answers. There is, of course, the risk that what you proposed will not work and there's a price for that.

6. After all your efforts getting ready, you may not even get the opportunity to speak. Take the risk anyway.

Not everyone with something worthwhile to say is heard. Nor is everyone on the agenda allotted sufficient time to fully present his or her views. Agendas at meetings rarely run on time or allocate speaking and question time equitably. If what you have to say is important negotiate an agenda with the powers that be that provide you the best time and place to be heard.

After all your effort in preparing a coherent, focused presentation you may not even get sufficient opportunity to speak for reasons beyond your control. I have made such unforeseen foreshortened presentations many times and know how frustrating that can be. I have also suffered the privilege of making a potentially career-changing presentation to group of high-level executives in a meeting room adjoining a jackhammer renovation project. Bad luck. The chance to make that presentation to these high-level executives never recurred.

Being heard is the product of negotiation. It does not happen just because you deserve it or want it. It is a privilege earned by building pleasant ongoing relations with others and a willingness to concede something of yourself in return. Winning the attention of your group is always difficult. Like any scarce commodity, it is in short supply.

II. LEVERAGING YOUR BEING HEARD POWER

One cannot control the extent to which one's point of view or idea will be heard and listened to in presentations or meetings. Much depends on attendees, the time of day and the subject under discussion. Yet there are some things we can do to enhance our power to be heard and to encourage others in attendance to want to share our views.

One important thing we can do to bolster our being heard power is to gain a reputation in the group not as a criticizer of ideas but as a partner in developing solutions, a facilitator of new proposals who makes them better through discussion and collaboration. Criticizers and impeders who get in the way through internal politics or position are plentiful. Facilitators are rare, better heard and well-regarded.

There is another path to being heard and listened to. A road that rests on the kind of information that one can now bring to the attention of others in the organization. It is based on telling them things they don't already know about the global economy they live in and the changes taking place daily that affect their work and lives.

Those whose work brings them close to the new frontiers of technology and the global marketplace will be listened to if they exchange what they learn and open these frontiers to others. Exhibit 6, which follows, describes six frontier areas where our "being heard" power may be leveraged for all to listen to and benefit from.

LEVERAGING YOUR BEING HEARD POWER

1. BEING CLOSE TO THE GLOBAL MARKET AND NEW TECHNOLOGY.
2. UNDERSTANDING AND EMBRACING THE INTERNET'S POTENTIAL FOR COMPETITIVE ADVANTAGE.
3. CONVERTING IDEAS OR PRODUCTS INTO UP-TO-DATE IMAGES, WORDS OR METAPHORS HELPS YOU BE HEARD.
4. ABILITY TO COMMUNICATE COMFORTABLY WITH OTHER CULTURES.
5. ABILITY TO EXTRACT COMPLEX INFORMATION THROUGH ANALYSIS AND CONSULTATION OF DIVERSE SYSTEMS.
6. "TELL ME SOMETHING I DON'T KNOW."

Exhibit 6

1. Being close to the global market and to new technology.

In the give and take of being heard and influencing others, those whose work intersects with the global economy, technology or image-making activities are in a good position to win the attention of others. The team or group's competitive edge lies in what those on the forefront learn as advance scouts about the ever-changing world outside and their willingness to impart it to others. Those who work on the frontiers of our new economy are, for the rest of us, our early warning system of trends to come that will soon affect our success and lives.

Every business and institution is now affected by the global marketplace. We have seen American banks rise or fall on what takes place in France or Thailand. A salesperson enjoying a casual conversation may learn in Chicago that intense competition from China is soon to threaten her product line or that the price of everything they sell will fall because Indonesian businessmen are planning to expand market share. When people tell us something we don't already know that we need to know, we listen. It matters not if the messenger is new or recently on the job, or higher or lower on the organization pyramid, our self-interest lies in listening.

This is also the case with respect to current technological changes. Advancements in new products are occurring at a remarkable speed. Somebody, somewhere, at this moment, is developing a better, faster, more efficient way to do whatever your organization is best at. Only if you develop and harness internal and external avenues to gather information and listen, can your organization keep up.

2. Understanding and embracing the internet's potential for competitive advantage.

In the company I am associated with we have one person who has a special understanding of the entrepreneurial power of the internet and how we can use it for competitive advantage. While there are others in the firm adept at using the internet for e-mail messaging and routine search requirements, this person goes beyond the rest.

He keeps current with every server change and upgrade, studies the latest online advertising techniques and pricing, searches web page improvement techniques and studies how best to mine the huge and expanding customer information base. When he says, "I'd like to tell you about something new on the internet and how we can use it," we stop everything to listen; we are awed by the many changes. He has embraced the medium while most of us are still playing with it or just sending e-mails.

3. Converting ideas or products into up-to-date images, words or metaphors helps you be heard.

Those able to convert ideas into appealing up-to-date images or metaphors command our new communication world. I've known Henry since he was a baby. Only 24 now, he graduated from the University of California Los Angeles two years ago. Henry majored in nothing in particular, spending most of his time playing on his computer and electric guitar. Very bright, he got almost all A's without much work and even wrote two songs that attracted some attention. Upon graduation he floated around with small graphic arts and advertising contracts to pay the rent. The son of a surgeon, he chose to find his voice elsewhere. Then he did.

He found a small, low-paying job with a company that didn't exist three years ago. What they specialized in was writing advertising copy for independent films. They are just one of many Hollywood firms hoping to find a place in the movie business. His job was to capture the essence of the scripts he read and the movies he viewed in a few words or images. To do so he had to rapid-read books and scripts and watch a multitude of yet-unnamed movies. His goal: to convey the value of a product, book or DVD in only a few words and tell them why they should buy it.

Henry found the voice he didn't know he had. In less than a year the owner of his company raised his salary to $250,000 a year.

My guess is that Henry's knack for converting ideas and images into catchy phrases and metaphors will soon reach the huge ears of the movie and political leaders who also demand to be heard with catchy images and words.

4. Ability to communicate comfortably with other cultures.

The office and factory floor will never be the same as what it was only a decade ago. Working side-by-side in Los Angeles and New York City are people from every race, religion and worldly culture. These giant cities are today leading the United States in professional and manufacturing workplace diversity. The rest of the country will soon follow. Creating a harmonious and productive symphony of these multicultural talents and backgrounds will not be easy, but Americans have been practicing integrating people from everywhere since Columbus landed. We are better at it than most. Those who can speak to the problem of making diversity work better will have a ready platform in every organization, large or small.

Clara has that platform in her company. Late in the 1990s, the Silicon Valley insurance firm she worked for decided to open an office in India to train people there to do the sophisticated analysis and programming then being done in California. Clara, a graduate of Stanford University, was assigned to open the New Delhi office and meld her colleagues into a talented team. As a student from Stanford, she studied beside talented others from India, China and the Near East on projects in business school. It was good practice for the world that was soon to follow.

The New Delhi office went well and another opened in Mumbai soon after. The Indian programmers learned to work collaboratively with associates in California. After six months in India, Clara returned to California and further trained the American programmers to work even more effectively with their associates a world away. The India offices are today as large as those in the United States. She is still recruiting and teaching others how to work patiently and productively with people different from themselves. Clara has mastered a vital skill that everyone will need to have as our world becomes more diverse.

5. Ability to extract complex information through analysis and consultation of diverse systems.

A relatively new profession, technological-economic consulting has emerged with vigor. It is born of the need to integrate highly technical computer specializations and systems into an economic whole. A Wal-Mart buyer in Bentonville, Arkansas can determine how many blue men's bathing suits are selling in Boise, Idaho or Beijing, China; how many are in the store inventory and the nearest warehouse; when the next shipment will arrive somewhere; how many he or she should order from the factory and when they will be ready. This could not have been done a few years ago. Now, with supply-chain consultants integrating the disciplines of marketing, purchasing, logistics, transportation and the internet, supply chain management is a reality worldwide. We, as consumers, click our mouse in New York and learn that the United Parcel Service package we sent yesterday just arrived at the railroad depot in Milan and will be delivered at nine in the morning to the Milan office on Garibaldi Street.

Consultants and system integrators, proficient in science, medicine, computers, electronics and business, command our attention as never before both within our organizations and in our dealings with others outside. Those who embrace these new systems and are willing to help others master its use will gain an an ear in any group.

6. Having your finger on the pulse of changing trends and styles — "Tell me something I don't know."

A political pundit we know from television conducts a panel discussion each Sunday morning. He closes the program by asking his panelists, "Tell me something I don't know." I always listen carefully to their answers because each comes up with a nugget of information that I am usually unaware of.

The same appetite for new tastes and ideas exists in the workplace. When you tell others something they don't already know they will listen. But like the panelists on the television program you'll have to do some extra work to deliver these useful nuggets. You will have to communicate with your associates and technical networks, both within and outside the organization, to mine the special information not available to them.

III. BEHAVIORS, HABITS AND APPROACHES THAT LEAD TO BEING HEARD AND LISTENED TO

In a world where people have little time to spare and short attention spans, it's not easy to be heard even when your ideas are good. You have to earn the right to be heard through the give and take process of negotiating with others. The behaviors, habits and approaches suggested below will set the stage for being heard and listened to in your own organization and beyond:

Don't shoot from the hip. When someone at a meeting asks for your opinion or position on the subject under discussion and you are not ready to comment, have the courage to say so. We pay too high a price for expressing ourselves before we think things through. If we are wrong, our credibility suffers and with it our power to influence.

People don't waste affection on those who habitually resist or say "No" to ideas proposed to them. They reciprocate by rejecting you or not listening when you speak. Criticizers are never appreciated. Those who don't get in the way and help move things along are welcomed.

Don't hope for the best. People will not accept your brilliant thoughts the moment you utter them. Give acceptance time a chance to work. Having others listen and be influenced takes time and repetition. Be prepared to say what you wish to impart several times at different meetings if you want to increase the probability of acceptance. People are reluctant to give up the "old friends" in their mind for your "new friends" on a moment's notice. Let "acceptance time" do some of the necessary work in changing their minds.

You have more influence than you think. Of course, those positioned at a higher level in the organization are better heard when they speak. It is an advantage but certainly not the only road to influence and power in today's world. Today, what captures the attention of others at work are the tools, techniques and trends that will provide a competitive advantage in the race for economic security and survival. Those closest to the frontiers of knowledge who are smart enough to impart it will be the best listened to. Theirs is the power to teach us how to use the new technology and the many applications they give birth to. Things we need to know.

The time to build good relationships with others is long before troubles arise. It's always easier to talk to those you like and trust, especially when difficulties arise. The problem is that things like trust, respect and good rapport take time to mature.

When in the course of arguing or debating your position, don't belabor the point you are trying to make. Too much of a good argument can reduce its effectiveness in persuading the other. Shakespeare said it best, using salt as a metaphor: "Whereas a little more than enough is by far too much."

For much the same reason, resist the impulse to rebut every negative point the other side makes. There will be other opportunities to raise exceptions after their views are fully heard. In the meantime, take notes and weigh the importance of each exception point you wish to make.

Your thoughts, however valuable, will not be heard when you or others at the meeting are angry or disturbed. Find a better time to make your presentation, or find ways to cool things down before proceeding.

Knowing how your organization or group works allows you to better contribute to its welfare and shape the message you intend to send. There are, in most organizations, if not all, a formal and informal organizational structure existing side by side. The informal organization is not easily seen but is often more important than the formal. Knowing who really talks to whom, makes decisions and allocates resources can help you focus the message for those who really lead.

It's a matter of give and take. If you allow others to speak, most will recognize your right to do so. Courtesy dictates that each party to a disagreement be permitted to complete their thoughts before the other starts. If they do not let you do so, you have the right to insist that they do.

"Tell me something I don't know." People don't listen to those who tell them what they already know. As a person who wants to be heard, you owe it to your colleagues to bring to their attention matters relevant to them and their problems, not yours. The conduit to their attention is your knowledge from experience, work and connections that can be of help to them.

How we express ourselves is as important as what we say. If you want others to give consideration to your thoughts and concerns, take the time to present them in a coherent, interesting way. That's part of the bargain we make with one another at work.

Those on the front line of knowledge by virtue of profession or function in the organization command our attention. Salespeople who, because they meet customers every day, perceive how tastes are changing or where the marketplace is heading are listened to and heard. Such information and knowledge used to move from the top-down, now it moves in the opposite direction.

When meeting to resolve any problem or disagreement give thought to the right time and place. If you fail to do so, your best ideas may fall on deaf ears.

Nobody is perfect. The next time you make a mistake or misspeak at a meeting don't fall apart or retreat from your viewpoint. Acknowledge the mistake and go on. Everybody is wrong once in a while. Defending an error or covering it up creates more problems than it solves.

Those who get involved in planning, strategy and systems always seem to know what is going to happen before it does. They also get closer to the people who make it happen. Get involved in planning whenever you can. When planning people speak, others are likely to hear them out.

Use simple words, phrases and examples to convey viewpoints you stand for. When an audience reads or hears something difficult to understand they immediately try to determine its meaning. They stop listening while sorting it out. President Reagan understood the persuasive power of simplicity. Never known as a great orator, he was nevertheless recognized as an outstanding communicator.

In every field of endeavor those who prepare do better. One of the best ways to prepare for a meeting is to present and defend your views to someone on your team who will act in the role of rebuffing your arguments and lead you to rebuff theirs. This "Devil's Advocate" technique works. Think back for a moment to the worst presentations you have made in the past. How much better would those presentations have been if you had prepared with a Devil's Advocate?

The ability to network with associates is a crucial skill in today's fast-changing economy. No matter how smart or competent you are, you cannot solve the problems that arise without rapport with others on the team and good connections with those who do similar work in your company or associations elsewhere. Part of your job description and value as a member of the group is to be a source of information and contact with others with similar problems and specialties.

Understand the big picture and your role in it. Know how you and others in your department fit into the company revenue and profit stream. This wide perspective will add weight to your arguments that others, without that perspective, do not have. This will also help you separate the small stuff from the larger when internal problems and differences between team members surface.

Things get done in the U.S. Congress the same way they get done in other organizations: through coalition-building rather than between individuals only. When members of a coalition speak they are more likely to be heard. Know how your organization works. Join the coalitions that best express the position you prefer. Coalitions have more "being heard" and bargaining power than individuals.

The experience of being heard becomes possible when you are knowledgeable, set a good example, act in reliable ways and demonstrate involved commitment to group goals. These positive attributes can mean as much or more in terms of influencing others than a lower or higher position on the organization chart.

Being heard and listened to is a negotiation. Set higher goals and you'll do better. Be prepared to do the extra work and take the risks that go with aiming higher. Aiming higher in this context can mean reaching for a larger or more powerful audience, broadening the scope of issues under discussion, asking for a wider range of actions or focusing your message not on a number of existing issues or problems but on the central matter that represents the single issue that is the heart of the matter; that is, the central problem requiring correction or elimination before the others can be fixed or improved.

When people try to negotiate some difference between them but fail, tension rises. I have found from experience that saying something as simple as, "Let's find a better way for both of us," helps reduce the level of tension, especially when I add, "There's always a better way if we look for it together."

It gets our collaborative energies moving in a creative direction and leads to both-win solutions because such outcomes are always possible if we search to find them.

You will sooner or later find yourself in a group or project where a member suffers from what some call "emotional incontinence." These are emotionally challenged people who show little tact or discretion in what they say or do. They create a climate of hostility and defensiveness that stifles productive effort. The team is well advised to rid themselves of such people as quickly as possible.

In the next chapter we will cover the next quadrant of the Virtuous Cycle; that is, the behaviors and approaches that lead to a better exchange of viewpoints, ideas and concerns between members of any team or project. The focus of this chapter will be on what we as members of the group can do to facilitate a candid and unimpeded flow of information and positions between participants.

6

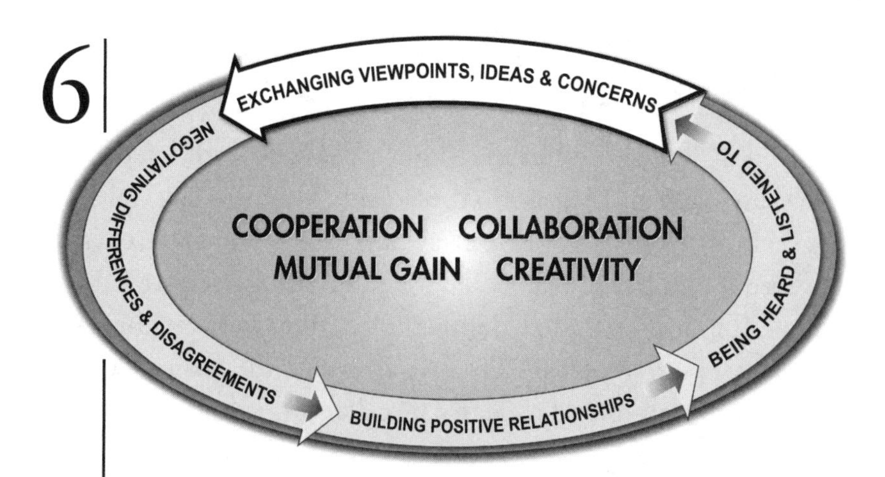

Exchanging Viewpoints, Ideas and Concerns Without Fear and Censure or Criticism

HELPING OTHERS ON BOTH SIDES OF AN ISSUE EXPRESS THEMSELVES

The exchange of information and ideas within an organization starts not with policies or directives from the highest level but with those who interact in solving the problems and differences that emerge. To encourage innovation and collaboration, we as participants must break down the barriers that impede the flow of information from person to person. This is especially important where ideas or differences are in direct conflict and tempers are high.

Let's start with the realities of today's workplace. As members of a modern team or group, we usually associate with people whose technical knowledge is so sophisticated and different from our own that we sometimes find ourselves bewildered by what they are saying. Many of these highly trained specialists have never learned at school or elsewhere how to express themselves in terms familiar to us. Like an international chorus trying to sing "The Star Spangled Banner" in a medley of languages, their voices are poorly heard. Yet, if we are to get the project completed successfully, all must be clearly heard and understood.

We work side-by-side with people who are unlike us in many ways: in terms of culture, language or religious belief. Some prefer to bring bags of food to work that, when opened, overwhelm our sense of smell. Some prefer to relax and speak to others who share their language and make us wonder what they are saying. Some, when expressing themselves, are so sensitive to their heavy accents that they talk in whispers as if wishing that by speaking so quietly they will avoid being contradicted. The American melting pot, more diverse than ever, meets face-to-face more closely on the workplace floor than in any other social setting. Solving the problem of communicating effectively is tethered to our economic well-being.

Whatever our position in the organization, our job responsibility calls for helping others express themselves. We depend on the knowledge of co-workers, suppliers and customers to compete in building our better mousetraps and economic future. Close collaboration is crucial to success.

Improved communication has long been studied and written about. Our focus in this book rests primarily on what we personally can do to facilitate collaboration and an improved flow of ideas and information between those who work together on team and group assignments. The responsibility to help others express themselves better, in my opinion, rests with us as well as with them.

The table below lists five approaches to improved communication that can be implemented by each of us as early as tomorrow. Each behavior and approach is designed to help those we work with express themselves more fully and more comfortably at meetings and group discussions. Both sides of the discussion are sure to gain by doing so.

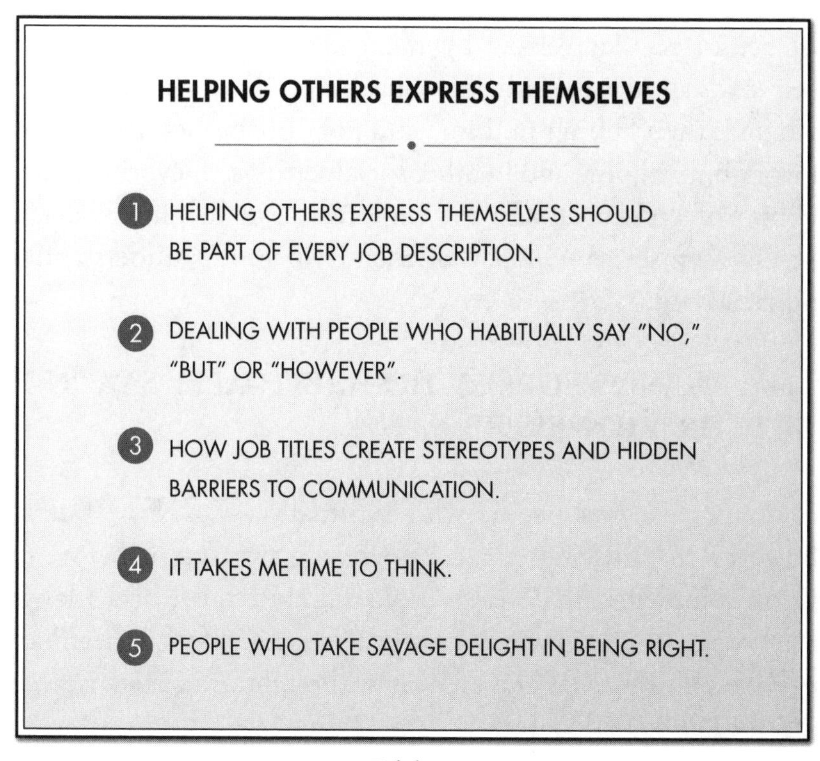
HELPING OTHERS EXPRESS THEMSELVES

1. HELPING OTHERS EXPRESS THEMSELVES SHOULD BE PART OF EVERY JOB DESCRIPTION.
2. DEALING WITH PEOPLE WHO HABITUALLY SAY "NO," "BUT" OR "HOWEVER".
3. HOW JOB TITLES CREATE STEREOTYPES AND HIDDEN BARRIERS TO COMMUNICATION.
4. IT TAKES ME TIME TO THINK.
5. PEOPLE WHO TAKE SAVAGE DELIGHT IN BEING RIGHT.

Exhibit 7

1. HELPING OTHERS EXPRESS THEMSELVES SHOULD BE PART OF EVERY JOB DESCRIPTION

One thing we can do to improve workplace communications immediately is add to every employee's job description the need to help others express themselves, even those with whom they disagree. By doing this we would be making that skill a crucial requirement in getting ahead, as important in some settings as technical competence, high intelligence or personal connections. Every performance review should consider whether the reviewed employee encourages others to express their viewpoints and ideas, and whether he or she is patient when others speak and listens attentively to what they say, however haltingly they may do so.

Subject to regular review by managers, most would improve their skills in helping others to speak up. They would begin to recognize their failings in this regard not only in their interactions at work but at home and in other social settings. Devoting a small portion of each review to the importance of helping associates express themselves will pay dividends in group understanding and creativity.

2. HANDLING PEOPLE WHO HABITUALLY SAY, "NO," "BUT" OR "HOWEVER"

All of us have met people who habitually say, "No," "but" or "however" to anything someone else suggests, often before the person completes their presentation. It's hard to live or work with such a person. Little wonder that their victims feel unheard and deeply resent the way their every new thought or idea is discarded without fair consideration.

There is a consultant in New York who specializes in freeing people from this troublesome habit of saying "No" too quickly. As reported in an article in the New Yorker magazine, he has been hired by corporations to train their most negative executives to behave in a more positive manner when dealing with others at meetings. The fee for this service is paid by the company and is presently restricted to talented higher-level executives who recognize they have a "No" problem and profess a wish to change. The consultant starts by asking the executive about their family and follows that by speaking to family members. Most executives believe that their negativity is confined to the office but are soon surprised to learn that their "No" is as rampant at home and other social settings. They wear their "No" hat almost everywhere.

To stop this habit the consultant imposes a $20 cash fine for each sentence the client speaks starting with the words "no," "but" or "however." One client who opened with a "No" was told, "That will be $20." The client responded immediately to the penalty by saying, "No, no, no." He was then told that this would cost him 40, 60, then 80 out-of-pocket dollars.

$420 in fines was incurred at that session. The executive soon began to recognize how costly this habit would be if he continued doing so. Only later, when the habit receded, did he recognize the high price he had paid at home and work for such negativity. Another insight proved valuable. These managers learned that their reputation for negativity continued long after they managed to control the habit. It was as though their reputation sat with them everywhere: at meetings, at negotiations, in casual conversations and even at social gatherings. People do not connect with those who wear "No" hats. As the consultant wrote in the New Yorker article, "The executive had to improve one hundred percent for his associates to perceive a ten percent positive change."

Those of us who are inclined to be negative can learn to be less so if we recognize this tendency in ourselves. We can pay attention to our words when saying "No," "But" or "However" in response to what someone is saying, and we can choose to stop that non-productive behavior. The more we resist saying these negative words, the easier it will be to drop them from our repertoire. Saying "No," "But" or "However" is a habit we can break by continuous observation and practice at home and at work.

3. HOW JOB TITLES CREATE STEREOTYPES AND HIDDEN BARRIERS TO COMMUNICATION

People at work and elsewhere have prejudices that serve to impede the flow of information between them. Among the worst barriers are those that take root in culture, race, religion or national origin. Much has been written elsewhere about these prejudices and their deleterious effects. Bad as they are, such prejudices are diminishing, to the benefit of all who value equal opportunity and free expression.

We will instead focus here on another, less recognized barrier to communication, and that is the attitudes and stereotypes people have about the jobs others do and the job titles associated with those jobs. We all know that people look up to some kinds of work and down on others. They tend to pay more attention and give greater consideration to those occupations held in higher regard. These hidden attitudes serve to distort the flow of ideas and therefore need to be addressed.

Unfortunately, it is the job titles that contribute in part to communication stereotypes and biases. The job titles people hold tend to elevate the influence of some co-workers and reduce the influence of others. In truth, what people think others do at work by virtue of their job title is usually far from what they really do. Job titles contribute to this disconnect.

I know someone in a high position on a major engineering project who thinks little of those who work in purchasing. In describing them, he says, "All they do is buy whatever and as much as they are told to buy." Instead of finding out what purchasing executives actually do and what is difficult about their work, this engineer scoffs at it to everyone's loss.

At project meetings he barely listens to what they say. He is wrong. I have worked with purchasing professionals in small and large corporations. Their job requires a high level of intelligence and business judgment. They engage in protracted and difficult negotiations over a wide spectrum of ideas, specifications and legal complexities. Supply management is a very important activity in most organizations. When those in supply and procurement speak, it's wise to hear them out.

This type of stereotyping at work applies to many occupations. Medical doctors fail to listen to nurses and technicians whose proximity to the patient provides insights that the doctor, skilled as he or she may be, may not have. I have attended meetings where the words of salespeople, closer than anyone to the marketplace, were dismissed because they were only "low-level salespersons." This casual dismissal of potentially important information would have been more difficult to do had they been sales directors or vice presidents. In that case they would have been heard. Nobody at the meeting could afterward remember that they had been told by the salesperson that the customer had warned that the product line was in jeopardy because a competitor would soon be offering a superior product. Had we in charge listened better to that salesperson and acted quickly, the big account and product line might have been saved.

In today's global economy those closer to the frontier of change may know much more about what is going on than the chief executive officer. They have the information we need to know to survive, whatever their position in the organization or job title.

Few people take the time to learn about the actual work those alongside us do. We make assumptions based on their job titles that never tell the real story. This is especially difficult in the digital age where so much of what we do cannot be observed. Output is invisible. Work done by a team member today may not be recognized as successful until the project ends years from now. No job description or title can tell the story. Dig deeper to gain a more full understanding of what your co-workers really do.

Job titles and the stereotypes they create inhibit communication unless we dig deeper. The more we know about the work associates actually do and the more they know of ours the easier it will be to settle differences and make sound decisions. It will also help in building rapport and stronger long-term relationships. People generally enjoy talking about what they do if asked in a non-judgmental and casual manner.

4. IT TAKES ME TIME TO THINK

A friend told me this story about his son. When the boy was in the first grade the teacher called his parents to the office. The teacher, in the presence of the boy, told them that their son never answered when asked a question in class. Instead he looked at the teacher in embarrassed silence. When asked why, he said nothing; the boy looked down and refused to talk. Seeing this, the boy's mother tried to elicit why he didn't say a word when asked. He said in a whisper so low the teacher could not hear, "It takes me time to think."

It is now many years since that meeting. The boy, now a man of fifty, is a successful businessman. It still takes him time to think.

Associates, recognizing his intellect, give him plenty of time to think. It's worth the wait. He sees the world in ways most do not and that's what helps him do well.

Many, like this man, fail to express themselves for the same reason. By the time they muster their thoughts others have captured the stage. If such people are handled patiently, or provided an opportunity to think or plan in advance, they could give us the benefit of their really good ideas.

5. PEOPLE WHO TAKE SAVAGE DELIGHT IN BEING RIGHT

Recently I saw a cartoon the New Yorker that perfectly described a difficult person with whom I worked for years. The cartoon pictured an executive at a large desk surrounded by others seated at a meeting in his office. It showed the executive with a joyous smile on his face pounding a huge gong. Everyone at the meeting looked glum except him. One whispered to another, "Every time he's right, he smiles and hits that gong."

My co-worker Herb was like that. We were both managers in the contracts department of a major aerospace company. As peers we had many occasions to meet and lunch together. Herb was an exceptionally bright and disciplined person but awful to have lunch or work with. Those who directly reported to him were terribly unhappy.

Herb not only enjoyed being right but set the stage for his own success. With peers at meetings he moved the talks to subjects they were having problems with. With subordinates he challenged every estimate and assumption they made. At lunch with me he steered the conversation to areas of work where his section and mine required special coordination. The trouble was that I came to lunch to eat; he came, I believe, to experience the joy of telling me what I had to do. I always left lunch with a list of assignments written on soiled napkins and the feeling that future lunches or meetings were to be avoided.

Herb did this with everyone. It wasn't that he was often right. He was. His suggestions, if I can call them that, were mostly well-considered, correct and necessary. What bothered me and others was that he brought along that big gong and joyous smile whenever he was right. Why have a relationship or communicate with someone like that unless you absolutely have to. What amazes me so many years later is that Herb never recognized his problem and that none of us chose to tell him.

HELPING TO OPEN A WIDER EXCHANGE OF VIEWPOINTS: WHAT TEAM LEADERS AND GROUP MANAGERS CAN DO

Department managers and team or project leaders play a similar and challenging role in conducting effective group meetings. What they must strive for is a brisk exchange of relevant viewpoints. They want members to openly share ideas and discuss their concerns about the project and other matters that trouble them. Conducting such meetings requires preparation. The alternative to a high level of preparation is chaos and drift.

Meetings of the Los Angeles school board provide an example of such wasteful drift. A recent Los Angeles Times editorial describes a typical board meeting. As a long-time resident of this city I cannot help but wonder if our public schools will ever improve.

Board meetings, the editorial points out, are characterized mainly by drawn out debates over minutiae. Members indulge in long-winded repetitive speeches after spending long periods honoring people that few in the meeting have heard of or care about. As the meetings drag on, members of the board peer into their laptop computers, keep an eye on cell phones, look at tweets or check what has to be done for the rest of the day and what's new in the news. They have no qualms about interrupting speakers or whispering to each other on the side. Meetings generally start at 1 p.m. and drift slowly into evening. People who have come to speak cool their heels for hours before speaking or give up trying and leave.

The editorial goes on to say that it doesn't have to be this way. The Times then contrasts Boston school board meetings with those in Los Angeles. Boston meetings start at 6 p.m. and end in two hours. No e-mails, text messages or side conversations are allowed. Those who speak are expected to come to the point. Time is not wasted on non-business matters like meaningless anniversaries or celebrating people still living at 100 years of age. Interruptions are unacceptable except in emergencies.

Those in charge of meetings at work should run them like the Boston School Board. Their responsibility is to make efficient use of their associates' talents and time. By insisting on a high level of preparation, courtesy and self-discipline on the part of those attending, associates will feel they belong and are appreciated. They will in turn contribute their thoughts more candidly. Trust and respect are likely to grow in such a climate along with creativity.

Creativity, in my opinion, is born of necessity and disagreement as to how and what needs to be done and how. Ready agreement between people and commands from above on how to solve problems do not lead to inventiveness. Team leaders and department managers who welcome collaboration and are unafraid of dissent will enjoy a higher level of group creativity than those who dampen differences or wish them away. Leaders who criticize, preach or judge associates in front of others, or behind their backs, also serve to reduce the flow of creative energy and group contribution to innovative solutions.

LEARNING FROM THE CHINESE – WAYS TO SAY "NO" WITHOUT CLOSING THE TALKS

Business people in the Western world tend to say "No" too quickly when confronted with an idea or offer they do not like. The Chinese, like the Japanese, are not so inclined. They rarely say "No" directly to any request, idea or proposal and resist in less confrontational ways that encourage the flow of information and later allow for compromise or accommodation without loss of face. The Chinese are especially wary of jeopardizing relationships that have taken years to build.

What follows are a number of approaches to saying "No" or showing resistance without threatening existing relationships or closing the door to further consideration. To say that these techniques are exclusively Chinese or Japanese in origin would be incorrect, but it would be accurate to notice that they have been developed to an extraordinary degree by both cultures would be accurate.

Here are 17 ways in which the Chinese traditionally say "No" without saying it.

- They attribute their negativity to themselves rather than to the other's proposal by saying, "I can't afford to do it that way," or, "It does not suit our organization's product mix," or, "We are over-invested in other projects at this time and cannot afford that approach."

- They acknowledge the other's position or proposal with a considered response; that is, they stop talking, write or calculate something on a piece of paper, nod their head and say, "It's hard to see how we can work it out that way."

- They attribute resistance to higher authority or pass it on for further consideration.

- They raise a question about something related to the matter under discussion that entails a lengthy, complicated answer and invites further inquiry.

- When others in the organization are concerned, as they always are, they use phrases like "We cannot," or, "It will be difficult for us," instead of, "I cannot" or, "It will be difficult for me."

- They point out, to paraphrase Ben Franklin, "I can see how, under certain circumstances, what you propose can be so, but it does not appear that it applies well to this situation."

- They sometimes change the subject to something else, relevant or not.

- They remain silent and wait for the other to fill the void. I am familiar with a well-known consultant who mailed a services proposal to an Admiral in the Navy who had earlier indicated some enthusiasm for his ideas. It was a relatively complex project involving two million dollars in fees. The Admiral never acknowledged the proposal by saying "No," nor did he answer by phone or letter. When the consultant called he was told that the Admiral was on the road but still considering the offer. The consultant called several times to no avail, and then tried something else. He revised the proposed price downward by twenty percent and mailed it once again. It was then that the Admiral responded and invited him to San Diego for further negotiations. After protracted talks they settled at $1.3 million.

- They respond to the design proposal or offer with an ambiguous phrase such as, "That's interesting," or, "That appears possible or correct." Or they say "Maybe" or "Perhaps" without elaborating or explaining precisely what they mean.

- They say nothing but let their body language reveal discomfort and negative leanings.

- They respond negatively by slowly shaking their head, but add a ray of hope by saying, "That script might be possible if we could get Bill Clinton to play the president's part," or, "If you were to pay 40 million dollars extra perhaps we might agree." Both parties to the negotiation then recognize that what has been suggested is not possible to work out.

- They show they understand our position but nod their head in a sign of sadness to indicate that it can't be helped.

- They say "No" or show resistance by ignoring your request or offer. Rather than saying "No," they repeat their prior position as though your request had never been spoken. North Korea did this on a daily basis for years in negotiations with the Americans during the Korean War. It drove our diplomats half mad.

- Whatever they say that implies "No" is usually contradicted by the trace of a smile of regret or a touch of "We wish we could but cannot."

- They reschedule the matter for later consideration and do so again and again.

- They find among the proposed mix of ideas and designs a few that might be possible and ignore those that do not fit.

- They whistle lightly through their teeth or say, "tsk."

At first glance it might appear to us in the Western world that the Chinese aversion to saying "No" is merely a tactical approach to dealing with others. I believe it to be far more than that. I believe that it serves a beneficial purpose in their business and social affairs. Instead of narrowing or closing doors to further discourse, as the word "No" does, the Chinese approach says, "Tell me more and I may be able to see it your way." It leaves negotiating space for give and take and Both-Win® ideas that a firm "No" closes off. It helps preserve the relationship by reducing loss of face for the other side.

As trade between East and West grows, we can expect that Chinese and Western attitudes toward saying "No" will become more similar. Yet, it seems to me that the fundamental values the Chinese strive to achieve by avoiding a direct "No" will be increasingly accepted over time by western men and women as a more effective, less confrontational way of conducting business or negotiating diplomatic affairs.

HOW BEST TO PROMOTE THE EXCHANGE OF IDEAS – ADVICE FROM BEN FRANKLIN

Ben Franklin was a street-smart businessman as well as politician. As a youth he was prone to making overly strong assertions in promoting positions. Later he learned to modify his assertions to gain wider acceptance. What he advised over two hundred years ago is relevant today.

> "I make it a rule to forbear all direct contradictions to the sentiments of others, and all positive assertion of my own. I even forbade myself the use of every word or expression in the language that imported a fix'd opinion, such as 'certainly,' 'undoubtedly,' etc., and I adopted instead of them, 'I conceive,' 'I apprehend,' or 'I imagine' a thing to be so or so; or 'it appears to me at present.' When another asserted something that I thought an error, I deny'd myself the pleasure of contradicting him abruptly, and of showing immediately some absurdity in his proposition; and in answering I began by observing that in certain cases or circumstances his opinion would be right but in the present case there appear'd or seem'd to me some difference.
>
> I soon found the advantage of this change in my manner; the conversations I engag'd in went on more pleasantly. The modest way in which I propos'd my opinions procur'd them a readier reception and less contradiction; I had less mortification when I was found to be in the wrong, and I

more easily prevail'd with others to give up their mistakes and join with me when I happened to be in the right.

And this mode, which I at first put on with some violence to natural inclination, became at length so easy, and so habitual to me, that perhaps for these fifty years past no one has ever heard a dogmatical expression escape me. And to this habit (after my character of integrity) I think it principally owing that I had early so much weight with my fellow citizens when I proposed new institutions, or alterations in the old, and so much influence in public councils when I became a member; for I was but a bad speaker, never eloquent, subject to much hesitation in my choice of words, hardly correct in language, and yet I generally carried my points."

As Ben Franklin makes clear, the art of winning agreement and building relationships with others he disagreed with was not a skill he was blessed with. Rather, it was a learned discipline born of necessity and a discipline we are all capable of acquiring through practice.

I will now suggest a number of behaviors and approaches that lead to better communication and understanding in the workplace. Both persons involved in a dispute or difference of opinion stand to gain when each encourages and help the other to express himself or herself more effectively.

BEHAVIORS, HABITS AND APPROACHES THAT ENCOURAGE OTHERS TO EXPRESS THEMSELVES

1. Even a single person acting alone in a group can exert a positive or negative effect on how the entire group will listen and exchange

views. When interruptions or cross talk occur, that person can insist that the person speaking be accorded full attention or, by allowing the disruption to go unchecked, make matters worse. If you want others to express themselves well, offer them a ready audience and platform to do so.

2. Getting others to speak up and express their views fully is a negotiation. If you want them to expand their views about some matter, ask them to do so. They may be reluctant to tell all they know because they are shy or apprehensive about whether you are interested. A comment like, "Tell me more," "Help me understand," or, "Please explain that," may be helpful in getting a better explanation. As for those in the group or team who are reluctant to speak at all, a good way to get them started is to ask their opinion of the matter at hand. As in any negotiation, if you don't ask for something, you're not likely to get it.

3. The higher the ratio of pleasant and positive interactions between team members to negative ones, the more team members will feel free to express themselves. Simple social actions such as a welcoming smile, a warm hello or an occasional lunch together serve to show respectful attention and regard. Each interaction adds to the others and strengthens the milieu in which open expression thrives.

4. Too many people use and manipulate what other people say as a springboard to speak about what they themselves want to say. They do it in two ways. Either they wait until the speaker says something that allows them to divert the conversation in their preferred direction, or they jump in with questions that are really statements leading into their own preferred positions. Both trespass on the speaker's space and should be avoided.

5. Another habit that cuts the flow of ideas at a meeting may originate with the person in charge who gives only casual attention to the issues under consideration as it quickly becomes obvious that he or she has already made up their mind about what is to be done. Once this bias becomes apparent, others lose interest in expressing alternatives. I've wasted time at many such meetings and resented being used that way.

6. Be patient. If people are given more time to think and get prepared they do a better job of expressing their thoughts. No matter how smart someone appears to be, it takes them time to put together what they want to say and to decide what their position is on any matter. Some, of course, are quicker than others, but that in itself does not ensure that their input will be more valuable. Those who are slower and more methodical may have the best ideas. Without time to sort out their thoughts they may choose to say nothing. Be patient.

7. Benjamin Disraeli, Prime Minister of Great Britain under Queen Victoria, once said, "Good rules make it easier to do right." His advice applies as much to international conferences as it does to dealing with associates at business meetings. Among the rules that keep order at meetings are agreement among participants that interruptions not be permitted, that emails and phone calls be avoided, that text messages not be sent or answered and that questions be saved until the speaker or team leader designates.

Resist the impulse to rebut or answer every point the other person makes with which you disagree. Many points will disappear from their thinking or lose importance without a word from you. Some can be put into another context later and then be better handled. Your opportunity to express opposition or support won't be lost forever.

8. The stronger the relationship between parties prior to a meeting, the more forthright their exchange of viewpoints and concerns will be. One of the great joys of work is sharing ideas with someone you get along with. It's a habit that builds upon itself even when your ideas differ.

9. Trust and mutual respect are the catalysts that allow people in a group to share ideas and express their views and concerns. These attitudes are especially important when the project is complex and diverse opinions essential for making sound decisions. Without mutual trust and respect people will not risk speaking out.

10. Members of a team who have deep accents or are otherwise hard to understand are reluctant to speak in group settings for two good reasons: not only do they find it hard to formulate their thoughts in a new and less familiar language, they are also fearful they will be turned off by the very listeners they wish to please. The best approach when dealing with those so challenged is to accord them an extra measure of patience. As for those who have heavy accents, they owe it to the group and to themselves to improve as quickly as possible rather than retreat in silence, anger or despair.

11. Expressing oneself clearly and succinctly is hard enough. Speaking to someone who thinks he knows what you are going to say and says it for you before you do makes matters worse. I worked for a boss like that and disliked every meeting we had to be together.

He did it with me and with others in the department. Whenever we made a presentation or said something in the course of a meeting he would not let us finish. He would pick up on something we were saying and carry on in his own words. It quickly became his presentation, not ours. If what he said was not what we had in mind, it became difficult to openly contradict him.

12. Interruptions of meetings by people who are trying to be funny also impede the flow of ideas. I, like most of you, am all for humor in business. What I find disturbing are those who cannot resist the impulse to make humorous remarks that are out of context. If your joke or remark is good but out of context then tell it later or elsewhere so that it won't impede the flow of the meeting.

13. Nothing cuts the flow of ideas like criticism. Criticism is never welcome and generally does more harm than good. Frequent praise and infrequent criticism are keys to better communication and stronger relationships.

14. Fully involved listening acknowledges that the other has reasons for taking the positions they choose. These reasons deserve understanding even when you do not agree. This is a major concession we can all afford to make.

15. In order to speak out fully without fear of criticism one must feel accepted by the team or group. Without acceptance and the sense of group cohesion that goes with it, the best ideas are likely to be left unspoken. Acceptance has been called the "fertile soil that brings ideas to light."

16. Your body language sends a powerful signal to those wishing to express themselves. It can cut them off or encourage them. Rubbing your nose, frowning, folding your arms, nodding your head in drowsiness or signifying "No" by shrugging your shoulders impedes the flow of ideas. Those of us who have spoken before

audiences know how sensitive we are to body clues, both positive and negative.

17. When introducing someone new to the project or asking them to speak, give them a good introduction that adds stature to their work and position. It will not only encourage others to listen closely to what they say and better appreciate their contributions, it will also better connect them to the group.

18. Hostile questions have no place in internal negotiations or discussions. Neither do television show questions requiring "Yes" or "No" answers, such as those used in some of the television courtroom performances. Both serve to threaten rather than promote exposition. Far better are inquiries that show genuine interest in the subject and an eagerness to know more of the story surrounding the issue or matter under review.

19. A negotiated pre-meeting agenda kept on track creates the best opportunity for all viewpoints to be heard.

20. Rational discourse stops when people argue or scream at one another. Nobody wins an argument, nor can much be learned from it. The personification of issues that usually follows from argument makes it harder to reach agreement.

7 The Art of Softening Disagreements Before They Harden

Sandra Day O'Connor, the first woman justice of the United States Supreme Court, was once asked by a television talk-show host, "Did you find it hard as a woman to deal with the other justices, all men?" She said, "It was not easy because I was the odd justice of the nine. The eight were evenly balanced in many cases. In different ways we were all somewhat odd. I had to learn in the twenty-six years of working with them every day to disagree agreeably." Upon retirement, Justice O'Connor won great respect for doing so well with such a difficult and talented group. This chapter is about how to disagree agreeably.

Making organizational choices, whether in budgeting resources or designing new products, invariably involves informed argument between strong individuals with differing backgrounds, perspectives and motivations. The quality of such decisions depends on whether diverse viewpoints can freely emerge and how disagreements between participants are handled to reach consensus.

Informed and well-explored disagreement that allows for self-aware exploration of the issues at hand is the key to making better and more creative group decisions. Executives and team leaders should embrace, indeed welcome, informed disagreement. This sets the stage for a courteous exchange of member perspectives and concerns at meetings, which in turn will improve the participation level and creativity of the entire group.

The difficulty in fostering creative disagreement in the workplace arises when those who disagree harden their differences by becoming disagreeable as they argue points of view. What too often ensues is acrimony and divisiveness as things get out of control. The illustration that follows shows how a small disagreement in our office became a real problem in a short time.

It happened this way. An advertising agency handles our brochure work. Brochure designers at the agency work in teams of two consisting of a copywriter and an artist skilled not only in drawing but computer graphics. Both are creative people who work with us to find suitable brochure themes. Once a theme is selected they come up with words, ideas, layouts and graphic images to match the selected theme. Some of their ideas are really wild, others humorous, still others purely informational. Generally, we at the office review their suggestions, make changes and, after several iterations, make a decision. Disagreements between them and us frequently arise but are usually manageable. We are rarely privy to differences between them and within their organization.

Not this time. It wasn't as though the copywriter and graphic artist hadn't worked together as a team before. They had collaborated for three years. Their disagreement with us arose regarding their choice of brochure photos to represent attendees at typical seminars. While we had all previously agreed that the brochure would contain pictures of attendees listening to a speaker, nothing had been decided as to exactly what was to be pictured. We awaited their recommendations and sample photos.

The moment our meeting with the agency started they began to argue among themselves. The graphic artist insisted that the choice of photo composition fell into his domain, not that of the copywriter. He believed that a picture showing the face and torso of several male and female executives at a table listening intently to someone unseen speaking was perfect for our brochure. The copywriter replied tartly that he favored a photo showing two men or women at the water cooler disagreeing about which report was best. Suddenly, to our consternation as customers, the style and composition of the photos and brochure was not the problem. Their dislike for one another was.

It got worse. The copywriter continued to say that the other always put him and his ideas down. He shouted that the graphic artist was completely "nuts"; his choice of drawings, photos and ideas were a waste of time. He insisted that the graphic artist was in this case dead wrong, and had missed the theme of our program entirely.

Frankly, we were embarrassed at the outburst. A simple difference of opinion had exploded into open conflict, recrimination and criticism. Personal slights with origins in the past had intruded into what was, from our perspective, a simple disagreement. The past is always partner to any dispute and, as in most situations like this, only made things worse.

After further shouting, we helped redirect the matter by specifying in greater detail what we wanted: one or two pictures of attendees at a seminar listening to a speaker, and two or three photos of male and female executives at a conference table speaking to one another while trying to settle a pricing, design or budget difference.

The next day the advertising agency found some archive photos that matched our needs and incorporated them into our brochure. Looking back at the affair, I think that the best picture might well have been a before and after photograph of the two advertising men actually arguing then settling this dispute in our office. It's too late now for that picture.

In the past, differences and disagreements in the workplace were discouraged or buried. Today's executives are more willing to expose conflicting ideas to open and rational debate. The problem is that those involved tend all too soon to add strong emotional content to the issues under contention, thereby heating the debate. Instead of focusing on the merits of opposing positions, each side attacks and disparages the opposition. By doing so they make it harder to reach agreement.

This, of course, is counterproductive. Disagreements between people at work can be softened long before and even after they arise if we recognize the danger of hardening differences and take steps to avoid it. We will start with how the Chinese do so and then consider the question of criticism from two points of view: first, its negative effects; second, how to speak constructively if we have to criticize at all.

HOW THE CHINESE SOFTEN DIFFERENCES BEFORE AND AFTER THEY ARISE

The Chinese place great value on the development of interpersonal harmony and trust long before differences arise. This heavy investment in building strong relationships helps dissipate the heat of disagreement before it envelops them in dysfunctional animosity. In this section we will consider three approaches taken by the Chinese to manage disagreement to keep it from getting out of control.

THE QUANXI TRADITION

The Chinese investment in social harmony begins with what they call the QUANXI tradition, a tradition that began millennia before the current Chinese industrial revolution. Friendship and allegiance to the family were promoted and developed at an early age. Each person in the immediate and extended family including uncles, aunts and cousins as well as second and third extensions were governed by widely accepted standards as to what constituted proper courtesy and tact in dealing with one another. The "QUANXI" culture emphasized the importance of obedience and deferral to those above you, not only in family affairs but also in business and social matters. In effect, the rules established in dealing with others were well-understood and accepted in a wide variety of circumstances.

Today, in China's complex industrial economy, QUANXI is less frequently attributed to family relationships but lives on in business-based connections, relationships or networks based on trust and reliability. Chinese business people invest significant time in getting close to those they deal with.

They build ongoing relationships not only on a company-to-company level but also on a personal basis both prior to a sale and long afterward. Networks with intersecting entities like banks, suppliers, customers, trade networks and governments are nurtured, knowing that the QUANXI tradition of mutual "back-scratching" and exchange of favors will help them reduce bureaucratic friction and win more business later.

QUANXI, whether in family affairs or business, makes it easier to cope with discord and conflict by setting limits on the dysfunctional aspects of disagreement. Differences in status, age, gender, connections, intellect and motivation are recognized and afforded courtesy and consideration. Emotional outbursts, casual interruptions and disrespect are softened.

CHINESE ATTITUDES AND APPROACHES TOWARD THE PROCESS OF NEGOTIATING DIFFERENCES.

Chinese civilization flourished when we in the Western world still wore bearskins. Through millennia of prosperity and hard times they have learned to place great value on patience, perseverance, hard work and thrift. These values affect how they deal with each other in the marketplace and with foreign negotiators in international affairs.

Many of the negotiating approaches that the Chinese practice in business affairs serve to reduce disagreements before they become unmanageable. These approaches toward dealing with people are just as applicable when handling workplace disputes. They have evolved over the centuries as culturally acceptable techniques for resolving internal conflicts in a face-saving and friendlier way.

When negotiating a difficult or complex problem, the Chinese prefer to discuss issues at great length. They find it useful to haggle over less important matters and spend lots of time getting to know and trust one another on a personal level. The context of the deal and the conversations surrounding it substitute, in many ways, for the absence of a well-established Chinese legal system to settle contentious issues that may arise later. This differs markedly from the Western world, which relies on detailed written contracts and an adversarial legal system to settle disputes.

For the Chinese the process of negotiating is as important as the agreement, the ways of dealing as important as the ends; the give and take of bargaining, concessions, context and information exchange more important than the words in the contract. Long-term harmony is often more important than profit. Likewise, good relationships are more valuable than short-term outcome.

Most American business executives prefer not to spend much time on "non-task" talk when engaging in business with others. They generally consider time spent on lengthy dinners and all night heavy drinking sessions to be of limited value. Not so the Chinese. They feel that personal talk in social settings cements relationships and softens disagreements in ways that purely task-directed talk cannot.

The Chinese reluctance to saying "no" in almost any social or business situation was addressed in Chapter Six. In negotiation, the word "no" is rarely heard in response to any request, idea, viewpoint or proposal offered them no matter how much they dislike it. Americans, on the other hand, say "no" too quickly, sometimes before they even understand what has been expressed.

THE SPECIAL ROLE OF SAVING FACE IN CHINESE CULTURE.

The Chinese place a high value on face-saving in both negotiation and everyday affairs. They try to leave the other a graceful way to retreat from any position taken. They take the time to frame their opposition in such a way that the other can agree without losing the good regard of associates. They do this in several ways.

The key to leaving the other side a face-saving way to retreat from their position lies not in manipulation or the clever phraseology of a demand or offer. It rests on conditioning the request for concession or other benefit on the motivations of the concession-maker and the values they wish to achieve.

For example, a buyer asking a seller for a further concession or benefit to close a deal might say, "I know from past experience that you are a fair and reasonable person, a person who believes that good business depends on a well-satisfied customer who benefits from the exchange. Your offer to sell at that price is appreciated but leaves us little room for healthy growth. We believe a lower price will benefit both of us because it would allow us to sell more to our customers and therefore buy more from you." The seller who concedes to such a request does so without loss of face.

Another way to save face for those they oppose is by handling threats carefully. When, in the heat of negotiation, they are tempted to threaten someone, they avoid it. Threat, whether carried out or not, demeans the other. It treats them like a child. Threat, not carried out, results in loss of face for the threatener.

On the other hand, when threatened, they respond by making light of it by saying, "You wouldn't do a thing like that to someone like us." Such a remark makes it easier for the threatener to later desist with little loss of face.

A third way to soften loss of face for the other and yourself lies in following Ben Franklin's advice as shown in Chapter Six. Ben Franklin opens his essay, "I make it a rule to forbear all direct contradictions to the sentiments of others, and all positive assertion of my own." He summarizes at the close with these words: "And to this habit I think it principally owing that I had early so much weight with my fellow citizens when I proposed new institutions and so much influence in public councils." Ben Franklin was from an early age extraordinarily sensitive to saving face for others and himself.

In conclusion, the Chinese, in their desire for social and business harmony, have built strong defenses against dysfunctional disagreement. Most important are the "QUANXI" tradition that provides family and friendship channels that serve to reduce the level of dissension in business, social and family affairs, as well as the tradition of "saving face," which allows for gracious give and take, and retreat in place of continued discord.

Because both sides share deep-seated cultural roots governing tact and courtesy, and have developed trusted connections who are readily available to act as mediators, they are better able to resolve disputes that might otherwise be intractable.

CRITICISM AND ITS NEGATIVE EFFECTS

In his best-selling book, Benjamin Franklin; An American Life, Walter Isaacson describes Franklin's little known contribution to the Declaration of Independence. His role tells us much about constructive criticism and Franklin's wisdom.

Thomas Jefferson was selected by the Continental Congress delegates to write the Declaration of Independence in June 1776 after John Adams and Ben Franklin chose not to. On June 21, after incorporating changes from Adams, Thomas Jefferson sent a draft to Franklin asking him to suggest possible changes.

Franklin made only one major change and a few very small ones. The major change concerned Jefferson's phrase in the draft, "We hold these truths to be sacred and undeniable." Franklin favored, "We hold these truths to be self-evident," as an assertion based on rationality rather than religion.

Members of the Continental Congress voted for independence on July 2 after which they further edited Jefferson's declaration draft. Five paragraphs were deleted as well as several entire sections, much to Jefferson's chagrin. The final document as we know it was adopted on July 4, 1776.

Franklin was well aware that others in the Continental Congress would take pains to further edit Jefferson's draft. He also knew that Jefferson took great pride in his ability to write well. After many years as editor and publisher of his own newspaper, Franklin was certainly able to recognize the excesses in Thomas Jefferson's draft.

Yet, he chose to alter only three words, a change he could defend on rational and philosophical grounds. His criticism was as minimal as possible and based on sound reasoning. He understood the sensitivity of his friend Jefferson to criticism and sought to soften its sting.

Few of us are as wise as Ben Franklin. Yet, as managers, peers or supervisors, we are often placed in the position of taking exception to how or what another person or subordinate is doing. It is not a pleasant role, one that if poorly handled can reap havoc with any relationship, even a good one. The rest of this chapter will concern itself with constructive feedback: how best to criticize if you have to.

Most managers see criticism as a necessary part of their job responsibility in getting what needs to be done completed within designated quality, time and cost standards. What they wish to do is encourage subordinates or others to do the work in a better manner or to rid themselves of a certain dysfunctional habit that impedes their effectiveness. They generally do not wish to punish the person criticized, but instead view their action as constructive and appropriate.

Some people criticize for unconstructive purposes. They seek not to improve but to raise their own self-respect at the expense of another. By finding fault or lashing out in anger at imperfections, they strive to establish their own dominance or superiority. I have even attended professional conferences where people criticized other professionals by pointing out petty errors in their reasoning or analysis for no reason but to look good. Criticism for these purposes is never constructive, guaranteed to do more harm than good to both recipient and sender.

Whatever the reason, well-intended or not, there is far more criticism at work than need be. Most psychologists agree that criticism does not lead people to change behavior. Instead it creates anger and defensiveness on the part of the person criticized. Communication between the parties is shackled, and positive relationships impeded.

Yet, we are left with a paradox. On the one hand criticism is ineffective, if not harmful. On the other hand, some criticism at work is certainly part of the habitual interaction of managers and subordinates everywhere. People at work do indeed fail to follow directions or make mistakes and need guidance in doing work correctly.

The trouble is that, as managers, we may unintentionally provide negative feedback to another even when we try to help them change as carefully as possible. For reasons beyond our control, the other may interpret our best intentions as faultfinding and resent both message and messenger. Constructive criticism that minimizes resentment is a difficult act to balance.

CRITICISM AND THE PSYCHOLOGICAL FLYWHEEL

In Chapter Four we introduced the Psychological Flywheel and described how its rate of spin affected self-confidence and well-being. When we are criticized, our psychological flywheel begins to spin more slowly. If someone we work with, be it our boss or peer, takes fault with our work, it slows our wheel. If they do so over and over again our flywheel almost comes to a standstill. We become depressed and retaliate by finding subtle ways to do less or to absent ourselves from the problem.

Being criticized in front of others has an even more devastating effect. The humiliation of public loss of face is never forgotten. It waits to be avenged overtly or in whispers when opportunity arises.

Every few months we read of an office or factory worker gone berserk. They return to the workplace after being terminated or otherwise humiliated by their boss or co-workers for long periods of time with guns ablaze killing everyone in sight. It is as though their psychological flywheel has reached its limit. Sufficiently distressed, not only has the flywheel slowed down and stopped, it has begun to spin violently out of control or in reverse.

Criticism, even when done in private, slows the flywheel. A friend, a good writer with far better than average skills in expressing herself, told me of a supervisor she worked for. A fussy boss, he criticized her reports not only for analytical content but also for irrelevant grammatical matters. Angered by this constant criticism, but needing the job, she gradually changed her approach. The reports became less analytical, the sentences shorter, the words one syllable in length. Little was left to find fault with. She left the firm soon after for a job that better appreciated her talents and allowed her to sort these matters out for herself. Now, two years later and vice president of the firm, her flywheel spins well.

That's the way frequent criticism works not only on writers but also on medical doctors, engineers, computer programmers and factory employees. Not only does it reduce their creativity and inclination to do good work, it leads them to retreat in search of emotional security.

Criticism also plays a harmful role at team meetings. What we want as managers or team leaders are associates who feel free to express their ideas and concerns without fear of censure. What we get instead is the opposite: brilliant engineers or scientists who are apprehensive about speaking up because they are cowed by others more forceful, articulate or blatantly critical of anything they disagree with.

Most of us have attended weekly department meetings and heard door-closing expressions like "That's crazy," "That won't work," "That's way off," or, "We tried that last year and it failed." These door-closers, directed at the person proposing a new approach or idea, act to stop the flow of information in its tracks. Not only does it serve to stop the person under attack, it tends to mute others in the room as well. Who would want to go through such an inquisition when it could so easily be avoided by keeping quiet?

What should be our role as an associate or member of the project team? It is to recognize the negative effects of criticism and "door-closing" expressions on those speaking, and to support the leader in quieting such expressions the moment they take place. Our role is also to encourage the leader to negotiate and stick to an agenda that allows the presenters to fully express themselves and gets associates the answers they need. Unless meeting leaders have the full support of the group, they will fail to develop the collaboration necessary to create the new products and services we sorely need to compete on a world stage.

WHEN CONSTRUCTIVE FEEDBACK WORKS BEST

When a subordinate does something wrong or fails to follow directions, most managers feel justified correcting their behavior by speaking to them in a constructive manner. If this constructive feedback is done well the individual may move toward positive change. If done poorly it will leave a trail of hurt feelings and result in little or no behavioral change. In the balance of this chapter we will explore several approaches to constructive feedback designed to help others move in a positive direction.

WHEN CONSTRUCTIVE FEEDBACK WORKS BEST

1. WHEN YOU MAINTAIN A HIGH RATIO OF POSITIVE TO NEGATIVE INTERACTIONS
2. WHEN YOUR RELATIONSHIP WITH THE OTHER IS GOOD
3. WHEN IT IS ASKED FOR – BUT
4. WHEN IT IS ACCEPTED AS PART OF THE TRAINING PROCESS
5. WHEN THE CRITICISM OR ADVICE IS SPECIFIC AND TIMELY
6. WHEN BOTH PARTIES ARE INVOLVED IN HELPING TO SOLVE THE PROBLEM TOGETHER
7. WHEN THE FEEDBACK IS PRECEDED BY STRONG POSITIVES
8. WHEN THE ADVICE ALLOWS THE OTHER TO SORT THINGS OUT FOR THEMSELVES

Exhibit 8

1. WHEN YOU MAINTAIN A HIGH RATIO OF POSITIVE TO NEGATIVE INTERACTIONS.

One of the worst managers I ever worked for was Harry. The only time I heard from Harry was when I did something wrong or when our weekly reports indicated some failure to meet an objective. When things went well, as it did most of the time, not a word was heard from him.

Anyone who has worked for such a person knows how you feel when they approach. You say to yourself, "What now?" and wait for the worst. Their criticism is deeply resented. You can't wait for them to finish with you and go on to someone else. And they do, because chronic criticizing is a bad habit; being somewhat addictive, it can be very hard to break.

Whatever your position in the organization hierarchy today, you will someday be in charge of others and their work. Situations will arise in which your constructive feedback will be called for. The manager who maintains a high ratio of positive to negative feedback will find their peers and subordinates more receptive to change. Later, by maintaining a good ratio over time, your words of advice when things go wrong will fall on friendlier ears.

2. WHEN YOUR RELATIONSHIP WITH THE OTHER IS GOOD.

Criticism, even when directed with the best of intentions, is hard to take. When the relationship between parties is strained, it is rarely effective and certain to be resented. The rule is simple: the stronger the bond between the parties the higher the probability the feedback will be accepted and acted upon.

If you want subordinates to pay attention to your advice and feedback, put goodwill into the bank long before criticism is necessary. A smile, an acknowledgement or a few minutes of small talk goes a long way. Knowing a little about their family and their interests helps. If they know you care and respect their contributions they will be more open to your help and suggestions when things go wrong.

As stated above, building relationships based on respect, trust and appreciation is part of your job description no matter how busy you are.

3. WHEN IT IS ASKED FOR – BUT.

When the other party requests your suggestions or advice it is generally wise to offer it, but be careful. What they might really want is not your honest opinion but some positive affirmation or approval instead. Knowing what they want and limiting its scope can make a big difference in how your feedback will be countenanced or accepted. Remember what Ben Franklin did when Thomas Jefferson asked him to edit his draft of the Declaration of Independence: he changed as little as necessary and gave good reason for it.

If what they are looking for from you is a good opinion of their work, then you may find yourself in the difficult position of being the bearer of bad news. You may find yourself punished for doing so. Worse yet, if the recipient of such unwelcome criticism happens to be hypersensitive to this challenge to their work you may lose them as a friend. Criticism or feedback, solicited or not, is something done only with prudence, tact and forethought.

4. WHEN IT IS ACCEPTED AS PART OF THE TRAINING PROCESS.

Constructive advice is accepted when it is provided as training. Once the training period is over, people tend to perceive further feedback not as training but as criticism. Instead of welcoming new suggestions they resent both the message and messenger.

Feedback made after the formal learning experience concludes is better accepted if those being trained expect it as routine. Where the program includes subsequent follow-up sessions and hot-line personal assistance, later feedback will be perceived in a more positive way, provided it does not highlight the trainee's mistakes in front of others.

5. WHEN THE CRITICISM OR ADVICE IS SPECIFIC AND TIMELY.

Feedback provided for performance problems that took place in the past is far worse than none at all. Such feedback is destructive because it is likely to cause bickering and faultfinding rather than improvement.

To be useful, feedback must not only be expressed soon after the problem arises but must also be focused on the specific task to be corrected. It cannot be general nor can its scope exceed what the other person can attain. Feedback that fails the test of timeliness, specificity and personal limitations will lead only to bickering and anger.

6. WHEN BOTH PARTIES ARE INVOLVED IN SOLVING THE PROBLEM TOGETHER.

The more associates have worked together to solve joint problems the less they will view their differences and associates' corrections as criticism or ego-threatening.

Prior experience in working together to find a better way leads the parties to recognize that acceptance time has a role to play in helping others and themselves accept new ideas that may at first appear intrusive or hostile. It helps them to remain patient with one another and thereby permits successful solutions to emerge that might otherwise be lost. If the other doesn't accept your advice immediately, then give acceptance time a chance to do its work.

7. WHEN THE FEEDBACK IS PRECEDED BY STRONG POSITIVES.

If you find it necessary to criticize another the better way to do so is to start with positive things the other person has done and follow that with one (yes, one) specific and timely matter requiring improvement.

Constructive feedback is enhanced when positive accomplishments are recognized and appreciated before negative matters are discussed. Suggestions are more likely to be accepted if restricted to the main dish rather than a smorgasbord of large and small problems.

8. WHEN THE ADVICE ALLOWS THE OTHER TO SORT THINGS OUT FOR THEMSELVES.

The more you leave others free to work in their own way the more responsible they will be to your suggestions.

Change your "feedback given" to "leave them alone" ratio. Decrease the number of times you give advice and increase the number of occasions you grit your teeth and let them sort it out for themselves. This, probably even more than direct praise, allows those who work with you to feel that you have confidence in them and helps them view occasional admonishment as being for their benefit.

A special note for dealing with highly sensitive people in the workplace: I have learned from experience that a surprising number of professionals and skilled craftsmen are, despite their competence, hypersensitive to even the mildest form of what they perceive as criticism. They resent being told what to do or how to do anything. This is especially so if, on occasion, they are wrong. For such individuals, it is better to let them persevere and find their own way. On balance, I believe that both you and they will be better off unless the lapse in performance is likely to lead to a catastrophic outcome if uncorrected.

TO BURY OR SURFACE DIVISIVE MATTERS?

Matters frequently arise at work that cause personal discomfort to persons involved. Yet, despite discomfort, many prefer to submerge differences rather than resolve them through open negotiation and compromise. Whether one should bury such issues or allow them to surface requires good judgment because the resolution of even smaller differences is rarely achieved without conflict and risk to one or both parties. Unintended consequences are hard to predict.

Burying the matter for another day is a choice. Some difficult issues do disappear over time even when nothing is done. Yet, an emotional price is paid when we avoid confronting a painful issue. Such matters generally fester and grow harder to cope with when submerged. When we avoid negotiation now, underlying tensions may explode in fury later.

To confront or not is not an easy personal decision. Some years ago I was employed at a large aerospace firm when a rift flared between two senior engineering managers in separate but adjoining design sections of the company. The trouble was that one manager had a bad habit. He not only made suggestions to the other's subordinates as to how to design certain electronic components, but also prodded them about when the components had to be scheduled for use on the assembly line. He could not resist giving advice and acting as manager to a group of engineers over whom he had no jurisdiction.

This blatant type of territorial infringement had gone on for six months and was deeply resented by the manager whose authority was being challenged. Admonishments to his own people to pay no attention to the intruder helped little to change the other's behavior. Despite some occasional sharp words between them, the trespassing continued unabated.

When the offended manager and I had lunch together, he told me of his anger at the situation created by the other. When I asked why he chose to be silent, he said that it might blow up in such a way that one or both of them might have to leave the company. The general economy was not strong at that time and, as uncomfortable as the matter was, he was not willing to risk losing a good job due to this issue. He preferred to do nothing and wait the matter out.

A few months later the matter came to a head. One of the offended manager's subordinates was pressured into a design change suggested by the intruding manager. The improperly authorized change did not work, and delayed completion of the component by almost a month. When the offended manager finally confronted the issue it was too late. Higher authority became involved. Both managers suffered what proved to be permanent loss in status: one as a troublemaker, the other as someone who could easily be pushed around for tolerating the infringement of his authority for so long. Neither, from that point on, went far in the company and, within a year, both left.

With all the dangers inherent in submerging or burying internal differences, why do people do so? As managers we should understand their reasons. Some choose to tolerate disturbing annoyances in the hope that the other person will leave the job, be assigned to another position elsewhere or come to their senses that their actions are harmful and hurting people. Though rare, these serendipitous events do occasionally happen.

Some continue to tolerate the strange behavior of others because they are simply too busy with more important matters. Others do so because the offending person has been on the job longer than they or has tenure or political clout.

Many in the workplace live with distressing situations because they doubt that relief is possible. The situation is often partially attributable to external systemic factors such as chronic computer breakdowns, inadequate systems and procedures or systemic organizational problems. When this is the case it seems a waste of time to negotiate in hopes of a resolution. The best that the two individuals at odds can do is to work together to gain the attention of those higher in the organization who can do something to repair the failing system, or can try to help each other live as well as possible under imposed limitations. With patience and collaboration a better way can be found even when structural boundaries or impediments exist.

As we can see, there are good reasons for choosing to submerge or postpone difficult issues for another time but the price is high.

Those of us who have for one reason or another done so know how hard it is to remain quiet for long periods while our anger boils. It's no surprise that one day, like a volcano, we explode and express in a moment what has been on our mind for years.

Unfortunately, by then the damage is done. Like Humpty Dumpty and his great fall, the better relationship we so need cannot be put together. The relationship, bad as it was, is now likely to be worse than ever, possibly beyond repair. Living with buried issues is much like living in California over a major earthquake fault. Sooner or later it will erupt and destroy much in its path.

There is, however, a prudent option available in contrast to submerging painful differences and hoping for the best. My advice is to open such issues to negotiation between the parties in the most tactful and courteous way possible. Let the "Effective Negotiating® Virtuous Cycle" and its four guiding factors be your guide. Work together to search for a collaborative Both-Win® solution to overcome the difficulty separating you. But, most of all, be sensitive to the psychological dangers and unintended consequences attendant to opening difficult matters. Good judgment and preparation are essential. Choosing the right time and place to talk, as simple as that seems, is critical.

There are positive benefits available only to those who open difficult issues to the light of negotiation. Opportunities for mutual gain solutions can always be found when two people search for them together. Relationships between them improve the moment they strive to find a joint solution in a respectful manner. The very fact that each is heard and listened to instead of arguing has a positive effect on both. The pattern of working jointly to find a better way on one problem sets the stage for reconciling future differences.

The decision to negotiate differences rather than submerge them is difficult. In my opinion, the tendency most people seem to have toward submerging interpersonal differences should be tempered in favor of taking somewhat greater risks, not only at work but also with those we live with at home.

I believe that differences and problems exposed to quiet, polite, reasoned and open discussion lead to better results and relationships in the long run. They allow the process of cooperative, collaborative negotiation to lead us to lasting agreements that are more creative and satisfying. And, despite its initial difficulties, open discussion ultimately moves us toward more stable relationships with which to weather future storms. Effective Negotiating® is something we get better at the more we learn about it and practice it well.

In Part III of the book we will deal with the fundamentals of negotiating: what you have to know in any bargaining situation be it with someone in your own organization or with the seller of goods and services. Those who understand the basics and rules of negotiating will be in the best position to reach successful agreement and to negotiate anything with anybody at work.

PART III

FUNDAMENTALS OF NEGOTIATING: WHAT YOU NEED TO KNOW

PART III

8

The Five Modes of Negotiation and How They Lead to Better Outcomes

Why is this chapter on negotiating so important? Doesn't almost everyone know what negotiation is from their personal experience as buyers or sellers in the marketplace? In my opinion, what they know, while partially correct, is too limited to enable them to negotiate effectively. This chapter will open the way to more satisfying agreements whenever people bargain or settle their differences.

Most view negotiation as a contest between two parties, one of whom offers or indicates a willingness to do or sell something for a price or other consideration while the other expresses some willingness to accept the offering of the price or consideration as set or altered to a lower or more satisfactory level. In such negotiations both sides are primarily focused on their own competitive self-interest. They want to leave no more than necessary in the other's pocket. When people in this frame of mind negotiate, they typically model their interaction on the conventional competitive or transactional aspect of bargaining.

What most people fail to recognize, even as it is well-accepted by experienced negotiators, is that in every bargaining situation there are not one but five negotiations taking place at the same time. Knowing this allows them to be effective in closing better agreements not only for themselves but also for both parties.

Good negotiators use these five modes as tools to move talks in the direction of mutually satisfying settlement. Each mode and its potential for making better agreements will now be described and discussed.

THE FIVE MODES OF NEGOTIATION

1. **THE CONVENTIONAL COMPETITIVE OR TRANSACTIONAL MODE**
   (distributive-oppositional)
2. **THE COLLABORATIVE BOTH-WIN® MODE**
   (cooperative-mutual gain)
3. **THE RELATIONSHIP MODE**
   (attitudinal-connection)
4. **THE ORGANIZATIONAL MODE**
   (structural-collective)
5. **THE PERSONAL ISSUE MODE**
   (individual satisfaction)

Exhibit 9

The five modes of negotiation are analogous to a set of golf clubs in a golfer's bag. A skilled golfer would not dream of playing the course with less than a full set of clubs. Not only do they know which clubs to use under certain circumstances, they also understand how to handle each to greatest effect. This helps them to succeed in difficult situations.

They would not choose a putter to drive the golf ball three hundred yards or use a driver ten feet off the green. The golfer knows that the proper choice of club and skill in handling all of them in concert creates the best results. So also does the effective negotiator understand the importance of each bargaining tool or mode in his or her quest for a good agreement. We will begin with the conventional competitive mode because that is where most disagreements start: with both sides sitting on opposing sides of the table.

MODE #1 – THE CONVENTIONAL COMPETITIVE MODE (distributive-oppositional)

Elements of competition and collaboration exist in every negotiation including those that occur in the workplace. People bargain with one another because they want some satisfaction from the other that they believe the other may be persuaded to grant if sufficiently rewarded. A difference exists between their positions that they hope to close by negotiating. Each wants to improve their level of satisfaction by influencing the other to exchange their package of contributions for benefits or considerations offered in exchange.

The conventional competitive mode of negotiating is dominant in typical buy-sell transactions. The literature on negotiation is usually focused on how to do well for yourself in such bargaining. The strategies and tactics of competitive negotiation have been researched and documented. They have proven themselves to be effective since the dawn of human history.

Workplace negotiations, though different in some important ways from buy-sell bargaining, also have competitive factors associated with the give and take process. Each side in a workplace dispute has a point of view or position they wish to favor. Many rules of successful competitive bargaining apply to negotiating in one's own organization. But there is one essential not-to-be-forgotten difference. Internal negotiations must always be relationship-based in principle, never based on manipulation, bluffing or lying as strategies for success.

In the workplace we must work together cooperatively or nothing will get done. Positive relationships are critical. Respect, trust, credibility and good faith are essential. Of course these attitudes are beneficial in commercial buy-sell negotiations but not essential to transactional success.

The four basic rules of competitive negotiation that follow meet the relationship-based test. They will protect your interests and move the issue in your favor without jeopardizing your relationship with the other party or your ability to work collaboratively with them during the negotiating process and long into the future.

RULE 1 - Competitive Mode
Fight the fear of negotiating

Few people look forward to negotiating. Most dislike it intensely. Even experienced negotiators admit that they are apprehensive in advance of talks. Negotiating with peers, subordinates or superiors at work is rarely fun.

There are good reasons for this aversion to negotiating. The process always involves some degree of conflict between parties. There is some risk that relationships between them may grow worse if agreement is not achieved or is reached in rancor. The final outcome of any bargaining situation is never certain. Second guessers in your organization may enjoy a field day. Those higher or lower in the organization may criticize the agreement even if those at the table are convinced that it was the best they could have achieved.

Yet, whether we like negotiation or not, it is important that each of us fight this fear of negotiating. In business, as in work or life, you don't get what you deserve, you get what you negotiate. If you don't ask for what you want, you're not likely to get it.

RULE 2 - Competitive Mode
Leave some room for give and take when negotiating

This rule is controversial in workplace negotiating, although far less so in external buy-sell bargaining where leaving space is generally accepted as good practice. There, the rule is simple: leave as much room as you can reasonably justify if challenged by the other side.

When discussing this matter at Effective Negotiating® seminar programs, I usually add that research by others and myself supports the finding that the more a competitive negotiator asks for, the more they are apt to get. The danger of leaving too much room, of course, is that those who do so invite increased hostility. They also experience more deadlock when they do so because they may appear exploitative or frivolous by asking for too much.

Why then do I propose that one leave room or space to negotiate in workplace dealings? Is that not in conflict with the need to be fair and open with those you work with? No, I believe that leaving bargaining space is not only necessary for effective internal negotiating but, if done properly, actually reduces conflict between parties. What I propose is that, by leaving room, you create the negotiating space necessary to assure that the talks will encourage sound reasoning and argument on the part of both sides.

Both sides need negotiating space and time to search for compromise and collaboration. Without negotiating space they could face deadlock from the start. It would be as though one party had opened with a firm "Take-it-or-leave-it," leaving neither side with any place to go from there. Effective Negotiating® cannot take place unless both sides have space to talk, persuade, discover and explore alternatives.

How much room is appropriate? Unlike buy-sell negotiations, where I suggest leaving all the room you can justify without losing credibility, in the workplace I suggest a more moderate relationship-based approach. Negotiators should feel free to leave room for contingencies that may arise and for estimates they make that may prove wrong. Leave room for promised support by other departments or personnel that may prove less qualified or able than expected, or be provided by them later than promised. These things happen in the real world and must be accounted for and discussed in your internal bargaining demands and offers.

You have every right to leave room for contingencies, problems and errors you anticipate possibly emerging on your side. Your role in negotiation is to ask for what you need and to defend your viewpoint honestly and openly when questioned. That is the road to a prudent and better deal for both parties. Not leaving room for contingent needs leads to deadlock and hard feelings unless these needs are fully discussed and evaluated by both parties.

RULE 3 - Competitive Mode
Ask for something in return when you make a concession.

The French do not make unilateral concessions. They give nothing without asking for something in return. Americans, as a rule, do not like to tie strings to their concessions. They consider it bad taste to give with one hand and take with the other. From a negotiating standpoint, that's a mistake. Open your mind to the French rule of "QUID-PRO-QUO." Always consider asking for something in return when making a concession.

For example, you are a member of the accounting team negotiating with the organization's head of information technology (IT) on a project you are responsible for. You have asked IT for three extra programmers for three weeks to make changes to an existing report. The IT head has countered with an offer of two people for two weeks that she believes adequate for the job.

From past experience with your IT people you believe that two programmers can get the work done in three weeks if both are senior programmers who are already familiar with the report from previous work on it. You offer to settle for a three-week completion date only if John and Mary are assigned, since both are well-versed on your needs.

You have made a concession but tied a string to it. Four benefits accrue by doing so:

1. You have added value to your concession to accept two programmers instead of the three you initially asked for. Without the string your offer to accept two might have been less appreciated by the IT manager.

2. If the IT head rejects your offer by saying that John or Mary are not available then you are back to your initial request for three people for three weeks. You have made no concession. You have also not lost face or shown weakness, or in any way lost credibility, by offering to move back from three to two programmers.

3. By asking for something in return you have created negotiating space for other possibilities to be explored.

4. You may, by tying a string to the concession, learn more than you expect about the IT staff, its ability to perform and its capacity to outsource work. A better agreement for both sides might then be discovered.

Is it any wonder that the French rarely make a concession without asking for something in return? They have much to gain and little to lose by doing so.

RULE 4 - Competitive Mode
Give in slowly and in small increments when making concessions.

Most negotiations end in compromise. Concessions that are poorly made can serve to further separate the parties rather than bringing them together. A concession may inadvertently serve to raise the expectations of the other if they interpret it as a sign of weakness or further softness. How and when a concession is made is often as important as its size or amount.

Everything you do in a bargaining situation affects the other's expectations. Your initial demands set the stage. Your persistence in holding firm to a position or idea you favor tells others how you feel about it. Then, as you move to agreement, the rate and time of compromise has an effect in raising or lowering their aspirations.

The benefits of concessions offered in small increments over an extended period of time are well-supported by research and experience. Those who do so provide the negotiating space necessary for fair and reasonable agreements to be reached and for the parties to learn about each other and explore alternative proposals. Small concessions, slowly given, leave each side room for testing unrealistic expectations and assumptions. Such concessions are easier to explain than large ones and leave one's credibility and face intact.

The research is sound. People who are patient and concede in smaller increments when negotiating do better because it leads to greater mutual understanding, more prudent outcomes and greater satisfaction when the settlement is reached.

More will be said about the strategies and tactics of competitive bargaining in Chapter Twelve. Many workplace negotiations such as those involving resource allocation, budgets, funding, facilities, office space and the equitable sharing of workload have competitive aspects to them. Our role in these negotiations is to remember at all times that our chosen strategies and approaches must be relationship-based rather than exploitative or self-centered. An internal negotiation which diminishes or destroys relationships between parties is one in which both parties lose whatever the outcome.

MODE #2 – THE COLLABORATIVE BOTH-WIN® MODE (cooperative-mutual gain)

The Collaborative Both-Win® Negotiating Mode is the key to success in dealing with others at work. It is, in my opinion, the most important of the five modes—the one that best leads to a resolution of internal differences and the building of stronger, more innovative relationships.

Let us assume that our negotiation with an associate, be they subordinate, peer or superior, has gone on for a while. After considerable talk and give and take we are still apart. An impasse is likely if nothing more is done. It is, I believe, this need to do something or risk creating a deadlock that provides the opportunity for both parties to develop, through collaboration, creative ideas and alternatives not previously considered or thought possible. It has been said, "Necessity is the mother of invention." The analogy that follows illustrates how collaborative Both-Win® negotiating does its magic in creating new alternatives and breaking impending deadlocks.

Imagine for a moment a special 10" diameter pie cut into ten pieces. You and I are bargaining over how many pieces each of us will get. If you get seven, I'll get three. If I get eight, you get two. How we share this special pie is important because we intend to celebrate Fridays at the office from now on by baking our favorite pie, sharing it with associates and taking leftovers home to the family.

The negotiation begins with you offering me three pieces. You think that is fair because not only is it your special recipe, but it is you doing all the work baking the pie in your deluxe oven at home. I object to your offer of three because I sincerely believe a share of five pieces fair. It is I who purchased all the ingredients and invested sixty percent of the money required. You are initially adamant but later raise your offer to four pieces. If we deadlock there will be no Friday celebrations. Worse yet, our presently superb relationship may suffer.

Both of us want to reach agreement because we have invested a lot of personal time and energy in this Friday celebration idea. We decide to put our minds together to bridge the gap that exists, and to find a better way to close the deal in a fair and reasonable way.

Before long, through collaboration and an open exchange of information, we find ways to combine our resources, purchasing power and culinary skills in a new and innovative manner. We create a 12" pie that is bigger and tastier than the original 10" pie. We can cut this new pie in twelve pieces and share it more easily than the original smaller, less delicious one. This pie costs the same or only slightly more than the other. Would it not be easier to share twelve pieces of a larger pie than ten pieces of the smaller one that didn't taste as good?

As stretched as this analogy may be, it illustrates a governing principle of negotiation; that, through collaboration, there is ALWAYS a bigger and better deal possible for both sides if they are willing to search for it together. Both negotiators have the power to increase mutual satisfaction by working together, often at little or no expense to the other. They can make the negotiating pie larger, better and easier to share. ALWAYS.

We will further expand on these ideas in Chapter Thirteen, "Collaborative Both-Win® Negotiation – Moving Together to a More Creative, Higher Value Agreement." We will show how best to implement such an agreement in any negotiation, especially one between associates in an organization bargaining over differences.

MODE #3 – THE RELATIONSHIP MODE (attitudinal-connection)

Two or more team members enter into a negotiation. They are trying to reach consensus on how to resolve a problem or decision facing them. Their viewpoints differ. Each specializes in something different. Each is motivated in part by personal interests. Both would like to resolve the matter dividing them and complete the project successfully.

Why should we care so much about their relationship to one another? What does this have to do with hammering out an agreement that will work and reconcile their differences? This is what two negotiation theorists, R.E. Walton and R.B. McKersie wrote in their groundbreaking book, A Behavioral Theory of Labor Relations, almost fifty years ago. It is as applicable today as then in any bargaining situation.

> "Two parties negotiate. The negotiating process shapes the division of the product of their joint efforts. The negotiation process also facilitates the resolution of joint problems and the integration of their interests. A third result of the negotiation process is a maintenance or restructuring of the relationship of the participants toward each other."

Whatever the issue, the parties come to the negotiation with attitudes toward one another. The bargaining process is affected by their relationship, be it good or bad. Whether they like, trust and respect each other mediates their every offer and counteroffer, their responses and positions, and of course their strategies and approaches.

How they treat each other as the negotiating session proceeds then affects their initial relationship for better or worse. Negotiators wary of each other as talks start may change if the other person is candid and open during the process. Respect can grow or diminish as each party exchanges viewpoints. How they move to agreement or to deadlock can alter their relationship not only at the table but for years to come.

A negotiation within a negotiation is taking place as they talk. The parties, while discussing and exchanging ideas on the issues, are re-establishing their relationship. At the end of the process they may think well of the other or wish never to work with them again.

Three basic rules govern the relationship mode and deserve a place in a negotiator's planning and preparation kit.

1. The relationship that exists between the parties affects how they will act at the table and the behaviors, strategies and tactics they will employ.

2. What one or the other does or says during the talks has an effect on the attitude and behavior of the other as talks progress.

3. The relationship between parties not only affects the outcome of their bargaining but also, in a reciprocal way, the outcome

and how it was reached affect their willingness to abide by the agreement and their future negotiations.

MODE #4 – THE ORGANIZATIONAL MODE (structural-collective)

This mode rests on the premise that in every negotiation, large or small, there are unseen others at the table with a stake in the outcome, people who are affected by the issues under consideration.

How issues are resolved in the privacy of bargaining has a profound effect on those outside whose workload, productivity or job satisfaction may change in ways not clearly understood by the bargainers themselves. What goes on at the bargaining table always affects others behind the negotiators. And, what goes on deep in the organization affects the negotiators at the table. Negotiators who fail to factor the organization and its motivations into their planning are less likely to reach agreements that stand the test of time.

There is good reason for this. Agreements reached by negotiators in the privacy of their office are, in my opinion, fragile even if carefully wrought and signed. They will not work if others in the organization do not favor them. Both sides need a "Yes" from their respective constituents or the deal will fall apart.

Figure 6 depicts a typical organizational situation. A and B are negotiating in a small conference room. Surrounding them but not at the table are others who have an interest in the deal.

THE ORGANIZATIONAL MODE OF NEGOTIATION

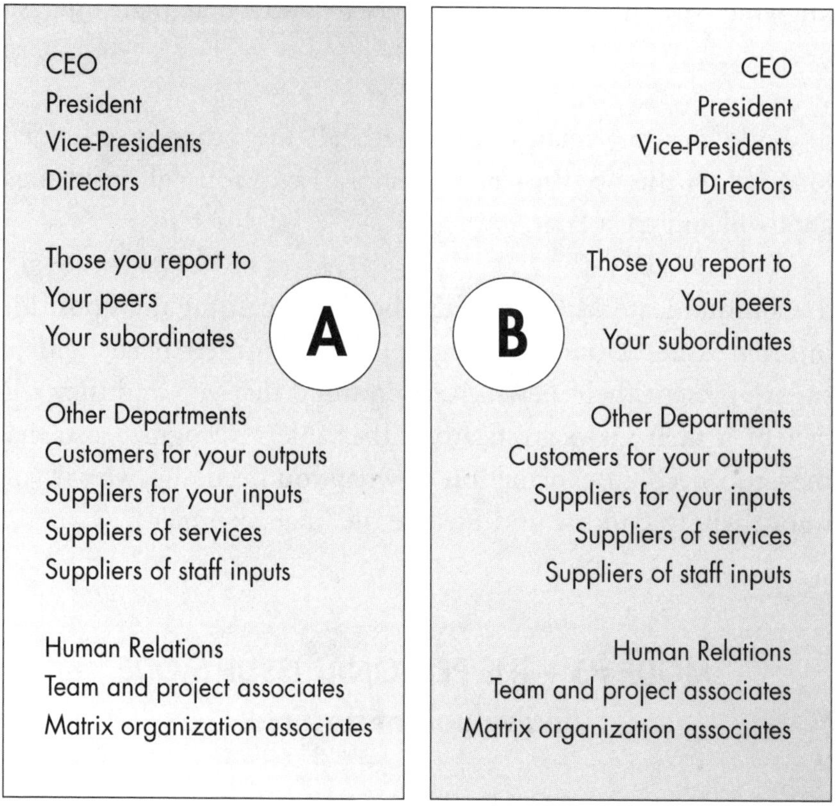

Figure 6

As the diagram illustrates, the network surrounding negotiators A and B includes their superiors, subordinates and peers. Rarely can a change in procedure, program, process or relationship be made without affecting someone working close by. In summary, there are four organizational factors that we should consider in preparing for any negotiation, be it internal or external. They are:

1. Recognize that others in the organization have a seat at the table whether present at the negotiation or not.

2. Understand that an important part of preparation consists of knowing who the other stakeholders are and where their interests lie.

3. Build positive relationships with all the other stakeholders long before the need for negotiation arises. You will need their goodwill and trust later.

4. Communicate with other stakeholders regarding their position on each issue before talks begin. Listen to their needs and be sure to present their views. Keep in mind that you and they will benefit if their views are heard at the table. Recognize also that they also need an explanation of what you need and why if you want them to endorse and execute the final agreement.

MODE #5 – THE PERSONAL ISSUE MODE (individual satisfaction)

What are the satisfiers that people look for in a negotiation? Of course they want what they ask for: a higher budget, more time to complete a task, enough space to work, new equipment to get the job done well and the service necessary to keep things running smoothly. These tangible satisfiers are brought openly to the bargaining session as issues in contention.

There are other issues below the surface that neither party can easily bring to light; that is, intangible personal matters demanding satisfaction. These needs usually go unspoken. Whatever the negotiating situation, it is important to recognize that the person you are negotiating with has needs they cannot or will not put into words.

Negotiators in the workplace must be sensitive to these intangible issues and how they motivate the other party. They know that if these unspoken needs are satisfied, then a "Yes" answer will follow. They also know from intuition or experience that people who have lost face, or whose unspoken ego needs have been demeaned or threatened, often choose to say "No" even to offers that would otherwise benefit them.

Below are personal issues that neither side will speak of but which loom large in their workplace thinking:

1. They want to feel good about themselves.

2. They want to be recognized and accepted by associates.

3. They want to keep their job and be considered for promotion.

4. They want to work easier, not harder.

5. They want to meet their personal ambitions without violating their integrity.

6. They want to know and feel that what they are doing matters.

7. They want to avoid the insecurity that comes from unpleasant surprises and changes.

8. They want to be treated fairly.

9. They want to be heard and listened to.

10. They want to be treated with dignity.

11. They want to share in the excitement, fun and social warmth that work with others offers.

12. They want to be liked and belong.

13. They want to resolve differences and disagreements without rancor or hard feelings.

14. They want to be told and know the truth.

15. They want to be thought of as honest, fair, kind and responsible.

16. They want reasonable control of their work and how it should be done.

17. They do not want to be hassled or picked on.

18. They want some participation in the decision process if it affects them.

19. They want to maintain peaceful relations with those they work with.

20. They want no one to trespass on their workspace, their job responsibilities, their possessions, their budget allocation or the people assigned to work for them.

Like the golfer with a set of clubs we now have five tools or modes of negotiation to help us move to better agreements. Like each club to a golfer, each mode serves a different purpose. Each leads to a more comprehensive and satisfying negotiating outcome, not only for one's self but for all parties involved. They have a place in everybody's negotiation golf bag.

9

Thirteen Rules for Relationship-Based Negotiating in Your Own Organization

This chapter is concerned with basic rules of negotiating applicable to the workplace. All thirteen are primarily relationship-based, that is, aimed at building positive connections between negotiators while bargaining assertively for what you want and need. The rules are also designed to foster understanding and open discourse between parties in order to set the stage for collaborative mutual-gain agreements. Each rule has an important place in raising your effectiveness in dealing and working with others.

THE THIRTEEN RULES OF RELATIONSHIP-BASED NEGOTIATION

1. You have more power than you think.

2. Understanding your sources of power and influence.

3. Knowing the difference between wants and needs facilitates

agreement.

4. Good notes and frequent summaries build power and foster amity.

5. Don't hope for the best.

6. There is always a story.

7. Covering-up differences won't work.

8. Your assumptions are probably wrong.

9. Important negotiations call for a devil's advocate.

10. Avoid threat, bluff or bluster.

11. Workplace agreements are always brittle.

12. Never open with a chip on your shoulder.

13. Collaborative both-win negotiation is the most powerful strategy in your arsenal.

1. YOU HAVE MORE POWER THAN YOU THINK

Experienced negotiators know that negotiating power is one of the most, if not the most, important factors influencing outcome. Experiments confirm this. Yet experiments also show that negotiators, even experienced ones, often under-estimate and under-value the strengths they have in dealing with others. Knowing how to assess your strengths and to understand the limits of an opposer's power is essential to getting ready for any negotiation, be it internal or external.

Power may be defined as the ability of one person or party to control the resources and benefits accruing to the other. To the extent one can control what the other needs, that person holds the balance of power. Our goal in dealing with associates at work is certainly not to control what they need or to take advantage of their weaknesses or constraints.

What we want in relation-based internal negotiations, be it about budgets, system designs or conflicting scientific viewpoints, is for each participant to express their viewpoints or proposals in the best way possible without fear of censure or personal criticism. We want each person on the team to present its arguments in a rational, coherent manner. Only in that way will the project or collaborative group emerge from the meeting with better ideas and solutions.

Our contention is that in negotiation, you usually have more power than you think. In developing this thesis we well consider the sources and limitations of bargaining power. We believe that those who walk into a negotiation more confident of their bargaining position will present their positions more assertively and positively. They will also be less averse to taking the risks that go with every negotiation and better prepared for the emotional frustrations that so often surface when people feel strongly about their positions and ideas.

Power in negotiation is not what it appears to be. The other party, like yourself, has constraints on their power that you are unlikely to be aware of. They also have needs exerting pressure on them that they are cognizant of although you are not. In most negotiations you will be far more aware of the pressures on yourself than those of the other side. That's why you will gain a measure of power by taking the time to discover the pressures and limits on them rather than dwelling on your own constraints.

Another factor that leads to a negotiator undervaluing their own strengths is that they recognize the troubles and losses they may experience if deadlock occurs. They are, however, unaware of the other's aversion to deadlock. The other side may well be more concerned with the consequences of breakdown than you are.

Both parties in a negotiation have constraints that limit their actions, even when they are strong. These limits may be legal or moral, economic or physical, imagined or real. Whatever the reason, these factors reduce their ability to use all the power they possess.

We at Karrass have tested the "You have more power than you think" hypothesis many times at practice negotiations conducted at programs worldwide. We do it by providing each attendee with a private information fact sheet prior to negotiation. This sheet includes their strengths and weaknesses as well as facts related to the other's power position. Then, during the practice negotiation, the parties bargain to reach agreement.

Outcomes are then posted for all to see. A critique and discussion follows that almost always reveals that most participants dwell on their own weaknesses and pay less attention to their strengths. They focus on what the other can do to them if they fail to agree rather than the reverse. As a result of this negative thinking, participants tend to take an opening position by asking for less than they otherwise might. After the critique discussions end, participants are always surprised that they dwelled so much on their weaknesses rather than focusing on their strengths.

From now on, when you prepare for any negotiation make a list of your strengths and what you believe to be the other person's limitations. You'll approach the talks in a more confident manner and strive to test your assumptions as the negotiation progresses. Another thing you can do before getting into a negotiation is to review the six principles of power that follow. They will open your mind to aspects of power and influence that might easily be overlooked.

> First, the exercise of power always involves cost and risk. Those with power who are unable or unwilling to incur cost or risk abdicate their strength.
>
> Second, power may be real or only apparent or assumed. Organization charts rarely determine where the real power lies. Those with power unwilling to exercise their strength do not have power unless you assume they will use it. For example, someone in a higher position has the power to punish a subordinate. If, for practical or ethical reasons, the superior has no intention of punishing the subordinate, then that power is for all practical purposes nullified. On the other hand if the subordinate believes he or she will be punished, that source of power remains intact.
>
> Third, power changes over time. The balance of power moves as the balance of contributions and benefits between the parties changes. Good negotiators compensate for such changes in the balance of power by incorporating such changes into their agreements to keep them from failing over time. If one party to a negotiation has little power at the start of a project they may have considerably more as the project moves along and

their work or expertise becomes essential.

Fourth, the ends of power cannot be separated from means. Good and lasting relationships cannot be built from manipulative tactics.

Fifth, power is always limited. Its range depends upon the specific situation, the general economy, the government or such structural matters as policies, company regulations, ethical standards and present or future consequences, whether known or assumed.

Sixth, power is always relative. Rarely, if ever, does one side enjoy complete power over the other. Understanding the sources of power and making the most of them will add credibility to your position and confidence in your assertions.

2. UNDERSTANDING THE SOURCES OF POWER AND INFLUENCE

The Power of Time

Time is a key factor in bargaining strength. If one party has time to reach an agreement and the other doesn't, the one who does is in a stronger position. The problem with evaluating time as a factor is that we tend to underestimate our strength because we are more aware of the time pressures on ourselves than on the other person.

Below are five ideas to build time power.

1. Leave time to negotiate. When forced to decide quickly you won't do well.

2. Be on time or early for the meeting. Getting there with time to spare will help talks get started in a more relaxed manner.

3. Be prepared. Don't just hope for the best. Too many people go into negotiations with little or no preparation and pay a high price for that luxury. Leave enough time to plan.

4. Pick the right time and place to talk if you possibly can. If the time or place is wrong, negotiate a better venue.

5. Give yourself time to think. Caucus often. Take breaks.

The Power of Legitimacy

Habit, precedent and custom exert power, often without uttering a word. The past exerts pressure on present and future behavior. Past dealings affect future agreements. When a public agreement establishes a 5% raise for teachers, wage negotiations in the private sector are affected by that percentage change.

We are surrounded by policies, procedures, rules and company standards or practices that set focal points on intra-organizational bargaining between peers, subordinates and those in charge. If you want the other party to look favorably at your position, find a good rule or regulation to support it. Legitimacy adds strength and credibility to your position. They allow you to take the high ground.

The Power of Risk-Taking and Courage

Risk is a factor in every negotiation. It is a factor we confront at every step of the process. A negotiator's willingness to accept risk or avoid it may determine outcome as much or more than other sources. Here are a few of the formidable risks you will be required to take in the process of negotiating.

- We take risk when we decide to negotiate rather than accept what has been offered. Many fear to negotiate or dislike it so much that they risk paying a high asking price merely to avoid negotiating. The risks incurred by negotiating are like those in war. One cannot predict with accuracy the intended or unintended consequences of a negotiation and its outcome.

- Should we take the time to plan before getting into negotiation? Of course the answer is "Yes." But planning doesn't always pay off. It certainly takes time from other things more pleasant or important. And if we decide to get ready, how far should the preparation go?

- When an offer is received that is reasonable or favorable, should we accept it? Most good negotiators would say that it is wise not to accept the offer too quickly, that doing so diminishes the value of your "Yes" to the other party. That's true, but good offers are sometimes withdrawn in the give and take of further talk and consideration. Continued talk takes time and work. Saying "Yes" allows you to go on to something more important, or fun, than the conflict inherent in continued bargaining.

- Effective Negotiating®, especially in the workplace, requires an open exchange of information. Deciding how much should be said and when always involves risk. The admonition, "Everything you say may be held against you," applies to everything you reveal in dealing with those in your own organization.

- It is well-known that setting higher targets in negotiation generally results in achieving higher outcomes, but that is not always so. Setting higher targets often leads to deadlock. It may also lengthen the negotiating process beyond what is worthwhile or beyond what makes for better relationships between the parties.

- Accepting the final terms and conditions of an agreement always involves risk. One can never be certain that the other side will perform as agreed or will be around long enough to do so. Everything changes over time. Whether time will reinforce the agreement or tear it apart remains to be seen.

Both sides are to a considerable extent aware of the risks to themselves inherent in negotiating. As a negotiator, you will be more aware of the risks on yourself than on the other. The important thing is to recognize that they are also under pressure. As you negotiate, dwell not on the risks you are taking but on the pressures on them. They may be less willing to accept these risks than you are, thereby shifting the balance of power in your direction.

The Power of Information and Knowledge

Knowledge and information determine power in negotiation. The surprising thing is that much of what you need to know is not too hard to get if you determine in advance what you want to know and where to look for it. What follows are some relatively simple questions that a negotiator should try to answer before talks begin or are in progress.

1. Who makes the decisions in the other person's organization? How does the other fit in with his or her associates?

2. Is there a pattern as to how they negotiate? How do they reach compromise positions? Are they people who tend to hold fast to positions, then give in all at once?

3. Do they live up to and abide by their agreements or renegotiate everything shortly afterward?

4. What do I know of their personal life that might be useful in forming a bond?

5. What are the time and work pressures that make their jobs difficult? How can I help relieve their pressures?

6. Why is this negotiation important to them? How are they appraised or judged by those higher in their organization?

7. How can I best make them amenable to working together with us to find a better outcome for both parties?

Now, more than ever, knowledge is power. The answers to these questions can often be learned directly from the other party if asked during lunch or casual, non-threatening conversation before differences arise. Some can be learned from associates who wish to reduce the level of dysfunction associated with unresolved disagreement. And, in today's exciting technological and information world, further information can be found on the internet with Google searches and applications that focus on what we want to know.

What we need to know in internal negotiations is information that will help us make an equitable settlement, we don't need prurient or personal bits of knowledge to manipulate or force agreement. The key to success in workplace negotiations lies in maintaining and building better relationships as a creative Both-Win® agreement is bridged.

The Power of Competition

One would not normally think of competition as a factor in workplace negotiations. It's not like bargaining in the outside world where a single buyer with a large order has the advantage of six anxious salespeople ready to give in on the buyer's every demand to win the contract. Yet competition is an important factor even in internal negotiations.

One or both opposing parties have many competitive interests they must keep in balance. In almost every organization, one party or both are loaded down with work. Negotiation preparation and talk takes time, time that could be used in other ways. That competition is keenly felt especially if talks drag on.

Some negotiations are very important to one side but have little priority value to the other. In a situation like that, the competition in priority or value might favor the party with the higher issue value.

Negotiators often come to the bargaining table with one issue or another to be settled. Many other problems remain to be addressed back at the office. Getting the immediate negotiation over with quickly, for better or worse, may be a better choice than waiting for days for a superior outcome. At least that would be one problem out of the way.

And, of course, there is competition within the organization itself. Some supervisors always want a larger portion of the department budget, some want a more up-to-date laboratory, some want their staff to get higher raises and some feel that their good work warrants greater rewards.

Competition exists at every level and affects every internal negotiation in a direct or intangible manner. Understanding the competition that exists and its likely effect on the balance of power between negotiators is part of the preparation process.

3. KNOWING THE DIFFERENCE BETWEEN NEEDS AND WANTS MAKES IT EASIER TO REACH AGREEMENT

Some years ago I had a date with Charlene, at that time the world's most famous marriage broker. I can tell you, Charlene knew a lot about life, love and negotiating.

She helped me to see the difference between wants and needs by telling me about her business. When unmarried people came to her seeking help in finding a partner, she asked them what they wanted. Each specified a long list of personality and character traits as well as sporting and cultural interests they wanted in a prospective spouse.

When I asked her if she met their specifications, she responded, "My job as a marriage broker is to listen to what they want and then discover what they really need. When I give them what they need, they forget about what they want."

I thought about it. Was Charlene being cynical? I don't think so. She was doing what we do when negotiating.

In any fairly complex negotiation, both parties start with all kinds of demands they would like to have met. Some are needs and some are wants. A need, according to one of Webster's definitions, is an urgent requirement for something essential that is lacking, something that is indispensable to a particular end or goal. Charlene explained that few of the wants in her clients' lists were indispensable; most were just nice to have. It's much the same in negotiation, where our job is to discover what the other says they want and what they really need.

There are many ways to fill a need. For example, when someone at the office complains that it is always too hot when the window is closed and asks that it be kept open, you as the supervisor have a problem. Others, quite satisfied with the temperature, want the window closed. You suggest that they negotiate to reach agreement.

Are there any other ways by which each side's needs can be satisfied other than by keeping the window open or closed as each wanted? Several come to mind as they negotiate.

They can choose to seat the person who wanted the window closed elsewhere where his or her comfort level needs are met. A window air conditioner with adjustable vents that provide variable temperatures in different areas might increase the satisfaction level for all. The discomfort level for both might be reduced by closing the window in the cool of the morning and raising it in the afternoon when it is warmer. Or the window could be open or closed on alternate days of the week. Lest we think this too simplistic, it was the way Israel and Egypt settled a serious border entry dispute.

As the example indicates, needs may be filled in many innovative ways. The next time someone in a negotiation says, "I want this or that," seek to discover what they need, then search for a satisfying solution based on that need. That's how creative Both-Win® deals emerge.

4. GOOD NOTES AND FREQUENT SUMMARIES BUILD POWER AND FOSTER AMITY

One of the smartest managers I ever worked for did something few others did. He kept better notes at meetings than anyone in the room. Then, before the meeting ended, he summarized from his notes whatever they had discussed and agreed to. He followed up in a short time with an e-mail summary to each attendee inviting their comments. When a dispute later emerged about what had been said or settled, his notes and summary tended to prevail.

Agreements are rarely written and signed by the parties in internal negotiations. Written agreements are, of course, common in external dealings. Yet, the problems in both internal and external bargaining are similar. Misunderstandings are common. People are so busy thinking about what they want to say they don't listen to what the other is saying. Words, ideas and responses come in a torrent, too fast to comprehend or integrate fully. Where different technological specialties and expertise are involved, what is said by one may be clear to them but as opaque as a foreign language to the other. Good notes and frequent summarization of where the parties stand reduce the risk of serious argument later.

We often forget how important good notes can be to a negotiator. Though informal rather than legal, they are nonetheless a source of legitimacy and power. Every negotiated agreement involves actions to be taken in the future by each side. Problems often arise. Good notes help resolve them.

It pays to keep track in writing of the things you do on an ordinary day that help to make an agreement work well. Special positive actions on behalf of the other party should not be taken for granted or discounted in value. Unless you make note of these good deeds they are likely to be forgotten later when the contract or arrangement is renegotiated or when a problem arises. Good notes add strength to your position. They are like money in the bank.

5. DON'T HOPE FOR THE BEST

If there is one rule that doesn't change, it is this: don't hope for the best. Unfortunately, most of us continue to hope for the best when finding ourselves in negotiating situations.

Experiments verify that preparation before negotiation leads to better outcomes. Experience by others and myself confirms this. At the least, when entering a negotiation, it is wise to write down what you must have, what you would like to have and what issues you might ask for that are not as important. List these wants in order of priority. This minimal plan will prove helpful because it will lead you to negotiate with yourself.

Unless you negotiate with yourself and prioritize your wants, you will have trouble getting what you need. Nor will it be clear what you can live without. The problem is that knowing what you want is not as easy as it sounds. Few people approach an oncoming negotiation by bargaining with themselves about their own priorities, nor do they ask themselves the hard questions necessary to handle a well-prepared opposing negotiator. The Quick Planning Checklist in Chapter Ten is designed to help prepare effectively for what will soon lie ahead at the table.

6. THERE IS ALWAYS A STORY

In negotiation, there is always a story. If you don't take the time to understand the other side's story, you won't understand the final outcome reached and why and how it happened.

The way to get the story is, of course, by listening rather than talking. Unfortunately, too many negotiators limit their listening to what they want to hear rather than to what the other is actually saying or intimating. Others lose useful information because they are busy preparing how they plan to respond to some point made by the other side to which they take exception. Experiments confirm that most of us are poor listeners even when the negotiating stakes are high.

Listening is always a wise concession that gives much but costs little. Only if you are disciplined enough to listen without interruption or criticism will you learn the real story behind every position or concession the other party makes. You will also gain something more valuable: the respect of the other for listening. Good listeners are rare, quickly recognized and appreciated by those they deal with. That's why the words, "He or she is a good listener," commands our attention in a positive way.

7. COVERING-UP DIFFERENCES WON'T WORK

Negotiation involves conflict. We do not negotiate unless there is some difference that must be resolved. Because conflict is uncomfortable, too many people prefer to avoid negotiating or to paper over differences when they arise. The trouble is that covering up differences will not work. They will emerge soon after performance begins and fracture whatever agreement the parties sought to reach.

Most negotiations follow a path. Serious issues are raised by one or both sides and generally settled by compromise or give and take. As talks draw to a close a number of smaller differences come to the forefront. Details become important. Who should do exactly what? Exactly when will something be done and what exactly does the word "done" mean? How and by whom will progress by measured? It has been said that "The devil is in the details," and it is.

These small but crucial matters usually arise late in the negotiation process. By that time both parties are tired of talking and both are afraid to reopen issues already settled. Both hope for the best. So they paper over the difficult details, shake hands and go on to something else only to have the agreement fall apart later.

We pay a high price for papering over differences rather than facing them. We invite misunderstandings and misinterpretations that later lead to rancor or renegotiation. Agreements within the organization, unlike external ones, rarely have legal structure to determine the rights of the parties on matters left unclear. Internal agreements are very brittle and crack easily when challenged.

Workplace negotiations are likely to fail when agreements between parties are left vague. Settlements that contain words like, "My department will provide the necessary support to help you meet the schedule," will fail unless the support to be provided is carefully specified as to quantity, quality and timeliness. Papering over words like, "We will deliver in ten days," leads to needless argument and fault-finding about what was meant when delivery is late. Did the ten-day delivery promised include a partial delivery or all of it? Did the time specified include weekend days and a national holiday or just business days? Better to negotiate a bit longer and settle on, "We will deliver the complete program on February 17 or sooner."

8. YOUR ASSUMPTIONS ARE PROBABLY WRONG

Making assumptions about the other party and their negotiating position is a natural part of the bargaining process. We make assumptions before negotiations take place and revise them as new information is discovered along the way. Unfortunately, the very assumptions made to guide our actions at the table lead us astray because they are all too often incorrect.

The trouble with assumptions is that they are as likely to be wrong as right. What is in the mind and domain of the other person is hard to know. For us to forecast future trends, costs and problems is extremely difficult. Knowing what the other will do if confronted with deadlock is at best an educated guess. There is much we cannot know when assumptions are made about those we oppose and their future actions or behaviors under pressure. They themselves may not know.

Yet, whatever the issues at stake, assumptions must be made. We have to ask ourselves questions like, "Am I asking for enough (or too much) and why?" and, "What will the other side do in response to what I say or do?" and, "What can they live with, what's their bottom line?"

Time is a factor in negotiation. Assumptions must be made about time pressures facing the other party and how these pressures will affect their choices and decisions in dealing with us.

Negotiating effectively demands not only that assumptions be made, but also that they be tested in the light of what is learned at the table and elsewhere. How can we best do so?

We do so by creating 'negotiating space.' We leave room for talk and bargaining. We leave time for explanations to be provided by both parties for everything they demand and offer. We give in slowly and in small increments. We ask for something in return for offering concessions and learn from the other side's response. We explore by exchanging information to get a better picture of what they want and what they really need. We talk directly to them, both on and off the record, to discover what we need to know in testing our assumptions.

Our assumptions are like anchors. If they are wrong, and we believe them, they will hold us back from reality. If we test them carefully they can guide us to fair and reasonable agreements.

9. IMPORTANT NEGOTIATIONS CALL FOR A DEVIL'S ADVOCATE

Negotiating in the workplace is too important to be taken lightly or entered into without preparation. Not only are the issues and how they are settled important to your career, what others think of you is also at stake. How associates view your ability to persuade and defend your positions becomes an intrinsic part of your reputation. The acknowledgement by others that "he or she is a good negotiator" is almost everywhere accepted as exceptional praise.

Never enter an internal negotiation without taking at least some time to anticipate the other party's approach and arguments. If the bargaining stakes are high, find somebody who will help by acting in the role of adversary; that is, as your Devil's Advocate as they were called in religious tribunals of the Middle Ages. Lawyers, getting ready for big trials today, employ such advocates, as do presidential candidates preparing for public debate with opposing candidates. Using a Devil's Advocate to win agreement is a strategy that has worked for centuries and continues to work today.

Here are three "Devil's Advocate" approaches that work. The best by far for defending your position is what I call "the double defense." First, generate arguments in favor of your position, then allow a friend or associate to first offset your arguments and then present an opposing position. If you can handle their rebuttal to your position and cope with their arguments in support of their ideas you are well-prepared to negotiate.

Not as good, but less time consuming, is the single defense where you practice offsetting the anticipated arguments of the other side as anticipated by the Advocate. Least effective, but far better than nothing, is for your helper to find additional good reasons in defense of your position without regard to the counter-arguments of the other side.

The Devil's Advocate approach will make you a more effective negotiator. To do so two problems must be overcome. You will have to find a friend who has the time and cares to help. You will also have to commit yourself to do a lot of preparation work. If the stakes are high it's worth the extra effort.

10. AVOID THREAT, BLUFF OR BLUSTER

Threats, bluff and bluster, though risky, do have a place in commercial negotiations. They have no place in dealing with workplace associates. Research indicates that those who have the means to threaten tend to use it. It also shows that threat leaves a trail of hostility that does not fade from memory. Threats, even when not executed, destroy or jeopardize relationships. The negative consequences of threats are hard to predict but not likely benign.

Sometime in the future, you'll be tempted to use threats to gain your point in a workplace dispute or disagreement. Resist the impulse. The other will never fully trust you again. They may have the means to counter your threats with worse ones of their own. I've seen this happen with people who threaten lawsuits and later find themselves paying heavy legal fees they never intended to incur.

As for lying, if you have ever worked with anyone who lies or seeks to mislead by bluffing, you know how hard it is to believe anything they say. After a few experiences like that you avoid them as much as possible. Negotiating with such people is not apt to result in an agreement they will later honor. Lasting relationships with liars and bluffers is not possible.

Another trait that proves difficult in negotiation is dealing with people who conduct themselves in an arrogant or domineering manner. As a salesperson I have dealt with buyers who stormed into our conference room as though they were above anyone there. They made it clear that we were subservient to them and in the bargaining room only by their good graces. All they accomplished by putting us down by their arrogance was to set the stage for paying a higher price than they might otherwise have paid.

11. WORKPLACE AGREEMENTS ARE ALWAYS BRITTLE

All workplace agreements are brittle because they are unsupported by a formal legal structure and subject to inevitable organizational change over time. In almost all external dealings, agreements are put in writing and signed. When disagreements arise between buyer and seller about responsibilities and obligations the courts stand ready to decide. A formal legal system exists. The settlement of disputes is encouraged first by direct negotiation between parties, then informal off-the-record bargaining between attorneys, and finally if necessary in a court of law.

The key to reducing the problems inherent in workplace agreements lies in convincing both sides that they must reconcile themselves to frequent review and follow-up of all the issues agreed to. Without that, settlements will fall apart and be more difficult to rebuild. More will be said in Chapter Fourteen on how to reach workplace settlements that resist the rigors of time and change.

One more ever-present factor that causes the breakdown of internal dealings is change. Constant change occurs in every organization. People move from place to place, team to team, department to department. Those who negotiated the agreement in good faith may go on to a higher position or retire. Their replacements are rarely as committed to the agreement or its goals as those who initially settled the terms. Those affected by the initial negotiated outcome are replaced by strangers with no institutional memory of how the agreement came about or why.

Priorities change over time, as do budgets, needs and motivations. All workplace agreements are brittle. They must respond to the realities of change and renegotiation to stay alive.

12. NEVER OPEN WITH A CHIP ON YOUR SHOULDER

This is especially relevant in internal negotiations where relationships play a very large role in reaching satisfactory outcomes. Never start with a chip on your shoulder. There is no point in criticizing, abusing or otherwise chastening the other party. Such attack serves only to harden resistance.

Negotiators jeopardize their objectives by attacking another person's dignity or invalidating their self-worth. The other party will respond by harnessing their energies to protect their interests and ego from assault. Hostility breeds hostility.

Far better, if you are angry, is to write a long letter to the other fully expressing your feelings. Then be sure to tear it up. An angry e-mail message is not recommended because it's so easy to send off. I know many who inadvertently sent off messages they wish they hadn't. Abe Lincoln wrote many angry letters to relieve his frustrations during the Civil War, but was careful not to mail them.

13. COLLABORATIVE BOTH-WIN® NEGOTIATION IS THE MOST POWERFUL STRATEGY IN YOUR ARSENAL

Collaborative negotiating® for mutual gain is the most powerful strategy in a negotiator's arsenal. It rests on the premise that a better deal or arrangement can be found for both parties if they search for it together. Collaboration makes differences and disagreements easier to settle.

Chapter Thirteen will show how best to forge collaborative settlements and keep them working effectively. It will describe in detail the strategies and techniques of relationship-based collaborative negotiation, strategies that can move any workplace difference from discord to mutual gain while building strong connections.

PART IV

COLLABORATIVE BOTH-WIN® NEGOTIATING

How to Reach Agreement and Negotiate Anything with Anybody at Work

PART IV

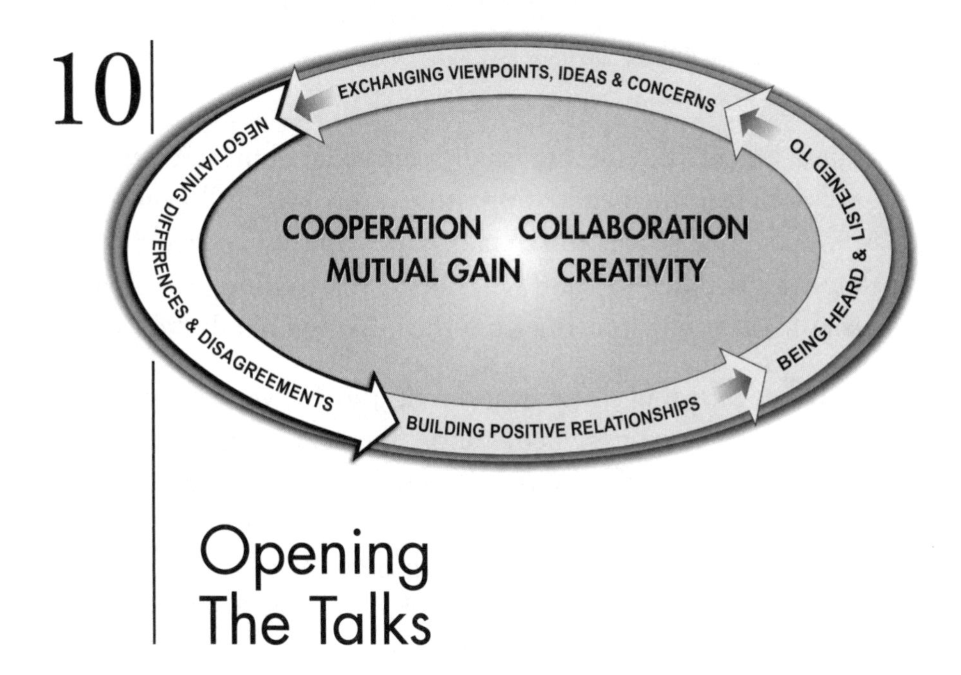

Opening The Talks

Preceding chapters of this book explored behaviors that move people with opposing views to work together productively and harmoniously. We reasoned in our model, "The Effective Negotiating® Virtuous Cycle," that when associates build stronger relationships, listen to one another and exchange viewpoints and concerns, they will find it easier to resolve conflict. People who do so will move from getting in the way of new ideas to facilitating and improving them through collaboration.

We will now focus on the strategies and techniques of Collaborative Both-Win® negotiating, the fourth factor of the Virtuous Cycle. Success in resolving differences in the workplace comes not only from satisfying the needs of the parties, but from something more, an integrative process that enables them to work closely to develop innovative Both-Win® ideas. When people work together to find new ways to solve problems or bridge disagreements they gain respect and warmth for one another. This growing regard also makes it easier for them to resolve new problems when they come up later, as they often do.

Francis Bacon, the eminent English diplomat of the 17th century, once described the negotiating process this way: "All negotiation is to work, to discover and to take risks." In the five chapters that follow we will develop and describe the bargaining process in an operational way by moving from the initiation of talks to closure.

As we move through the negotiating process we will introduce the reader to strategies, tactics and approaches that have worked for centuries. We will also present a number of entirely new ideas and concepts designed to help those at work to negotiate with associates above, below or level with them in the organizational hierarchy, in ways that achieve Both-Win®, mutually beneficial settlements and lasting relationships.

THE POWER OF PLANNING AND PREPARATION

Effective Negotiating® starts with planning and preparation. Experiments confirm that preparation prior to a meeting pays dividends. Surprisingly, most people do very little planning even when they know the stakes are high. They go into the negotiating session hoping for the best. But the best rarely happens except for those willing to do the hard work that goes with being ready.

I am aware of how difficult it is to prepare for a negotiation, be it with a close associate or with an aggressive opponent. Not only is there not enough time to do it well, but one often finds that what has been prepared for doesn't play out as thought. Some parts of the planning always prove to be of marginal or little value due to unexpected circumstances or information learned at the meeting. Nevertheless, there is still strong reason to do at least a minimal amount of planning rather than the little or nothing most people do.

THE QUICK NEGOTIATION PREPARATION CHECKLIST

1. Identify the issues or differences you wish to resolve. Prioritize them. Identify the other's interests and priorities.
2. Which issues should we talk about? Which should be avoided—or maybe delayed to a later date?
3. What is the best time and place to negotiate? Can this matter wait for a better time, place or hearing?
4. List your sources of strength. What are their limits and constraints? You have more power than you think. Why?
5. How will you open the negotiation and best support the position you take?
6. Most negotiations are settled through compromise and concession. How should you do so? What concessions might you ask for in return for those you make?
7. How will you and the other party document or otherwise assure that what both have agreed to will be accepted as a commitment to execute the terms of the agreement?
8. The best way to reach a committed agreement is by jointly searching for and finding mutual gain solutions that resolve differences and problems. Write down some Both-Win® ideas before entering the meeting.
9. Consider asking an associate to play the role of a "Devil's Advocate." Let them defend the other person's position and rebut your viewpoint and arguments.
10. Cool the "hot potato." The more difficult the issue, the more important it is to cool off before dealing with it. Don't start with a chip on your shoulder or a hot potato in your hand: Wait. Wait.
11. What relationship do you now have with the other person? Can something be done to improve that relationship before negotiating? During the talks? After agreement?

Exhibit 10

The 'Quick Negotiation Preparation Checklist' above assures that you will ask yourself important questions even when time is short. What relationship do you now have with the other person? Can something be done to improve that relationship before negotiating? During the talks? After agreement?

As you can see, the checklist covers many of the salient points that in the end determine whether your negotiating session will go well. The value of the checklist is that, in the rush to negotiate, some of these points may well escape our attention and lead us to needless resistance or a failed agreement.

The checklist suggestions are for the most part self-explanatory. Several suggestions, because of their importance, require further consideration. Item number 4, listing your sources of strength, is such a point. Negotiating strength flows from a variety of sources that are often forgotten or taken for granted by those who possess them.

In dealing with associates there are several attributes that carry weight in any workplace interaction. Among your special strengths is experience on the job and the things you do well every day. Your ability to express yourself well exerts power in any negotiation, as do your presentation and analytical skills when opposing demands and offers cross the negotiating table. Don't assume that everyone has these strengths. They don't.

Your reputation as a team player and responsible person who cares differentiates you from many who lack these qualities. You will find more power than you think if you take the time to consider even your smaller positive attributes and traits. Don't just take them for granted at your next compensation or performance review, or when dealing with a stubborn associate. For more about building your strength review Chapter Nine in the section related to power and its sources.

Other points in the checklist have been considered elsewhere in the book; however, point 11, the admonition to cool hot issues before trying to resolve them, is based on the personal experience and regret of many like myself who have occasionally failed to do so and suffered the consequences. Few of us are trained diplomats with "stiff upper lips" in the face of heavy pressure. Few are capable of controlling themselves when very angry or frustrated. Under the stress of severe criticism or rebuff we are apt to respond with words or gestures guaranteed to make things worse. Hot potato issues bring out the worst in us. They are better handled later when things cool off.

Many scoff at checklists, but research clearly indicates that those who use them make fewer mistakes and omissions. Every major airline now requires its pilots to go over a detailed checklist before taking off. The 'Quick Preparation Negotiation Checklist' is different but designed for a similar reason. It improves your chances of enjoying a safe trip.

GETTING OFF TO A GOOD START

Negotiations that get off to a good start are apt to end better. I've attended negotiations where the atmosphere was so loaded with hostility and distrust that fruitful bargaining was not possible. Moments after the parties met, recriminations for past shortcomings dominated the discussion and triggered deepening anger. Further talk to quiet both sides fell on deaf ears.

It's helpful to open with "non-task" talk. Talk about anything that will establish modest ties together. Speak of the weather, a recent sports event, a current movie, a breaking news story on the internet, or something funny that someone on television said. Also helpful is small talk about mutual friends and acquaintances that open the relationship door between parties in non-threatening ways. Inquiries as to the health and welfare of family members and children are usually welcome if done with discretion. "Non-task" talk is not a waste of time as some think; it is a catalyst that makes difficult bargaining flow more smoothly.

Occasionally you will deal with someone who won't abide with small talk. They are strictly business. They may not appreciate or reciprocate your attempts to establish rapport. I recall negotiating with such an executive once; he was the controller of a large corporation I worked for. He was as austere a person as I have ever dealt with: devoted only to facts and figures, rules and regulations. Negotiating a budget for my department with him was a nightmare.

Later, after several years, I found that dealing with him was not as difficult as first appeared. Two things softened the relationship; both were the result of working together on several semi-annual budgets. The first was a by-product of the bargaining process itself. As each of us learned and understood the other's needs we ceased to battle so strongly over each issue. We understood where concessions needed to be made and where we could hold fast. The battle over each issue no longer became a war.

The second thing learned over time was that he softened a bit as talks progressed at each session. After three or four hours of tedious work together he seemed to welcome a bit of "non-task" talk especially about his favorite charity, food pantries for the poor. There he served not only as financial advisor, but also as someone who personally solicited food markets for surplus items.

In addition he physically stacked the pantry shelves and handed out the groceries. Negotiating with him was never easy but improved as we learned to talk of things other than work.

"Non-task" conversation is an important part of the negotiating process. The paradox is that it is all the more necessary when the parties do not enjoy a strong relationship prior to entering into negotiations. When they already have a good relationship, light talk develops in a natural way and smoothes the path to agreement even when differences are wide.

Another action we can take to make it easier to negotiate is to break bread or meet with others on a regular basis long before difficulties occur. Good rapport with associates is something we should deposit in our relationship savings account. Regular lunch meetings are better than sporadic ones. When too much time passes between each lunch it becomes hard to re-establish the level of rapport that existed earlier. "Let's meet for lunch next week" is not nearly as good as, "Let's have lunch on Mondays every two weeks." Regularity is important.

It was perhaps for that reason that Mr. Coombs, the best manager I ever worked for, urged me to schedule regular lunches with those in other departments who were, one might say, customers for our output. He knew that sooner or later there would be differences that we would have to reconcile with them. Getting to know them early was a pleasant way to set the stage for later, more difficult talks.

It is also good to open talks with verbal assurances about your strong desire to reach a fair and reasonable agreement. Bill Van Allen, a superb high-level executive and negotiator at Hughes Aircraft, always opened his negotiations by personally assuring the other side of his regard for their relationship and of how much he valued a fair and reasonable settlement. He told them in no uncertain terms that he was open to anything they had to say and would do all he could to achieve a mutually satisfactory outcome.

When he later became vice president and was placed in charge of all significant corporate negotiations, he continued the practice. He personally opened every important session by joining with his counterpart in the other company to address those whose job it was to do the actual negotiating. His message was simple but important: higher management expected the negotiators to maintain their strong relationship and to reach a fair agreement. These joint high-level addresses softened what might otherwise have been contentious confrontations by those at the table.

In the Middle East, negotiations begin in an especially pleasant way. Guests are provided a bounteous feast of treats and goodies to nibble on. Special teas are served by gracious hosts; sweets, fruits, rare nuts, cookies, chocolates and dates abound. Negotiators are seated in comfortable chairs arranged around the room: not as teams in opposition, but like friends sitting side-by-side as they would at a get-together at home. To top it all, pleasant surprises and small gifts are given to each visitor along the way.

Being treated so nicely stays with you during the negotiation and long afterward, whatever the outcome. Contrast that, if you will, with those who negotiate by tactlessly saying what they please, making you uncomfortable or criticizing everything you say. There are people who negotiate that way, especially when they have power. Such discourtesy and intimidation has no place in the workplace where relationships are so crucial to long-term success.

CREATING A NEGOTIATING CLIMATE CONDUCIVE TO RELATIONSHIP-BASED COMPROMISE AND COLLABORATION

Differences are rarely easy to settle even when both sides have the best intentions. They are, however, easier to settle if an enabling climate of negotiation exists. Three factors play a major role in creating such a climate: where and when the talks occur, how emotional factors are handled and the degree to which those at the table are heard and listened to. If these factors are implemented, the meeting will go better. If not, differences between the parties grow rather than diminish.

A quiet, appropriate place and time to talk is essential. One would think that such a suggestion is only common sense. But I have seen some career-tipping internal negotiations conducted in the midst of clattering machinery, on stairways with other employees busy going up and down and in crowded offices surrounded by curious but embarrassed listeners. Important meetings in today's busy world are often subject to frequent cell phone interruptions, constant text messages and urgent e-mails delivered by lap-top computers, or personally by assistants who require immediate answers. That setting, I hope you'll agree, is no place to negotiate or decide anything. Yet, all too often, that's where the give and take of choosing between difficult alternatives takes place.

Sufficient time must be set aside to discuss major issues. Left to fare for itself, time will follow the 90-10 rule. Ninety percent of the time will be spent on minor points and ten percent on important matters. Time must be managed at any negotiation. Where critical matters are at stake an agenda should be negotiated and agreed to in advance. Some things, too hot to be discussed, should, if possible, be shelved for now or covered later in the talks. It takes good management skill to set up and run an effective session. Participants immediately sense the difference between team leaders and managers who conduct productive meetings and those who do not.

Carpet merchants in Morocco know how to set the stage for a "Yes" answer when tourists step through their door. They take lots of time to make customers feel at home. Small talk, warm tea and cookies lead to happier negotiation outcomes. The Arabs are deservedly recognized as exceptional bargainers in worldwide commercial and international affairs.

Not surprising to the carpet merchants would be a recent research study at Yale University in which two psychologists found that people holding a warm rather than iced coffee mug are more likely to perceive another person as "warm" or "friendly". Another study relevant to creating a quiet thinking space was completed at the University of Michigan where they found that people who took a walk in the park were better able to focus attention on details than those walking on busy streets downtown. A meeting space that allows for quiet listening and concentration surely favors a better exchange of ideas.

A good negotiating climate must also deal with controlling emotional outbursts and temper tantrums. Emotional outbursts are not uncommon in the workplace but occur more often in commercial buy-sell transactions. There, people feel less constrained to say what they please than in the office where they have to work with others on a daily basis. Nevertheless, unwelcome outbursts do occur at meetings and workplace negotiations that serve to disrupt ongoing dealings by making it difficult to resolve problems or differences peacefully. Managers and group leaders must find ways to reduce these bursts of anger and vituperation.

Team leaders as well as all team members have a crucial role in diminishing emotional impediments. They must jointly insist that any outburst stop immediately regardless of whose side or view is favored. The time to silence such outbursts is the moment harsh words and accusations arise. When members of the group collectively accept responsibility for keeping control of outbursts they will cease before they damage everyone there.

The same can be said for insisting that everyone who has something to say is given the opportunity to do so. Each person at the meeting has a part in assuring that the right of others to be listened to not be impinged upon by snide remarks, glances from side to side, text messages or body language gestures conveying inattention or disdain. All at the session have a role in cutting highly emotional behavior short, not just the leader.

If organizers fail to actively structure the time and place of talks, the issues to be covered, steps to diffuse dysfunctional emotional outbursts and techniques that foster open communication, then the climate of negotiation inevitably has a reduced chance of achieving meaningful results.

QUICK DEALS ARE DANGEROUS

Research indicates that quick negotiations, while dangerous for both sides, are worse for one party than the other. Those prepared win better settlements in quick negotiations, as do negotiators who are more skilled and possessing greater bargaining power. These laboratory studies have been confirmed by real experience. Quick deals should be abstained from where a fair and reasonable outcome is sought and creative collaboration is the goal.

Quick negotiations are risky and best avoided in the workplace. If at all possible, hurried talks should be postponed for later when ample time is available. Matters of compensation, budget allocations, performance and schedule commitment are too important for both sides to be settled under the pressure of time. Your career and reputation are at stake if the agreement reached leaves inadequate resources or time to effectively complete the assignment under consideration.

Mistakes happen when people fail to give themselves enough time to process information and make thoughtful decisions. Omissions are common. You think of all the brilliant things you should have said or asked for after the meeting has taken place.

Contingencies that mar plans often occur but are overlooked. Simple calculations go wrong in quick deals. Under the pressure of quick decision-making, listening is difficult and sensible rebuttals are hard to formulate. When time is short, opportunities for collaboration are absent. Discovering creative alternatives together becomes very unlikely. Quick deals lead to outcomes that are at best marginal, and at worst disastrous.

It is far better to set aside enough time for uninterrupted talk by both sides, enough time for all viewpoints to be aired and for creative alternatives to be explored. Little is gained by reaching agreements that fall apart or fail to provide the satisfactions sought.

When time is short, have the courage to face into it. Renegotiate another meeting. There is no rule that says you cannot meet later. A change in time or venue would be far better than a quick deal that results in shortsighted settlement.

LET ACCEPTANCE TIME DO ITS WORK

Two people at work decide to settle a difference between them. Each hopes the negotiation won't be too hard or acrimonious. Both enter the session with somewhat unrealistic perceptions and assumptions. The process of negotiating is itself an awakening. The easy settlement they hoped for is not quickly at hand. There's lots of give and take still to be done if a mutually satisfactory outcome is to be achieved.

The session begins. Proposals are offered, demands and offers exchanged. Phrases like "No," "I can't" and "I won't" are heard. Then something is submitted that one side believes fair or generous. To their surprise it is unceremoniously rejected by the other. Have they no sense? Is getting to agreement even possible? That's where "Acceptance Time" does its work in negotiation. People need time to accept anything new or different. Offering the other side something they are not prepared to take, or perhaps have not even thought of, is like asking them to give up the old friends in their head for the new friends you propose. Resistance to change is universal. It takes time to get used to new ways that are foreign or possibly unpleasant. Acceptance time is an important factor in life as it is in negotiation.

The human resources department of a mid-sized company with which I am familiar recently developed a sorely-needed improved health care plan for its employees. After considerable study and extensive negotiation with competing providers the new proposed plan was presented to its employees, first by e-mail and then by question and answer sessions in groups of fifty. The human resources team wished to ensure that all understood the proposed plan and its improved benefits.

The human resources department felt they were on firm ground: while employee contribution rates would go up slightly, benefits would improve much more. The team expected some resistance but not much. Within moments after the plan was presented an explosion of dissent followed. The human resources department was challenged to explain whether one plan or another was better than the proposed one, whether retirees were adequately covered, whether the increased contribution was necessary and whether the selected provider would be in business five years from now. The employees demanded further study before the company committed itself. As good as the plan and team presentation were, the new health plan was not accepted.

Then, slowly, over a two-week period, a change took place among employees. They began to discuss the plan and its details. They made their own comparisons. Each matched the new benefits to their personal needs. Acceptance time began to play a role in their decision process. A few weeks later, a slightly revised plan was presented, approved and implemented.

Acceptance time works that way. People need time to accept changes to their usual way of doing things or to new ideas. You cannot expect that they will give up what were in effect their old friends or ideas for the new friends you are introducing to them. Acceptance time has the same role in negotiation. The next time you make a proposal or present a better way to do something, no matter how good it appears to you, don't be surprised if the other person resists your magnificent idea. Let acceptance time do its work for you.

SIX ACTIONS THAT MOVE TALKS TOWARD SETTLEMENT FROM THE START

Among the fundamental rules of negotiation covered in Chapter Nine are six that apply closely to the early stages of bargaining. They are briefly described below for your consideration in opening talks. Which you choose depends on whom you are dealing with and the issues or viewpoints under discussion.

Negotiation is in part theatrics, even when it takes place within your own organization. How you present your first offer, where, when and how you back it up can move the other person to favor or oppose your ideas.

Experiments indicate that those who enter negotiations with inadequate or questionable backup in defense of their position raise the aspirations or expectations of the other side. The same happens when one's body language or vocal tone reveals lack of confidence in the position taken. Your opening offer and its presentation affect the entire negotiation process and the final agreement. Take the time to bring good support and be ready to present it well.

All negotiation involves risk and a measure of courage. It takes courage to resist the apprehension that goes with trying to negotiate a difference or disagreement. It takes courage to be patient and persistent in the face of strong resistance and a firm "No."

It certainly takes courage to say "No" and, paradoxically, to say "Yes." In the case of a "No," the bird in hand that has been offered may disappear and not be available later. In the case of

"Yes," you may later learn that a far better deal would have been possible had you waited only a little more. In both situations, every organization has "Monday Morning Quarterbacks" ready to challenge whatever you do, be it "Yes" or "No." Not being at the negotiating table in the heat of discussion gives these Monday Morning Quarterbacks the freedom to second-guess or criticize whatever outcome was achieved.

Four hundred years ago, Sir Francis Bacon said, "All negotiation is to work, to discover and to take risk." It still is.

Don't start with your last and final position. Leave some reasonable room to negotiate in your opening offer but not so much as to impair your relationship with the other side when challenged. Cover contingencies and changes that may arise. Be prepared to defend and explain whatever room you have provided for yourself. Have credible reasons and adequate backup for doing so.

In most commercial buy-sell negotiations both parties open with demands and offers that leave room for further talk and compromise. They usually allow space to make concessions despite expressing strong professions to the contrary early and throughout the talks. They leave as much room as they can credibly defend if questioned. They reveal as little as they must in explaining what they ask for or demand.

Workplace negotiators aware of the importance of relationships find it prudent to proceed differently. While they also leave room to negotiate they are prepared and willing to reveal their reasons for leaving the bargaining space they do. Everything they do or say during the exchange process is relationship-based. Deliberate exaggeration or obfuscation has no place in workplace give and take.

Your first offer is an important one. It should be made in a firm but courteous way. Much can be learned by observing how your opening position is received. The other person's body language may provide more insight than their words.

The other side's subsequent offers and concessions also tell a story. Most would interpret concessions made too quickly as a sign of weakness. A rate of concession-making that moves in the direction of ever-smaller increments transmits a message that further compromise will be limited or unavailable later. Whether these signs are real or only imagined depends on what is learned through further negotiation.

Surprises in the form of unexpected issues or negative information learned at the table are always hard to handle. When a surprise comes up, it's wise to find a reason to call a caucus or time-out as they do in basketball or football when things on the field go wrong.

When a question you are unprepared for is asked by the other, it is better to say that you are not ready to answer than it is to bluff your way through and be sorry later. Hardly a month goes by without some televised politician attempting to bluff a response to a difficult question and then spending the next month trying in vain to correct what was said in haste.

All good negotiators have an abundance of perseverance. When their great idea or well-analyzed viewpoint is rejected they do not falter or lose self-esteem. The perseverance rule is simple—when your proposal is rejected or laughed at, shape it in another way and return it to the table. Zhou Enlai, a famous Chinese diplomat under Chairman Mao once said, "If the other side resists my offer of a pizza cut in six pieces, I offer it later cut in eight."

As a recent Harvard Business Review article reported, perseverance may pay dividends in dealing with your boss. Jack Welsh described a technique that he used when Chairman of General Electric to test a subordinate's faith in the ideas that they proposed. He would reject their ideas a number of times to see if they would return with the idea after rejection.

After several re-submittals Mr. Welsh found that those who returned to him had greater faith in their proposals. They thought enough of their ideas to take on the boss. Like most decisions in business, when and whether to do this with your boss is a judgment call you'll have to make for yourself.

Perseverance works in negotiation. Its powerful partner is "Acceptance Time." Together they can help convince the other party that you are committed to your position in a thoughtful, disciplined way.

THE POSITIVE ROLE OF NEGATIVE PLANNING

We are told many times that positive thinking is the key to a more satisfying, successful life. That, I believe, is essentially true. Yet, in negotiation, be it in your own organization or with outside suppliers, there is value to be gained by proposing a positive role for negative planning and thinking. Why?

The path between what you want and what you settle for is replete with obstacles and frustrations. Your hopes for the best are not likely to be realized. Sitting opposite you is someone just as determined as you are to protect their interests, and just as convinced that their views prevail. With negative planning you can anticipate their arguments in a better way. With negative planning you can test your assumptions about what is achievable and what is not.

In a typical workplace negotiation, you open with an offer, a proposal, an idea or a design. Your position and viewpoint are clearly presented and amply supported by objective criteria and documentation. It is of course possible that the other person will say "Yes" quickly and all will be over. This is possible, but not likely.

More often they will flinch, gasp for breath or otherwise show their surprise or even disdain at your position. They will call it extreme and unwarranted despite your protestation that it is modest and in fact quite right. They will probably challenge everything you say.

Expect them to respond to your proposal by saying things like, "It won't work," or "It will cost more than you think," or "Absolutely not, it's not good enough." None of these responses are easy to cope with if unprepared. The best you can do is assume that the other side will be negative and protect yourself by rehearsing what you will do when they are.

The positive role of negative planning is to help us think about these negative reactions to our opening offer, however good it may be. Anticipating the negatives will move you to prepare for the onslaught of naysaying and abuse that your fine offer or viewpoint will endure.

In the next chapter we will focus on what to do when the other side opens talks with strong resistance to your position or ideas. Six hard-to-handle opposing responses will be considered ranging from dealing with a firm "No" to "Not now, but maybe later."

11

What To Do When the Other Side Opens Talks With Strong Resistance

Rarely does anyone making a proposal or offering a new idea find themself greeted with an immediate "Yes." More often they are confronted with a firm "No" or "But," or some other equally hard-to-handle negative response that indicates that strong resistance is sure to follow.

In this chapter we will discuss six negative responses you are likely to encounter and what to do when they occur. The better prepared you are, the more effective you will be in handling the response.

The first step in preparing for any workplace negotiation is to review the "Quick Negotiation Preparation Checklist" in Chapter Ten. Your review of this checklist will place you in a better position to consider the six negative responses that follow and the means you have available to you to deal with them.

SIX HARD-TO-HANDLE NEGATIVE RESPONSES AND HOW TO DEAL WITH THEM

1. THE FIRM "NO" RESPONSE
2. THE "BOGEY" RESPONSE
3. THE "YOU'VE GOTTA DO BETTER THAN THAT" RESPONSE
4. THE "FLINCH" RESPONSE
5. THE "GARBAGE ON THE LAWN" RESPONSE
6. THE "NOT NOW, BUT MAYBE LATER" RESPONSE

Exhibit 11

THE FIRM "NO" RESPONSE

There are people who respond to any new idea presented to them or any opening offer in negotiation with a firm "No." They usually do so with a view to reducing the other person's expectations or ending the talks as quickly as possible. Of course, both are legitimate negotiating objectives, even if they are not conducive to fostering better relations between the parties.

This firm "No" approach is sometimes used by buyers in commercial negotiations when they have considerable power and wish to leverage that strength to achieve a goal they have already decided on. The seller is told, "This is my final offer. Take-it-or-leave it." General Electric used the tactic successfully for more than twenty years in annual dealings with its union. The company, though forceful, was always careful to support its firm and final offer with detailed breakdowns and documentation. This radical approach worked until 1969 but left a residue of resentment on the part of labor. What followed in 1969 was the costliest strike in General Electric history—not just a strike but a holy war. The company never used "Take-It-Or-Leave-It" again.

We can learn from the General Electric experience. If you are going to respond to someone's idea or position with a firm opening "No," minimize the hostility they will surely feel. Never use the phrase, "Take-It-Or-Leave-It." It is unnecessarily incendiary and invites retribution. When a firm "No" is backed by facts, good precedents or history, it is less onerous. So also when the "No" is defended by existing organization policies, procedures or published constraints. Yet, however politely a firm "No" is rendered, it will be resented.

Time is also a factor in determining how the "No" will be accepted. If the other person is provided adequate time to present and defend their position or idea they will not resent the "No" as much. Whether a firm "No" is expressed early or late in the talks makes a difference. A "No" expressed late in the bargaining process is apt to be received with less bad feeling.

What can you do when the other opens talks with a firm "No" to your "great" idea or "reasonable" offer? My advice is: test the rejection hard. It may not be as rigid as appears.

Several options are available. The best, I believe, is to broaden the nature of the deal under discussion. Expand the problem or differences to be resolved to include other matters of interest to both sides such as service, work product or quality considerations not covered by the "No" response. Even those who take pride in saying "No" don't want to appear close-minded or unreasonable to everything that is suggested or under consideration.

In addition to broadening the matter or issue, you may test the "No" by using one, or several, of the ideas that follow:

1. Saying the words, "But it doesn't apply in this case," usually opens the door to further interest on the part of the other side. They cannot help wondering why the "No" doesn't apply in this specific case.

   You will, of course, have to spend time preparing for the "Why" and come up with some reasonably good reasons. When searching for appropriate "good" reasons as to why the firm "No" is not applicable in this case, it's well to recognize that every situation is different no matter how many precedents exist: that you are in some ways different from the general group; that your service, track record and loyalty are well established and that the rules and regulations governing this matter are not applicable in this case.

   The negotiating dialogue that follows once you start explaining why the "No" does not apply in this case will allow you to also discuss other aspects of your basic position. You will have opened negotiating space where there was little or none before and provided the person saying "No" with room or authority to move.

2. Another approach that works surprisingly well is to continue speaking as though you never heard the "No." You see this done often on television when two people are arguing about a

political or economic matter and one says to the other, "No, that's absolutely wrong." The other, instead of accepting the "No," goes on to say whatever he or she wished for as long as needed to complete the thought.

3. Find a face-saving way for the person who said "No" to retreat from their position. In a strange way, the person who says "No" in a rigid way has trapped themself into an awkward, inflexible position. They need a good way out or they won't retreat.

By far the best way to provide the other side with a face-saving avenue to move from "No" or any other strong position is to suggest a collaborative search for a better way by which both sides might benefit. If you can then offer one potential idea, they are likely to listen and come up with possibilities of their own.

THE BOGEY RESPONSE

The Bogey response in the hands of a courteous negotiator can serve to reduce the other side's expectations while it raises their hopes that a deal may be possible. I have seen the Bogey used frequently in buyer and contractor bargaining and just as often in workplace negotiations involving budgets, compensation and other resource distribution and allocation issues. People use the Bogey approach because it works and offends no one.

The best way to explain it is with an example. Some years ago as controller of the Control Data Division, a five-hundred-person division of a very large technology-based conglomerate, my responsibilities included negotiating an annual operating budget with the controller of corporate finance and accounting. While neither of us exercised any direct authority over the other, it was obvious that the corporate controller held a more influential position than I did.

We usually started talks with a few minutes of small talk. The corporate controller, more impatient on this day than usual, asked what my division needed for the year. I was prepared to go into considerable detail but was cut off after I made a request for $20 million, just a million more than the year before, and began to offer an explanation for the modest increase.

He responded immediately by saying, "We in corporate would love to give you the $20 million but we can't." He acknowledged that my department had done a good job the previous year, but that all the corporation could allot this year was $17 million because the company was under competitive pressure and outside capital and credit sources were drying up. He repeated, "$17 million is all we can do."

Frankly, my expectations fell. I had expected little or no resistance to our small increase over last year. A reduction would require cuts in staff and commitments. Neither side was happy with where we stood so we decided to meet at a later date. I brought my staff together to search for a way to handle the $17 million Bogey. Four approaches were discussed to bridge our differences with Corporate.

1. Test the bogey. Almost all budgets are flexible to some extent. Money can be shifted from one account to another, from one purpose to a second or from direct to overhead accounts. Working together we might find some relief that way.

2. The time shape of funding can be changed. If the other side doesn't have enough now, they may have it later or early next year. They may prefer to cover the budget shortfall by using investment or borrowed funds rather than direct revenue.

3. Change the time shape of performance. Not all work need be done between January 1 and December 31. Some parts can be completed later; some must be done early in the year. Changing the scope of work, leaving some things out, adding others and doing some later can serve to bridge the gap between parties in whole or in part.

4. Shift the work. If our department expects trouble meeting its responsibilities with the $17 million budget offer, we might offer to shift some work to other departments or to farm it out overseas. We could ask for temporary help or assistance to meet overload requirements. The lines of authority and responsibility between departments are never rigid over time. Some of our work could be done by another department if several of our people had to be transferred to meet the Bogey.

My staff and I met with the Corporate Controller once more. The negotiation between us closed with an $18.2 million settlement. Together we pared some costs, maintained our 3% salary increase target and transferred three people to an adjoining department. The corporate people accepted our reduced statement of work and the phasing of some parts to a later time. Overcoming the bogey by collaboration led us to a budget we could live with.

THE "YOU'VE GOTTA DO BETTER THAN THAT" RESPONSE

Several years ago we hired a young systems and computer specialist who was full of good ideas to reduce cost and upgrade our programs and reports. One of the first things that attracted his attention was a weekly sales report we had used for almost ten years. It had been designed by our present sales manager when he was only a junior sales representative. Ten years later it was still virtually unchanged.

When he received his first sales report the systems person found he couldn't quite understand it so he questioned several others on the distribution list. He asked what they used it for, whether the information provided was in their opinion accurate and how it might be improved. To his surprise, none of those queried read it carefully or understood the report. Several did say it gave them an approximate idea of how this year's sales compared to sales a year earlier.

Even the sales manager, when asked by the systems person for help in understanding the data, hemmed and hawed about the accuracy of the numbers and their relevance to present day operations. The systems person, unaware of the early history of the report, decided on his own to revise it. He was sure he could do it quickly.

He was right. It didn't take him long to develop a software program to do the work done by clerks and salespeople filling in the data required on the old forms. He eliminated portions nobody had an interest in and clarified other parts of it. Pleased with his work he arranged a meeting with the sales manager and sent him a copy of the new proposed report for review.

The systems person opened the discussion with, "I hope you like this new report and would appreciate any suggestions you have to improve it." The manager, an old timer, responded with just seven words, "You've gotta do better than that." The systems person was flustered, he asked, "What do you mean by better than that?" The manager replied once more, "You've got to do a lot better than that." He then handed back the new report and excused himself to go to another urgent meeting.

The new report never saw the light of day in the company. The system person's good idea and the brevity of his hearing left him angry and deflated. Like all good ideas, he knew that the proposed report was not perfect and could with effort be improved further. But where and by how much improvement was the question. Soon afterward other systems matters came up. The revised report was forgotten. To this day the old sales report is issued weekly to a broad distribution list that does not use or understand it.

In commercial negotiations between buyers and sellers we call this tactic the Krunch. A seller presents a proposal for $100,000 to a buyer for a package of goods and services. They document the proposal with customer references and product values designed to convince the buyer that the price is sound and the satisfaction to be gained assured. The buyer opens the negotiation with the Krunch, "You've gotta do better than that."

The buyer knows that almost every proposed project has some flexibility. They know that in the face of competition sellers always feel somewhat insecure. That's why the Krunch works better than it should.

The next time you hear the words, "You've gotta do better than that," don't panic. You can make an opportunity of it.

1. Whenever you are confronted with a general objection by the other side ask them to be specific. Ask in what specific way you must do better and why. Don't change your position, idea or viewpoint until the other person makes clear what exactly they are not pleased with.

2. Be persistent. Continue to present the values and benefits of your approach or idea despite the Krunch response.

3. Even when the other person comes up with specific objections to your position don't assume they will make their final decision based solely on the specific points in question. It rarely happens that way. Most decisions, especially complex ones, are a product of multiple factors, each with a varying weight of importance.

4. Specific objections can be handled. General objections cannot. When the other side takes objection to the quality of your output you have to find out what specific aspect of your quality they find inadequate. Only then can you offset the negatives associated with their position.

5. Take the time to build a sound relationship with the other side long before differences arise. If our systems person had done so he might have had more leverage in asking the sales manager to clarify his objections. I know from experience how hard it is to deny further clarification to someone to whom I've just said, "You've gotta do better than that," especially if I know them well and like them.

THE "FLINCH" RESPONSE

Several pages back we discussed the "Bogey" response and ways to handle it. You'll recall that as controller of my small division I requested a budget of $20 million, which I thought quite reasonable considering the effect of higher than usual inflation pressures on engineering salaries and technology-based materials. The other party responded with a $17 million counteroffer. That "Bogey" response with its low but friendly offer helped set the stage later for an amiable, mutually satisfactory agreement. What would I have done if, instead, he had "flinched" by saying in loud terms, "That's ridiculous," and offered nothing in response to my $20 million request? The negotiation might have gone differently.

I can assure you that a strong "flinch" would have reduced my expectations and made me wonder if any agreement was possible without large concessions. I've seen people "flinch" in many ways. One, in response to a price he didn't like, actually fell off his chair as it tipped backward. Others have screamed in anger, and still others, more polite, nod their heads sadly and say words like "Wow, that's awful," or "Are you kidding?" The effect of the flinch always leads you to think, "Coming to agreement is not going to be easy."

There is nothing unethical about the "flinch." Those who differ with your viewpoint, or proposal, have every right to express their disagreement by either flinching, remaining silent or quickly offering another opinion. Their flinch may, of course, be real or postured. It's hard to tell, but the effect is the same. The person facing the "flinch" feels they must relieve the concern of the "flincher" by explaining why their position or price is not unreasonable. Later, if the flinching resistance continues, concessions or alternate approaches may follow. Those who flinch know this.

The key to responding to the "flinch" is to recognize that it is an opportunity to express your position more fully. Instead of lowering your expectations it can serve as a springboard to exchange viewpoints and build a stronger relationship. The best way to handle the flinch is to tell your story as though the other person had said, "Please tell me more." Don't let it bother you or cause you to lose confidence in your position. Use it as an opportunity to explore Both-Win® possibilities.

THE "GARBAGE ON THE LAWN" RESPONSE

None of us is perfect. Even baseball stars hit safely only three times in ten. In a lifetime of investment most are lucky if half the stocks they pick turn out reasonably well. Not only does each of us have failings, there are always people around to tell us how imperfect we are. That's why the "garbage-on-the-lawn" response works as it does.

Recall for a moment the team we put together to develop our invention of a lifetime: the better mousetrap. Now, time has passed. The project has gone modestly well except in one important respect. Design engineering is six months behind schedule and holding up others on the team in getting their work done. The inexpensive computer chip device necessary to snap shut the trap has not performed properly. Engineering has completed a new design they feel will solve the problem. The new trap will be ready for full testing and production in four months at an additional cost to complete of $300,000.

At a special meeting, engineering has just completed a carefully prepared presentation and invited team questions. Unfortunately, everyone is skeptical of the engineering solution and forecast because this is the third time their design has failed. Most doubt that this fourth approach will work and believe that added costs will exceed $600,000 rather than $300,000 and take much longer to complete than four months.

No sooner is the new plan presented by engineering than a dissenting voice is heard. That voice is from the head of team quality control and testing. Her people have suffered most from past engineering errors. She is not about to let her doubts go unheard.

The head of testing responds to the presentation by saying, "Frankly, I think you've got it wrong again. This is your fourth try at a good design. Your first three failed miserably. Now, here we go again. I don't know what to do. Last time you promised to complete the work by June. I hired three lab techs to do the testing and data collection. I scheduled tests of the mousetraps at various locations around the United States, Asia and Africa to see how people around the world would look at and use our product. I wasted a lot of time and money. In the end I had to lay off two of these fine new hires. Why should I now build my plans and commitments around your flimsy promises?"

How do you think the head of engineering felt about his new design and schedule after hearing this response? He became unsure of his presentation. It showed in the tentative answers he gave to other questions. What he had experienced is what we in negotiation call the "garbage on the lawn" response. Such a response reduces our aspiration and confidence level. It prepares us for retreat and saps our energy.

"Garbage on the lawn" is commonly used by buyers to reduce a seller's proposed price. Early in the talks these negative remarks remind the salesperson about everything their company failed to do in the past year. Every late delivery is mentioned. Every defective product or service left undone is rendered with gusto. Deficiencies in quality even years back are reviewed in gruesome detail. No wonder the hapless salesperson is ready to reduce their price. They hope that by doing so they will retain the unhappy buyer's business. Internally in most organizations there is a lot of 'garbage dumping' every day. Relationships suffer.

The best way to handle "garbage on the lawn" is not to succumb to its implications: that you have failed before, are likely to fail again and now must pay a price for it. Preparation for this onslaught is necessary. Make a list of all that went well during the previous period such as special contributions to the group welfare and actions taken above ordinary expectations. List also ordinary things that went well. Too often what we do well day after day is taken for granted or forgotten. Don't let that happen when negotiating with anyone in your organization.

Finally, as a defense against "garbage on the lawn," it's well to remember that those who throw the garbage often bear a measure of responsibility for what went wrong in the past. History is rarely clear about such matters as fault and responsibility. The less we go into the past the better when it comes to faultfinding in negotiation.

THE "NOT NOW BUT MAYBE LATER" RESPONSE

There are few situations at work as difficult as negotiating with your boss about something they have no desire to discuss. That happened to a friend of mine who worked for someone who never wanted to negotiate about a problem that troubled her a great deal.

My friend was then a chemistry teacher at an elite private school in Chicago. She specialized in advanced college-level chemistry courses for students who were likely to attend Ivy-League universities. Her schedule of classes left little time for attending student sports activities, though doing so was part of her job description.

What made her workload worse was that the school, many years earlier, had inadvertently failed to provide hot water for its chemistry labs. These labs routinely require hundreds of test tubes, beakers and other glassware containers for qualitative, quantitative and physical chemistry requirements. Between classes and on weekends she found herself boiling water and cleaning glassware by hand. This, she soon decided, was unfair and intolerable.

A meeting with the headmaster was arranged. The headmaster himself was a kind man but harassed by the demands of this old but rapidly growing school. His day was filled with irate parents wanting to assure their children's access to Harvard or Yale, some of whom had social and relationship problems. Dealing with these parents and his staff of overworked teachers was hard enough. Negotiating with my friend about her need for hot water in a building built fifty years earlier seemed to be one of his lower priorities.

The headmaster, always polite, listened carefully to her plight. He understood it fully but said, "Not now but maybe later." Every six months at performance review and curriculum time she got another chance to plead her case. The response: "Not now but maybe later." He did explain that making changes in the building was expensive and that there were plans afoot to construct a new laboratory building in the future.

Every negotiation for the next several years went the same way. She complained, he listened and then said, "No, not now, maybe later." She continued to handwash the glassware. When I asked her why she did not leave, she explained that as a single mother she could not risk leaving the job. I asked her why she had not offered or asked for some compromise like getting a few hours of inexpensive help to clean test tubes in exchange for her proctoring monthly soccer games. She answered that, knowing the headmaster, she would end up proctoring the soccer games while the promised help was diverted for one reason or another from her lab.

To her surprise, after three years of fruitless talks, the headmaster assigned a part-time helper to assist with cleaning two hours a day for three days a week. A miracle. Two years later a costly piping and hot water system were installed and the problem washed away.

I believe my friend could have handled the "Not now but maybe later" negotiations better. Yes, I am aware that she needed the job, that getting another was difficult for a single mother with a child and that the possibility of antagonizing your boss is hazardous. Effective Negotiating® always involves a willingness to take risks. What could she have done better than she did? She could have assessed her power in a more positive way. Advanced chemistry teachers with high results on college advanced placements examinations are rare. Her students had all achieved a grade level of four or five, none less. This was outstanding. She never mentioned this to the headmaster though I'm certain he made much of it with prospective parents of students applying to the school. Her credentials in advanced chemistry were unusual. What she did not recognize was that she had more power in that school than she thought. She made light of her strengths and was overwhelmed by her constraints.

To her credit, she was persistent. That worked but all too slowly. Persistence pays dividends in negotiation when your position is sound. The passing of time worked in her favor. Time alters the balance of power for better or worse. In her case it paved the way for relief. So did "Acceptance Time."

Networking would have helped. Had she enjoyed better relationships with others in the science department she might have found that they also suffered similar problems. Together, they would have been in a better position to achieve their objectives. If, in addition, they were networking with professionals at science schools elsewhere, they might have found that those schools provided not only hot water but also special scrubbing devices and help tidying up. This would have given the headmaster good reason to request added funds from his Board of Trustees. Benchmarking what your peers are doing and networking with them not only adds information to your position, but also power.

12

Moving to Agreement Through Relationship-Based Compromise and Concession Exchange

Ideas, however creative or original, will not reach the global marketplace unless we as entrepreneurs learn to work together and make decisions in a better way. A report published recently in The Wall Street Journal made that point in no uncertain terms. The report, titled "Project Design," describes seven good ideas and how they moved to market, some successfully, others not. In the Editor's Note preceding the article, Lawrence Rout wrote:

> "It begins with an idea. A pair of women's jeans that fits well but won't cost a lot... a car that will appeal to consumers in both China and the U.S.... a watch that can be worn indoors but has a flashlight that makes it particularly useful at night." And then, Mr. Rout says, "It gets interesting. Because it's one thing to have a broad idea of what you want a product to be. It's something else to figure out how it will all be put together and what it's actually going to look like."

The report goes on to cover other products that reached the marketplace after considerable research and collaboration. In every case, it was teams of specialists who nursed these ideas to market, not individuals working by themselves in small laboratories or garages as in earlier times.

This chapter is titled, "Moving to Agreement Through Relationship-Based Compromise and Concession-Exchange" for two reasons. When bargaining for anything, we usually proceed toward agreement through a series of reciprocal concessions and compromises. Through the process of sharing information and give and take, we reconnoiter the possible settlement range and move to a fair and reasonable agreement that satisfies both parties. The negotiating and concession exchange process, while far from perfect, is a relatively fast and efficient way to reach agreement.

The words "relationship-based compromise and concession-exchange" in the chapter title are critically important in the context of negotiations taking place within our own organizations. In the workplace it is essential that all concession-making approaches take into account the significance of maintaining and advancing positive relationships between the parties. Unless we do so our ability to work together on a daily basis will result in little or nothing getting done.

Relationships are, of course, important in external negotiations such as those between diplomats of different countries or buyers and sellers. While important, they are not as crucial there as they are in internal dealings where interpersonal matters like respect, honesty, transparency, belonging and credibility play such a large role. We will now explore the difference between relationship-based negotiation and concession-exchange, and the conventional competitive techniques often employed in external give and take negotiations.

THE DIFFERENCE BETWEEN "RELATIONSHIP-BASED COMPROMISE" AND SELF-CENTERED COMPETITIVE COMPROMISE

People negotiate for good reason. They don't do so because they are lonely or have nothing else to do. A difference between them exists which one or both believe it best to resolve. At the very least they wish to protect their interests. At most, they wish to strike a deal that will best achieve what they want and need. Both realize that competition exists between their respective goals and both are defensive of their interest and positions. External and internal workplace negotiations are similar in those respects.

Yet, internal and external negotiations must be conducted in importantly different ways. Internal dealings are far more we-centered as a rule than external ones. Both sides are clearly members of the same organization and share similar organizational goals. Both must work together in a measure of harmony from task to task and day to day. Self-centered strategies and tactics are frowned upon within the organization and recognized as counterproductive in the long run.

Relationship-based approaches are paramount to building positive relations. Even when one's goals seek to promote one's interest through bargaining, the negotiator is best served when his or her inputs are recognized as being honest, respectful and worthy of trust. When those who oppose view the other person's actions or words as bluffing, threatening, manipulative, untruthful or secretive, their relationship diminishes.

The goal of relationship-based negotiators is to leave the table with a fair and reasonable agreement that commits both sides to work together cooperatively and collaboratively in the future; and, to forge an agreement that stands the test of time and can be resolved fairly when and if problems arise later. Such a settlement makes future negotiations easier and defuses problems and differences before they explode in anger.

Relationship-based negotiators recognize the strategies and approaches they cannot use. Borderline tactics, used all too often in external negotiations are shunned in workplace dealings. Tactics such as fait accompli, figure-finagling deception, bad guy-good guy, word play, devil in the details and deliberate escalation are never used. These and other tough borderline approaches are identified and explained in my book, In Business As In Life, You Don't Get What You Deserve, You Get What You Negotiate. These negotiating tactics are used by some in business or diplomatic dealings. They are, however, clearly counterproductive in workplace bargaining and dangerous to use in any negotiation because they incite anger and revenge in those who feel victimized by their use.

External negotiations are not so closely limited in what is said and done. Often the goal externally is to do as well as one can do, but not leave the other party so dissatisfied that they fail to perform as agreed. Self-interest is, of course, a motivator in most conventional transactions as it is in internal dealings. Good relationships are generally valued in both types of negotiation. But there is one major difference between workplace bargaining and that between buyer-seller or union-management representative. In most external negotiations, competitive self-interest, not relationships, dominates the exchange. Even there certain limits to action prevail. Strategies that are illegal, coercive, abusive or physically or psychologically intimidating are taboo there as they are in the workplace.

Relationship-based give and take rests on the premise that what one does and says at the negotiating table directly affects the relationship of the parties as much as the outcome itself. External negotiators, like commercial buyers and sellers, face one another at the table then go their mostly separate ways. Workplace negotiators have to face each other and work together every day. So when it comes to workplace negotiations good relations, rapport and open-honest dealing, matter a great deal. When these elements are missing, work will not get done effectively and creative collaboration becomes unlikely.

SIX NEED-TO-KNOW NEGOTIATING GUIDES OR CONCEPTS THAT HELP MOVE TALKS TO CLOSURE

The six negotiating guides or concepts that follow apply as well to the workplace as they do to external commercial bargaining. There comes a time in most negotiations when all that can be said has been said and little more can be added. Talks begin to sputter and stall. These concepts fill that gap and smooth the way to closure.

SIX RELATIONSHIP-BASED NEGOTIATING STRATEGY GUIDES THAT EASE TALKS TO CLOSURE

1. THE CONCEPT OF NEGOTIATING SPACE
2. HOW EXPECTATIONS RISE AND FALL IN A NEGOTIATOR'S HEAD
3. THE TIME TO THINK ACTION GUIDE
4. THE REAGAN KEEPING TRACK AND SUMMARIZATION APPROACH
5. THE CONCEPT OF SATISFACTION
6. THE COLLABORATIVE BOTH-WIN® CONCEPT

Exhibit 12

THE CONCEPT OF NEGOTIATING SPACE

The concept of negotiating space rests on the fact that we need more time and room to negotiate than we usually allot to making the best and most prudent deal possible for both sides. A manager I worked for at Hughes Aircraft used to say, "There's not much to negotiation, really. You make them an offer. They make you a counteroffer. You settle somewhere in the middle." Those of us who have negotiated extensively would differ. There's much more to it than that. To be successful one must create negotiation space to allow talks to move from point to point and to explore alternative possibilities.

Sir Francis Bacon, writing four hundred years ago, said, "All negotiation is to work, to discover and take risk." He understood this could not be done quickly or by merely splitting differences. Most negotiations are too complex for that, even relatively simple ones. What we need is negotiation space to talk, to test our assumptions, to learn about one another, to exchange ideas, to compromise wisely and to assure that what we promise to do will be done.

Some strategies leave negotiating space; others do not. Leaving some room to bargain, even a little, opens the door to further give and take. Leaving none says, "I don't have more to say or give – that's it." Making small concessions over time builds negotiating space by allowing you time to explain your position better and build bridges between each argument. What's the hurry anyway when getting the project done right or a reasonable budget allotment are at stake.

Negotiating space can be created by putting a string on your concessions. Asking for something in return when making a concession puts spirited new ideas and energy into quiet talks. It opens the door to varied responses on the part of both sides. Some responses to strings or conditions lead to clues about unspoken motivations. These provide spaces to explore further.

Negotiation space leaves room for the relationship to grow: space for each side to gain respect and trust in the other, to accept each other as partners rather than adversaries, to learn what each has in common and to understand what important differences really exist. Bargaining space allows attitudes and beliefs each side has about the other to change as each group reveals itself through the extended bargaining exchange.

HOW EXPECTATIONS RISE AND FALL IN A NEGOTIATOR'S HEAD

Almost everybody going into negotiation has some target or goal in mind. It may be based on reality or merely a hope for the best. It may be based on what the other party can live with or be far beyond their capacity to say "Yes." The validity of the estimated target will, in the end, be determined by the give and take of the process, the balance of power and each side's perception of it, as well as the bargaining skill of those involved.

Targets in a negotiator's head are not set in concrete. They rise or fall with the tides of success or failure based upon what is said and done at the bargaining table. Goals are set. Feedback follows. Every demand, concession, threat, delay, fact, explanation, deadline, or remark has an effect on the picture in a negotiator's head. The target moves up and down with each word and each new development.

How expectations change is important to those who negotiate and is summarized below:

1. Every concession can serve to raise the other side's expectations. Every "No" has the opposite effect. Small concessions, reluctantly and slowly given, are not likely to raise expectations very high. Large concessions do.

2. It takes a number of small failures to move expectations down. Saying "No" just once is not enough. It may take many "No's" to convince the other that you mean it. That's why persistence and repeating your viewpoint helps move the other to your position.

3. Research shows that those who ask for more in negotiation generally achieve more but they also suffer greater risk of deadlock and possible relationship risk. Good backup for your position and an open discussion of reasons reduces those risks.

THE TIME-TO-THINK ACTION GUIDE

No matter how intelligent you are, to be effective in negotiation you have to build time to think into the bargaining process. There is simply too much for any mind to process as talks progress. You have to listen, evaluate the other's arguments, observe their body language and gestures, get ready to present your ideas and rebut theirs. Is it any wonder that many brilliant people dislike or fear negotiating and consider themselves poor at it?

In this section we will consider five ways to incorporate time-to-think into the process. Let's start by recognizing the obvious: people think more clearly about matters related to their own field of expertise. What may be understood easily by the engineering member of the team may have far less meaning to the accounting person who manages project funding or the person responsible for chemical decisions.

That's why it is so important to assure that what is said at any meeting or negotiation is understood by all, not just a few. Only if all participants are aware of what is said and its implications can they contribute their knowledge and wisdom to the issue at hand. Helping all participants understand what you are saying is as much part of your presentation as its content and style.

We can learn much about the benefits of time-to-think from the sports world. Most sports provide clear rules for when a "timeout" can be exercised. A coach calls for a timeout when they wish to think about the next play or series of plays. They also do so when considering a change in strategy or whether to speed up to slow the game down. In basketball and football timeout is often called when one's team has lost momentum and the pace suddenly favors the other side. Timeout applies as much to negotiation as it does to sports. It gives us time to think.

Thinking time can be created by requesting time to locate necessary records or documentation to further support a position you take or by asking for time to consult with outside associates before agreeing on a point at issue. In international diplomacy, talks are commonly recessed for weeks or months to test the other's resolve or come up with alternate positions.

On a more mundane but practical level, lunch and dinner breaks provide thinking time. So also do bathroom and snack intermissions. Special breaks can be negotiated by the parties directly into the agenda. If more time is needed, ask for it. As we said before, "If you don't ask for something when negotiating, you'll not get it." I once attended a negotiation where the other person complained of diarrhea early in the talks. That gave them license to take as many breaks as desired later when the talks got intense.

Several other time-to-think approaches are helpful. One way is to let the other side present their position and documentation before you do. Listen, take notes and ask lots of questions. Then, when their presentation is complete, ask for an overnight or weekend to respectfully consider all you have heard and learned. I know from experience how hard it is to reject or postpone such a request when the other side does it courteously and everyone is tired.

Yet another approach is to advise the other party that you would like to propose an idea that will be better for both of you, but need an hour, a day or more to work it out completely. People are generally interested in new ideas and willing to wait to hear them, especially when talks are bogging down.

Asking questions that call for complex answers can often be rewarded with new information and lots of time to talk. I was once at a negotiation where the other side's engineer asked ours what he thought was a simple question, "What makes your GPS system as accurate as it is?" The answer took two hours. Much was learned that we didn't know about the strengths and weaknesses of their GPS system.

Effective Negotiating®, be it with associates at work or elsewhere is a difficult job. It requires clear thinking under pressure, something generally not found in one's ordinary work. Building in time-to-think when you need it should be part of every negotiator's planning kit.

THE REAGAN KEEPING TRACK AND SUMMARIZATION APPROACH

We can learn something about keeping track from President Ronald Reagan. Years before he was president, as governor of California, Mr. Reagan was called upon to settle a labor dispute between the bus drivers and the City of Los Angeles. A possible strike threatened to bring the city to a halt.

Reagan, then aiming for the presidency, flew to Los Angeles with great fanfare from television and the press. The Los Angeles Times reported that what he did was relatively simple: Reagan began by tracking the talks like a bookkeeper.

First he listed the issues agreed upon and the concessions made by both sides. Next he grouped the issues discussed but still open where the gap between them had been narrowed but not closed. Then he laid out remaining matters still in disagreement but not yet discussed. These he prioritized from easiest to settle to most difficult.

By repeatedly tracking and summarizing the status of the talks Reagan brought clarity to a complicated situation. Writing down settled and unsettled issues as well as recapitulating concessions exchanged served to focus on how much had been accomplished and how far the gap between them had narrowed. He did this again and again as talks went on. Tension diminished. Settlement followed not long after.

I have seen strange things happen in the heat of negotiation. I have seen bargainers make concessions that exceeded the demands of the other where the overlap went unnoticed until later when someone expressed confusion as to how much had really been agreed to. I have been to sessions when the negotiators shook hands in agreement only to learn soon after that they had settled on different amounts or terms than thought. Concessions given or accepted early in the day are often forgotten or remembered differently at noon, at the end of day or the following morning.

Keep track and review progress frequently. It helps both sides to listen and hear in a more focused manner. It moves the desired agreement along in a less chaotic, better-understood direction.

THE CONCEPT OF SATISFACTION

What we bargain for in negotiation is not money, goods or services. It is satisfaction. Satisfaction as Webster defines it is anything that brings gratification, pleasure or contentment. The trouble from a negotiator's standpoint is that satisfaction is subjective; by definition it is hard to measure. The value or utility received from money or services varies with each of us.

One person gets joy from a licorice ice cream cone. The other may hate it. Yet it is ice cream cones or their equivalent in goods, services or dollars that are the units of exchange we talk about when negotiating, not satisfaction. Satisfaction is too subjective to measure or exchange, yet that is what we really negotiate for.

As we have said, the most efficient road to agreement generally lies in the give and take of concessions between parties. Yet even that is complicated by the role of satisfaction. The satisfaction gained by a person receiving a concession is never equal to the satisfaction given up by the person making it. It may be more or less but not the same.

I have received concessions from the other side that lowered my level of satisfaction and led me to ask for more. Hoping to close, a salesperson who had been convincing me for hours that he could go no lower suddenly dropped his price more than I had expected. Encouraged by this large concession, I chose to continue the give and take process by asking and winning a still better agreement.

Concessions do not have to be matched in kind or amount. More can be exchanged for less, later for now, small issues for large ones, certainty for uncertainty, a quick payoff for one that flows regularly over a long time. Satisfaction is the common denominator in the negotiation equation despite the fact that it can't be measured.

There are four ways in which negotiators inadvertently reduce the satisfactions others receive: they give in too quickly and easily from earlier positions, they fail to learn in advance or during the bargaining what is really important to the other side, they do a poor job of explaining the benefits of their offerings or they fail to take into account what others within the organization will say, or feel, about the agreement once they learn its details. Worse even than reducing the other side's satisfaction is when you tell them, after the deal is made, that you would have given more had they asked. I've seen this done more than once. The recipient of that news never forgets.

Once, in a budget negotiation with my boss, I was offered and accepted a 5% increase for my department after being told that funds were short and 5% all that was available. I later learned that another department in our group had received 6%. Of course, my satisfaction fell. Why had not I been given an explanation? Did this affect my next budget negotiation? Yes, it certainly did. Our level of satisfaction with any agreement changes over time for better or worse. Much depends on what we learn while negotiating and afterward. Much depends on how commitments to perform are adhered to.

People do not always understand the benefits and satisfactions offered by a concession or offer. Those making concessions have a responsibility to make benefits clear to the party receiving them, and to explain benefits in terms familiar and important to the receiver. To say, "I will personally check the work before my staff delivers it on June 1," is not enough. Far better is to add that when we deliver our work you won't have to worry about it being perfect. It will be ready to please your most discriminating end-user or customer.

In the section later in this chapter, "How to Add Value and Credibility to Your Bargaining Responses," we will see how satisfaction can be added to your offer and counteroffer responses.

THE BEST APPROACH OF ALL: THE COLLABORATIVE BOTH-WIN® CONCEPT

The collaborative Both-Win® approach to negotiating is by far the most important concept in this book. How and why it works so well will be explored in the next chapter.

Collaborative Both-Win® Negotiating is the epitome of relationship-based bargaining: "It enlarges the spheres of mutual interdependence and interests of the parties and helps them discover benefits beyond what each negotiated for when talks began."

Collaboration between the parties is the most direct path to innovative negotiating outcomes. It frees the negotiators from merely protecting and promoting their self-interests to creating a framework for mutual gain and added value. Not only does it raise the stakes – it raises the level and content of the relationship between the parties. It generates new and additional satisfaction and value for them to share.

The road to success and creativity in dealing with others at work lies in collaborative Both-Win® negotiating. When two people actively search for a better way they will find it and mutually benefit. It is this concept that should guide workplace negotiations at all levels of the organization and lead to competitive advantage and success for the organization.

HOW TO ADD VALUE, CREDIBILITY AND SATISFACTION TO YOUR OFFER AND COUNTEROFFER RESPONSES AND CONCESSIONS

Negotiation involves work. People rarely bargain for the fun of it or because they have nothing better to do. They negotiate to gain satisfaction. What we will now consider are ways to increase the value of our responses to whatever the other party offers or concedes. Whether we say "Yes" or "No" to their offer it is important we do it right; that is, we must enhance their satisfaction and maintain a good relationship.

Concessions are normally made by both sides to bring the parties together. The person making the concession hopes to narrow or bridge the gap that separates them. How one handles the other side's offer can either set the stage for further movement or serve to harden disagreement.

Four time-tested approaches to adding value and credibility to your responses and counteroffers will be suggested. I call the first "The Considered Response." One of the best negotiators I ever encountered employed the "considered response" whenever he negotiated. It worked this way. Whenever the other side made a demand or concession his first reaction was to listen carefully and take notes. Then, when they were through, he would say nothing but make calculations on a sheet of paper. After what appeared to everyone to be a longer period of time than it was he would say, "I can't afford to accept your offer. It's simply not enough." His way of responding indicated to the other that he had seriously weighed their arguments and position, even though he had not agreed.

Frankly, I can't be sure that he really figured anything out on that sheet of paper. For all I know he might have been doodling. But I do know that his "considered response" gave his answer credibility and respect. It became, when negative, a stronger "No." And when he said "Yes," as he often did, the other person perceived it as a more satisfying "Yes."

The "considered response" is a powerful tool. By disciplining yourself not to shoot snap answers "from the hip," your strength as a negotiator will increase. The rule is this: The next time the other side makes a demand or offer, be it acceptable or not, don't respond to it with a "Yes" or "No" right away. Keep quiet and think about it for a while. Better yet, write down on a paper a few "pros and cons" and some calculations. Then answer "Yes" or "No" or whatever is appropriate. Your considered response will give greater weight to your answer and greater satisfaction to the other person, as well. Few negotiating behaviors provide as much time-to-think, negotiating space, response credibility and appreciation for the other's offer or concession as a considered response. Make it part of your response pattern.

The next suggestion is a bit risky but well worth considering. Learn to say "No" at least once more, even when you like and are willing to accept the other's offer. Then say "Yes." This is suggested not so much because you sometimes get a better offer but because it provides greater satisfaction to the other party than saying "Yes" immediately to what is an acceptable proposal. I will explain why I feel this way with a story told me by a then-prominent movie star.

Dinah Shore told me this as I waited to be introduced as a guest on her television show. Knowing that I was going to talk about negotiation, she said off camera, "I'm the world's worst negotiator." Whenever anyone says that, listen. A good story usually follows. Some years ago, when $500,000 was a very large sum of money, a Beverly Hills home was for sale at $500,000. The actress liked the house and offered $425,000. The buyer's broker immediately said, "We'll take it." Years later, despite the fact that the value of the house was already more than $1,000,000, she was still angry about the $425,000 agreement made earlier. Dinah Shore was convinced that her $425,000 offer was a foolish mistake because it had been immediately accepted. That's why she said, "I'm the world's worst negotiator." But was she really the world's worst negotiator, or was it the broker or seller?

If we wish to see how bad a mistake the broker made, we have only to imagine another scenario. What if the broker had said, upon hearing the offer, "I don't think my client will accept your offer, but I'll be glad to submit it." He could have returned in five minutes and explained that the client, because she was in a divorce action, was willing to take $440,000, still a real bargain. Suppose they then settled at $435,000. Would Dinah Shore have felt that she was a good negotiator or a bad one? Because of the delay in saying "Yes," she would have been more satisfied paying $435,000 than the $425,000 she actually paid!

It's ironic, isn't it? For Dinah Shore, paying $425,000 represented pain and dissatisfaction. Paying $435,000 would have meant the opposite. There is an underlying principle here: the other side will always appreciate the agreement price more if they believe they have worked for it and gotten closer to the bottom line. If not, their self-esteem will be bruised. They will be angry at you and angry at themselves for a long time.

One final note on why you should learn to say "No" a few times even when you are willing to settle. As many of you remember, Dinah Shore was a caring and giving person. If she had not been so nice, her anger about the deal might have caused her to make trouble for the seller in a number of ways.

If she were upset enough, she might have made an excuse to cancel the agreement before escrow or ask that expensive repairs or improvements be made. She might have demanded that the Persian rugs and fireplace accessories be included in the price. People do these things when they get a "Yes" answer too quickly. Like most people, rich or not, they hate to feel they were "taken" or that they foolishly left too much on the table.

A third approach to increasing the positive impact of what you say is repetition: standing firmly behind your argument or offer for a reasonable period of time. Few things wither a negotiator's position in the eyes of the other side so much as being seen as a person who quickly jumps from one view to another in the face of pressure. There is little question that the combination of repetition and perseverance serve to add a measure of conviction and resolve to a negotiator's words and actions.

Zhou Enlai, the famous diplomat and negotiator under Chairman Mao Zedong, Communist Premier of China, was not one to take another person's offer or "No" for an answer. For almost three long years during the Korean War Zhou Enlai repeated his offers day after day. His steadfastness led the less patient Americans to believe that his position was truly firm, and that concessions, if any, would be few and slow in coming. When he did make some concessions, albeit small ones, it was welcomed and celebrated as a major victory.

In a similar vein, Michael Eisner, for many years CEO of the ever-innovative Disney organization, used persistence and repetition as a filter to assess new ideas presented by his creative staff. He would deliberately reject the idea or ask that it be resubmitted later after considerable improvement. Creative artists and producers who had the passion and conviction to resubmit their proposals after multiple rejections were felt by Mr. Eisner to be worthy of another serious look. Repetition and persistence work like that if backed by good argument.

My fourth suggestion is that you learn to ask for something in return when making an offer or concession because it adds utility to any movement you make. It allows you to retreat from your concession if the other refuses to grant what was asked for. It permits you to do so without loss of face or power. Later, if you chose to drop the string attached to the concession, it will add extra value and satisfaction to what you then decide to concede. More will be said of this powerful approach in the next chapter.

NINE RELATIONSHIP-BASED CONCESSION TECHNIQUES APPLICABLE TO DEALING WITH OTHERS AT WORK

1. DON'T BE IN A HURRY TO MAKE THE FIRST CONCESSION
2. DON'T ORDER THE FISH UNTIL YOU –
3. LEAVE MORE ROOM FOR CONTINGENCIES WHEN OPENING TALKS
4. GIVE IN SLOWLY AND GRUDGINGLY
5. CONCESSIONS THAT GIVE SATISFACTION BUT COST LITTLE
6. CAUTION – YOUR CONCESSIONS WILL GET LARGER THAN NECESSARY AS DEADLINE NEARS
7. CIVILITY IS NOT A SIGN OF WEAKNESS
8. FUNNY WORK – FUNNY MONEY – FUNNY STUFF
9. INTERNAL AGREEMENTS ARE ONLY PROMISES SUBJECT TO A DISCOUNT RATE

Exhibit 13

RELATIONSHIP-BASED CONCESSION TECHNIQUES

The nine relationship-based concession techniques above work well in workplace negotiations because they minimize the conflict inherent in competitive, self-centered negotiating, and serve to maintain relationships rather than sever them.

These techniques set the stage for reaching a fair compromise based on an open exchange of viewpoints and concerns. When supported by logical principle, explainable contingencies, objective standards and sound backup, these relationship-based approaches build relationships and agreements that can endure even under severe organizational changes.

Don't Be In a Hurry to Make the First Concession

After the initial offer and counteroffer, the gap between parties is at its largest. The pressure on both sides is to say or do something that will bring them closer. Both, at this early stage, are somewhat apprehensive that the other will not respond by narrowing the gap in some way.

My advice at this point in the negotiation is to resist the pressure to make the first concession. By waiting you may learn how strongly the other side feels about the matter at hand. Those who make first concessions early in negotiation signal that they are overly concerned about settling the matter and anxious to move toward resolution.

I am reminded of a story in Robinson Crusoe by Daniel Defoe. Robinson, anxious to exchange what he possessed with a native for food, makes an offer. They talk and talk. The native shows no desire for Robinson's goods and makes no counteroffer in return. Robinson grows more anxious and makes his first concession. He describes how desperate he becomes at the native's reticence and disinterest. Later, when the native finally makes his first counteroffer, Robinson describes his intense relief at hearing the native's first glimmer of interest in possible exchange.

Your first concession is important, especially if it involves a major issue. On minor issues it is not as crucial. It may in fact be helpful to show that you are open-minded and flexible about your position or the difference at issue.

Don't Order the Fish Until You –

Once my son toured Italy. He came to a restaurant in a small town near the Mediterranean where a menu posted in the window indicated that the pricing was moderate. That, and the fact that it was full of local patrons, led him to sit down at the table.

The waiter soon came over and told him of today's specials. The best, he said, was a local fish that he described absolutely delicious. My son ordered the fish and it was indeed delicious. When the bill arrived, the special was priced at $140, far higher than the average of $40 for anything comparable on the menu.

The rule, when negotiating about anything, is don't order the fish until you know what it costs. That, of course, sounds simple but isn't. We do it many times when negotiating. Anxious to reach agreement and move on, we agree to something we do not fully understand.

The full cost of an agreement in terms of time, resources, people, or money is never simple to assess. What is included and what is not is rarely clear. When support or warranties begin and when they end are often obscure or buried in the details or fine print. In the workplace, agreements leave much out. They paper over sensitive areas like who will clean up after the work is done or who will repair work not good enough to pass and, for that matter, what the criteria for pass or fail really are.

The interesting thing is that the reasons why we do not ask 'the price of the fish special' are much the same as why we make agreements not well understood. As for the fish, my son assumed the average price of $40 would apply to the special. He was embarrassed at asking the waiter about something as crass as price after the waiter's raving fish review. He and the waiter were both in a hurry to get on with the meal. Holding up the food process with further questions and alternatives did not appear feasible. He hoped for the best as we all do when we think, "It will all work out I'm sure."

Those are the mistakes we also make in negotiation. Never agree to something you do not fully understand.

Leave More Room for Contingencies When Opening Talks

As we said earlier but wish to stress again, when negotiating with others in your organization, whatever the issue, leave room for contingencies, under-estimates and problems in your opening offer. Be certain that these contingencies can be fully explained and defended. Then, as you move to agreement, you will have room to offer further concessions as necessary.

Americans, as a rule, bargain less often in their daily lives than their counterparts in other cultures. They are uncomfortable making low offers when they buy and hesitant to build higher margins into proposals. These tendencies, in my opinion, hamper their capacity to negotiate effectively in business dealings, and serve to make workplace bargaining even more difficult.

Americans prefer to get to the point. Even in buying and selling they leave too little room. They don't like the give and take of bargaining, nor do they welcome the talk and repetition that is so much a part of the process. The conventional adage, "Time is money," appears to drive Americans more than businesspeople from other cultures. Yet, for negotiators everywhere, the reality is, the more time one gives to the process, the more will be learned and gained. For negotiators, "Time is money" means "Go slow." Where you start and how you give in is crucial to how well you will do. For many years I accumulated data on the results of practice negotiations among my seminar attendees. I consistently found that executives who started higher and made concessions in smaller increments did better. Other experiments confirm this.

The practical implications of these findings are clear especially for professional buyers and sellers in external negotiations. If you are a buyer, start quite low and be ready to defend that position. As a seller leave as much room as you can defend in your asking price. In both cases, ample room to negotiate is generally the key to better outcome in commercial dealings.

For those who deal internally with others in their organization to resolve workplace differences these admonishments to leave lots of room would not work well. Leaving a lot of room to negotiate could jeopardize hard-won relationships and result in the loss of long-term credibility. Working together cooperatively might later prove more difficult than before.

For internal negotiators, the rule is, leave enough room to cover contingencies and problems that may be expected. Be prepared to defend these matters in full detail. Leave room also for waste, inefficiencies and mistakes that require correction. Be ready to negotiate and defend each point with all the legitimacy you can muster. Some modest room to bargain is called for in relationship-based internal negotiations. Not to do so will leave you in an inflexible, take-it-or-leave-it position that has obvious problems of its own.

Give In Slowly and Grudgingly

Negotiations are lost when people cave in before they need to. As you negotiate, it is wise to make sure the other side is not certain as to whether you will back down further from your position. If you retreat too soon or too easily the other may be encouraged to try for more. Negotiators who concede quickly or make large concessions usually do so to move the agreement toward closure, but often drive the parties further apart by raising the other side's expectations to unrealistic levels.

Everything you do in a negotiating situation affects the expectation level in the other person's mind. Your initial demands set the stage. Your persistence in holding to a position leads the other party to wonder if their goals can be reached. The rate and timing of your concessions determine whether the other side's expectations will rise or fall. Your way of offering concessions will affect the overall satisfaction with the settlement. If concessions are small and grudgingly given, the other side is likely to be pleased because they will feel that little was left on the table.

As for making concessions grudgingly and slowly, the record is clear for workplace negotiators. People who are stingy with concessions come out better if they are consistent in making only small concessions and explaining them well. By giving slowly, negotiators add value to their movement and signal that there is little more to give. Concessions, carefully controlled, lead the other side toward closure and provide them with a higher level of satisfaction with the final outcome. These goals are also consistent with the objectives of relationship-based compromise in that they provide both parties with negotiating space and time to explore a better deal for everyone. Giving in slowly also leads to an increased flow of information and a better understanding of why the final settlement makes good sense.

Concessions That Give Satisfaction But Cost Little

It is not money, goods or services we negotiate for but satisfaction. Material things are only the visible spectrum of our dealings. Satisfaction is what we seek to gain and satisfaction can be created in some relatively simple ways.

Listening has a two-edged benefit. It provides the other party with great satisfaction and benefits the listener at the same time. Being courteous and tactful are concessions that quietly move the other side closer to agreement. Being respectful to the other person's views, whatever they are, helps them to be respectful to yours. Negotiators on opposite sides of the table tend to mirror each other for better or worse. Diplomats have known this for millennia and continue to act accordingly.

We, in our rush to personalize differences and settle everything quickly, have forgotten that to be an effective negotiator we must be a good diplomat.

Caution – Your Concessions Will Get Larger Than Necessary As Deadline Nears

A curious thing happens again and again in practice negotiations we conduct at seminars. Attendees are able to control their concession behavior through most of the bargaining. They make relatively modest concessions as give and take progresses. Then, when I announce that deadline is approaching, one party or the other cracks by making large concessions not reciprocated by the other. The party making smaller concessions as deadline approaches usually does better.

In my formal doctoral experiment at the University of Southern California with 120 professional negotiators, I found that both sides controlled their concession behavior for most of the session. Then things changed. As deadline approached and I began to announce, "three minutes to go," "two to go," "one to go" – a hush fell over the room. The tension mounted. Many participants settled only minutes or seconds before the final bell, although they'd had a full hour to do so.

It turned out that both skilled and unskilled negotiators made concessions as time ran out. Both caved in somewhat as they sought to reach settlement, but it was the unskilled who gave away the most.

A friend of mine, a psychiatrist, told me he wasn't surprised at these results. He has found that people make bad decisions under pressure; they behave in emotional rather than in rational ways. His belief for those who come to him as patients is that they are better off postponing a decision when under duress.

The next time you are in a negotiation, recognize that your tendency will be to give too much as deadline comes close. Discipline yourself to make smaller concessions and spread them out a bit longer. Learn to ask two simple questions as time runs out. First, "Why should I give so much in one lump sum right now?" And second, "Why not make these final concessions on the installment plan – a little now, a little later?" These reminders will help you avoid the deadline cave-in crisis. Remember also that most deadlines are themselves subject to negotiation. There is usually time enough to make another concession after you have renegotiated the deadline.

Civility Is Not a Sign of Weakness

This caveat applies to everyone but especially to those who negotiate from a higher position in the organization. I have worked for some managers who opened negotiations on a discourteous note and continued to do so throughout the talks. Subordinates may want to act that way but for obvious reasons do not.

President John F. Kennedy once said, "Civility is not a sign of weakness." There is no point to abusing the other side. An attack on a person's ego serves only to heighten resistance. They will harness their energies to protect not only their assets, rights and privileges, but also their self-importance. A negotiator endangers his or her objectives by attacking another's dignity or invalidating their self-worth.

Civility is not a sign of weakness but of strength.

Funny Work – Funny Money – Funny Stuff

I call it funny money. Funny money is money we give away by forgetting what it is in real money. Chips in Las Vegas are funny money. The gambling house knows we wouldn't bet as much if it were a twenty or hundred dollar bill we were putting on the gaming table. We, however, forget when all we have to wager with are plastic chips.

Credit cards are funny money for the same reason. They hypnotize us into spending money we don't have for things we don't need. The same is true for interest on a loan. One percent more isn't much, is it? Unless it is for a $500,000 loan for thirty years. A price increase of a penny a pound on a chemical isn't much unless you are a manufacturer buying or selling millions of pounds. Funny money transactions are everywhere. It leads us to agreements that later cause regret and aggravation.

In the workplace we talk of labor rates in dollars per hour, bonuses as a percent of profit or salary, production rates in terms of output per hour or shift, steel costs in dollars per ton and oil in dollars per barrel. Whenever we negotiate or talk in these terms we are dealing in and possibly being hypnotized by funny money. How much real money is involved depends on the quantities we buy, sell or deal with.

Budget deliberations always involve funny money chips on the table. Beware of agreements based on percentages, burden rates or learning curves, shares of stock, price per share or options with low probabilities. Know what you are dealing with in real money, not chips. Before you say something as conciliatory as, "Let's split the difference," know what the difference really is and what you are just about to give away.

Funny work is like funny money but even harder to recognize. In the workplace you are often asked by someone to do or stop doing something. Or perhaps you are asked to give up one or two of the additional people you requested in your budget because funds are scarce. The trouble with dropping the request for new people is that it affects not only the schedules you have committed to but also your group's workload distribution. Any time you are asked by an associate to cease doing something or requested to do something extra you are dealing in funny work. Somebody's workload will change in ways you had better assess before saying "Yes." Many hard-won internal relationships have floundered on concessions made involving funny work that were not thought through.

Whenever an engineering manager agrees to change a specification, he or she is dealing with funny work. I have seen managers agree to what at first appeared to be small, relatively easy changes in specification that turned into very difficult matters as other department personnel became involved. Implementation of these concessions later overloaded the manager's staff as it pulled them away from more productive work. Had the engineering manager recognized the funny work and its consequences on others it would not have engulfed her and so many on her staff who depended on her good judgment.

Funny stuff is a bit different from funny money. It occurs frequently in information technology (IT) activities. The IT manager is asked to develop a program for handling 100 company sales orders an hour each with five items per sale. As the program develops the 100 sales orders gradually grow from 100 to 105 to 110 and finally to 150 per hour and five to six to ten items each.

Changing the parameters and scope gradually to the increased statement of work is possible but takes lots of computer programming to do so. Each small increase from 100 to 150 in this case was not properly documented or accounted for by those involved. The initial budget and schedule agreed to was no longer appropriate. Later, when overruns occur, tempers flair and reputations suffer. That's how funny stuff takes over IT projects that have inadequate change control systems and fail to follow project progress regularly and systematically.

The next time an internal customer for IT services asks, "Can you change the program from 100 to 105 purchase orders per hour?"

be careful before you say "Yes." Figure out how much the change will cost the IT department and how long a time it will take. Then put it in writing and get their signature on the deal before starting on the 105 per hour target.

Funny work, funny money and funny stuff find their way into many workplace negotiations. The only way to deal with them is to recognize their nature and think it through in terms of real money, real work and real stuff before you get to "Yes."

Internal Agreements Are Only Promises Subject to a Discount Rate

A promise is a concession with a discount rate. Some are worth little, others at par or better. Much depends on the character of those making the promise and the situation or environment surrounding the participants. Added to the complexity of evaluating promises is the nature of the issues or differences involved.

Why as internal negotiators should we be interested in promises and their discount rate? Because most negotiations at work end in agreements that are promises to perform rather than written commitments. Business agreements between buyer and seller are documented by signed commitment. Later, when problems or disagreements arise, they are subject to commercial law. Internal agreements that fall apart are subject to settlement only by renegotiation or appeal to higher authority.

Is there something we can do to assure that internal agreements will be honored as negotiated, or do we just shake hands and hope for the best? The answer of course is that, with careful thought and action, we can raise the probability of promised performance, not guarantee it.

Internal negotiators who take notes of progress and agreements at the negotiating table, and summarize them with the other party as talks progress, raise the likelihood that what has been agreed to will be done. Good notes have power in the absence of a contract and, even when there is a contract, often pave the way for renegotiating subsequent misunderstandings. Taking copious notes and saving them for easy retrieval helps reduce disputes.

Agreements that include performance milestones, progress tracking and review procedures make promises more firm. Prior good relationships between negotiators and a history of mutual dependability raise the probability of workplace agreements. It also helps if others involved in the talks participate in and witness the agreement being made.

Agreements between those who negotiate in the workplace are fragile and prone to change and misinterpretation. In the end, the character and reputation of the persons promising performance and the stability of their respective organizations play a large role in determining its discount rate and present value.

13

Collaborative Both-Win® Negotiation - Moving Together to a More Creative Higher Value Agreement

This is the most important chapter of the book. When you reach the end you will be in a position to settle any workplace difference in an entirely new way. Collaborative Both-Win® negotiating allows negotiators to create new and previously untapped or unrecognized value for both sides to share. It fosters agreements that can make your daily work less burdensome and increase your and your organization's opportunities for growth and success.

Chapter Twelve discussed the strategies that move negotiation to agreement through relationship-based compromise and concession-making. We know from experience that compromise is usually the most direct route to settlement when differences or disagreements occur. But we also know that compromise is often not enough to bring us together. In this chapter we will see that there is something new we can do to close the gap when compromise fails. Collaborative Both-Win® negotiating is that path.

The magic of this new approach is that it opens previously unexplored avenues and alternatives for both to choose from: a smorgasbord of innovative ideas from which both sides can draw to forge a better deal.

When we speak of making a "better deal for both" it's important to recognize that the words mean something quite different in collaborative Both-Win® negotiating than it does in conventional competitive bargaining. In competitive negotiating we have limited goals; specifically, the pursuit by each side of its own interests and the satisfactory sharing of whatever is at issue or to be distributed or settled.

For example, let us imagine for a moment that we were bargaining for the sharing of a ten-piece pie. If one got six and the other found four satisfactory that would be sufficient for a conventional competitive agreement. The same would be true if the pieces shared were seven and three or eight and two as long as both sides found that satisfactory and acceptable.

Collaboration in a workplace negotiation can create profound economic and psychological benefits. It can reduce cost, make your work easier or relieve internal bickering by resolving problems or finding better ways to do things. On a higher level, collaboration has the potential to create new opportunities for growth and longer-lasting relationships. Collaborative negotiating is centered on enlarging value for mutual benefit. This leads to the successful resolution of differences and a better agreement for both parties.

To summarize, the magic of the collaborative process we propose is that it allows both parties to a workplace difference or dispute to work together to enlarge our hypothetical 10" pie to one that is now larger and at the same time tastier. These benefits make it easier to share and increase mutual satisfaction with the final distribution. The essence of collaborative Both-Win® negotiation is that there is always a better deal available if both parties invest the time to search for it together.

To illustrate the concept in graphic form two figures are presented below. They compare the conventional competitive mode (Figure 7) with the higher-level collaborative mode (Figure 8).

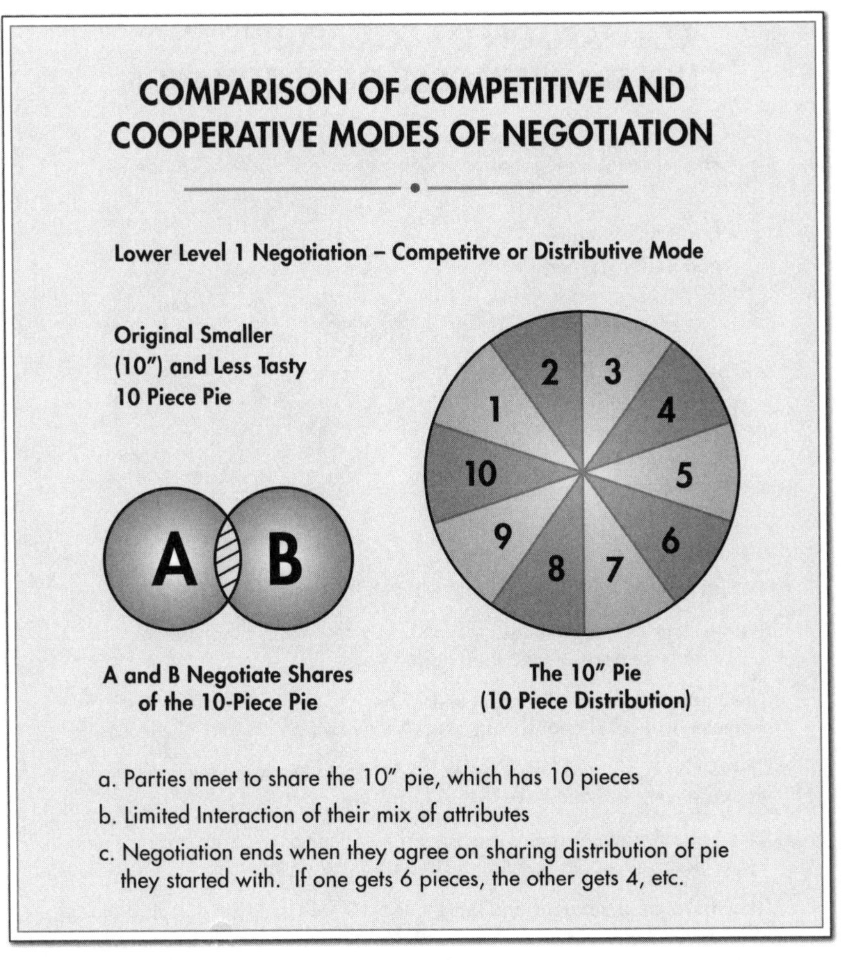

Figure 7

In Figure 7, the competitive model, we have two parties, (A and B), bargaining to share the 10" pie. Figure 7 also illustrates in the striped area (AB) that A and B have resources that the other needs. They would not be negotiating if this were not so. In this case, they are bargaining about one thing only, that is, how many pieces each should get. This is much like what we do at work when negotiating a budget or a larger share of the total company bonus pool.

COMPARISON OF COMPETITIVE AND COOPERATIVE MODES OF NEGOTIATION

Higher Level 2 Negotiation – Coorperative Both-Win® Mode

Customized Bigger (12") and Better (Tastier) Pie

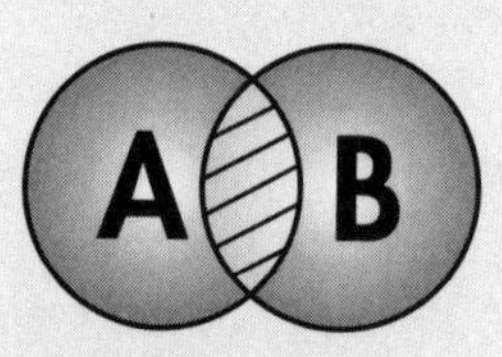

The Now 12" Pie

a. Parties meet to share the 10" pie, which has 10 pieces

b. Parties actively integrate their mix of attributes in ways that create innovation, previously untapped added value.

c. They make the pie bigger and better. The 10" pie becomes 12" in diameter, tastes better and costs less. It now can be cut into 12 pieces.

d. The pie is bigger and better, easier to distribute because they have worked cooperatively to make it so.

e. One person may now get 7 pieces and the other 5, but both are receiving more than they would had the pie been smaller or less tasty.

f. They make the pie bigger and better. The 10" pie becomes 12" in diameter, tastes better and costs less. It now can be cut into 12 pieces.

Figure 8

Figure 8, the collaborative Both-Win® model, shows that the pie, after collaboration, is now larger in diameter (12") and tastier than the original pie. It also shows in the enlarged striped portion (Area AB) that A and B have found more attributes and resources than before to blend together to create added value for both to share. The new pie, being larger and better than the original one, is now easier to distribute. Both have, through the collaborative process, gained by searching for and discovering innovative methods and solutions together.

DISTRIBUTING THE PIE BEFORE AND AFTER COLLABORATIVE BOTH-WIN® NEGOTIATION

To better follow the distribution of the pie before and after collaborative bargaining let's start with a story. A and B who work together entered talks with a plan to bake a pie each week at A's home and celebrate Fridays by sharing it in some proportion and enjoying the treat. Now the first 10" pie is done and ready to distribute. After exchanging some offers and counteroffers by each they have not settled on how much each should get. An impasse is close at hand. A has offered B only three pieces of the 10-piece pie. B refuses the offer because she believes it unreasonable in the light of her considerable economic contributions to the pie and its baking. Both A and B are now tense, their good relationship stressed.

A new approach is necessary to reach agreement. Both still want to share the pie and get on with enjoying it. Together they decide to pursue another path to agreement, that is, the collaborative Both-Win® track. Necessity, some say, is the mother of invention. In negotiation it is necessity that gives birth to collaboration, which in turn gives momentum to inventiveness and creativity.

Without necessity, the parties are less likely to collaborate, and without collaboration, creativity is less probable.

Having failed to agree, they choose to get together to break the impending impasse. The tension level of both A and B naturally begins to recede as they search as a team for a better approach. Negotiating to distribute a pie, an inheritance, a budget or any other limited resource is rarely free of stress. Where complex benefits or contributions by each party come into play it becomes far more difficult. Creativity is called for to make the distribution process most satisfactory for all involved. Only by collaboration and negotiation can it be done and accepted as equitable.

To continue, the parties collaborate by broadening the problem somewhat. Instead of talking about sharing the 10" pie they mutually decide to find a better way to bake future pies and share them fairly. They combine their strengths, limits and individual attributes in a new way. They use their financial assets, baking equipment, supplies, talents and old recipes to bake a bigger, better pie at a reduced total cost to benefit ratio and with less work to each of them.

Through collaboration they create a 12" pie larger and tastier than the original. This enlarged value, created from the creative mixing of joint attributes, resources and talents, was not likely or possible earlier, when the bargaining focused only on sharing the smaller pie through conventional competitive give and take.
Despite collaboration, there remains an obstacle to agreement that A and B must still resolve. Collaboration facilitates sharing but does not determine who gets what share. How are A and B to share the now larger, tastier 12" pie?

A begins by offering B a three-piece share as he proposed earlier.

After all, he reasons, the pie is now bigger and better, each portion more valuable than before. B responds by saying that the three-piece offer is unfair because of the extra work and money she spent going to the market to make the pie so good. A stands by his position because he sincerely believes he deserves more. He has spent hours at his special oven at home baking the pie. She answers that it took her days on the internet and in old files to locate the tasty recipe. Both are to some extent correct. After further negotiation they reach what each considers a fair and reasonable Both-Win® agreement on the bigger-better pie. Each has a substantial psychological equity and ownership in the final agreement.

This tale is, of course, far fetched; however, it reflects a collaborative Both-Win® negotiating process by which people with differences move together to a more creative, higher-value agreement than they would through conventional competitive bargaining.

BASICS OF COLLABORATIVE BOTH-WIN® NEGOTIATION – WHY IT WORKS

There is always a better deal possible for both parties in every negotiation. This may seem a bold statement but it is backed by considerable economic theory and research. About 150 years ago, Egardo Pareto, an Italian economist, theorized that any contract agreement between two individuals could be improved if the parties continued to work together to raise its value or utility. He proved, through contract utility analysis, that a gain in mutual satisfaction could be achieved at little or no loss to either party in a transaction. Subsequent economic theorists substantiated Pareto's theory and built on his findings.

Indeed, I am convinced that anything can be done better if people collaborate in doing so. When two negotiators work together to find a better way they will succeed if not limited or impeded by organizational, structural, legal or psychological constraints.

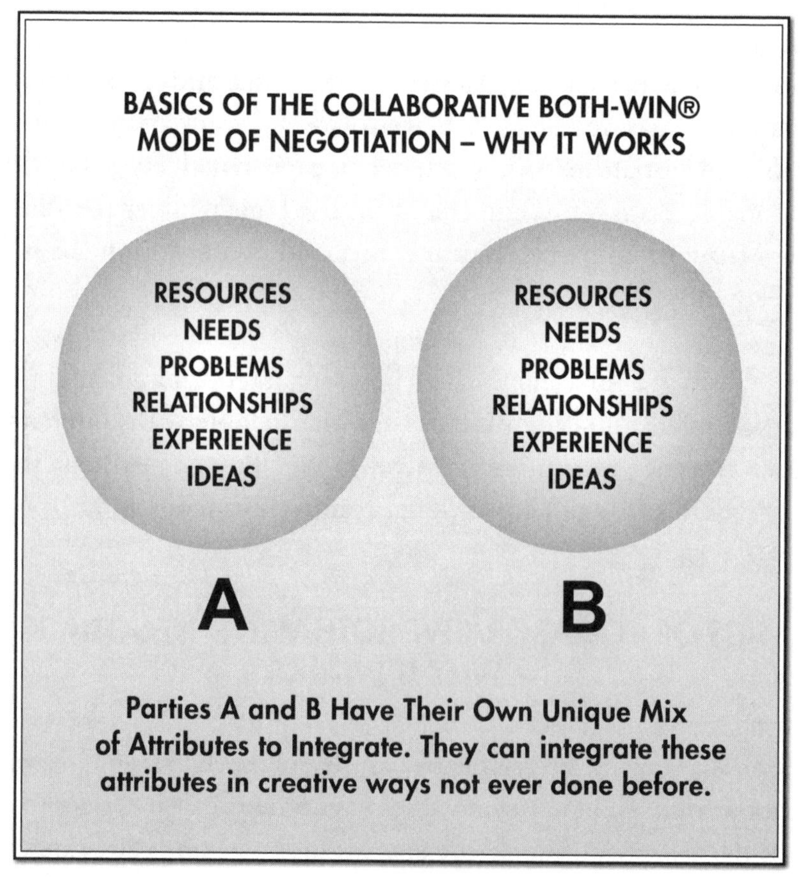

Figure 9

Collaborative Both-Win® negotiation is the path to better agreements. It is within the grasp of anyone to learn. Negotiators do not have to be geniuses to be creative and find a better way. To see why it works see Figure 9, "Basics of Collaborative Both-Win® Negotiation—Why It Works."

Two factors come into play to create mutual gain; first, each side comes to the table with their own unique aggregate of assets, ideas, needs, problems, experience and relationships; second, through collaboration both sides integrate their previously unconnected mix of attributes in ways that create enlarged joint satisfaction values not previously tapped or attainable by either party individually.

Exhibit 14, which follows, describes in greater detail the various factors that fall into each of the six major attribute categories shown in Figure 9. For example, under the category "Needs," such needs as power, money, growth, excitement, survival and others are listed. Each party has some inadequately fulfilled or unfulfilled needs within these needs attributes. This is also true for the other attribute categories. It is the integration and tradeoff of these attributes that paves the way for an innovative arrangement or agreement that enlarges satisfaction possibilities for both parties much as Pareto theorized.

MAKING COLLABORATIVE BOTH-WIN® AGREEMENTS
Attributes

RESOURCES OR ASSETS – finances, equipment, commodities, materials, real estate, information, human resources, proprietary rights, information, energy data, laboratories

NEEDS – growth, money, opportunities, security, excitement, power, recognition, belonging, ego satisfaction, respect, survival, wealth

PROBLEMS – debt, obsolescence, distribution, marketing, personnel, costs, taxes, legal, slow growth, decline, government, foes, competition, cash flow

RELATIONSHIPS – customers, suppliers, distribution, financial, technological, political, government, personnel, access to tastemakers, international, unions, friends

EXPERIENCE AND CONNECTIONS – knowledge, talents, technology, foreign, techniques, marketing, promotion, accounting, regulations, government, politics, communications, internet, legal, social networks

IDEAS – entrepreneurial, technical, marketing, design, impact of regulatory change, services, niches, advertising, new tastes, digital modeling and applications

Exhibit 14

To illustrate how the process of collaboration and the integration of each side's attributes help to produce a creative Both-Win® agreement we will describe two hypothetical negotiating situations. The first will focus on a buy-sell transaction involving a pizza storeowner and a movie producer in Malibu, California. The second will concern a negotiation aimed at resolving a rules and procedural disagreement between two departments of a company.

We will then supplement these two examples with one that occurred between the National Football League (NFL) and the National Broadcasting Corporation (NBC) only a few years ago. These examples illustrate that using collaborative Both-Win® negotiation as a strategy leads both parties to reach superior higher-value agreements than both thought possible when talks began.

THE MALIBU PIZZA NEGOTIATION

You are a movie producer living in Malibu, a wealthy community close to Los Angeles. You will soon be throwing a pizza party celebrating your son's fifteenth birthday. Two hundred boys and girls are expected. Your son is really excited about it.

Close to your home is a small pizza restaurant the family often visits. They sell a delicious crab topped pizza unavailable elsewhere. You want to buy 100 of these crab pizzas and 100 other mixed-topping pizza pies for these hungry teenagers.

Purchased one at a time or in small numbers these crab delights are $30 each, the mixed-top ones, $24. You request a price on the full order from the owner, who you know reasonable well. He thinks awhile, slowly calculates something on a piece of wrapping paper and says, "I'll give you a good deal, $4,900 for all 200 if you pick them up because I have no truck." You flinch. That's more than you want to pay. On the other hand nobody makes crab pizza like this man. There is no time to experiment with another source with the party only a week away. Many of the teenaged guests are children of movie stars, some of whom are business clients and associates.

You bargain with the owner and open with an offer of $4,200 to counter the asking price of $4,900. You believe that $4,400, that is, an average of $22 each, for such a large order is reasonable. After much hesitation and a long explanation about how expensive the ingredients are, the owner drops his price from $4,900 to $4,700, a two hundred dollar concession. You raise your offer to $4,400 believing he will accept it. He stands firm at $4,700, all the while reiterating how good his pies are and how expensive the ingredients have become. You are irritated with his adamance. He's beginning to feel the same about you. The good relationship between you is beginning to deteriorate.

You think to yourself, "It's not the $300." You're a movie producer who has negotiated hundred million dollar deals. $300 is peanuts, tipping change at top-flight restaurants. "It's not the $300," you think, "This guy is trying to exploit me." Yet, you can't walk away now. Better try some other approach.

You say to the owner, "Let's try to find a better way for both of us by working together." Both simmer down a bit as you start talking to each other in a collaborative rather than competitive way. He comes up with suggestions by asking in detail what all these pizzas are for. You in turn ask how pizzas are made and what problems arise when an order is so large and must be ready for single delivery. He tells you that he's never had such a large order and details the problems and extra costs he might have. These big problems and costs, he points out, have been built into his $4,700 price.

Before long the producer and pizza man jointly develop a number of Both-Win® ideas designed to reduce total cost and assure satisfaction. The owner will deliver the order by borrowing a nearby mobile lunch wagon from a driver-friend after 5 PM on party day when the wagon is normally unused. The producer will tip the wagon driver $100 for his help with the pizza order delivery.

The pizza shop owner, now more anxious to please the producer, advises that lobster costs him just a little more than crab this time of year but tastes a lot better. He suggests the order be changed to 100 lobster pies and guarantees that the kids will find them even more delicious than crab. To compensate for the slightly higher price of lobster they alter the ingredients on the mixed pizzas a bit.

Both then agree to have the maid at the producer's home cut the pies in six pieces immediately before they are served, and save the pizza shop owner the time and cost of cutting the pies. This will keep the pies warm longer. Finally, to cut costs further, the producer agrees to change the order to 95 lobster pizzas and 105 mixed. The owner, in an expansive mood, throws in 100 liter-sized soft drinks that he purchases normally at 40 cents a piece to seal the deal. The owner recognizes that the producer has many friends who also throw large pizza parties. He wants to have their business, too.

Instead of engaging in a competitive contest they have worked together to find a better deal for both. Their relationship has matured as each gained trust in the other. They have together managed to improve the pies and reduced the total cost. They have also found ways to deliver and serve the pizza more efficiently. That in a nutshell is the essence of collaborative Both-Win® negotiation. It mixes their previously unconnected unique attributes in ways that create new value and satisfaction. But there is more gain possible.

Because they have worked together to forge a joint-gain agreement their level of mutual respect has grown. Together, they come up with a really far-reaching idea. Why not open a nationwide pizza chain featuring the special crab and lobster topping? The movie producer says, "We'll call the franchise, 'UPPER CRUST PIZZA – THE VERY BEST.'" He beams with delight when the owner exclaims, "How did you ever think of that?"

Their attributes blend further. The owner has a lifetime of experience making delicious pizza. The producer can raise the needed funds among his many movie friends. Both find it exciting to work together on something new and challenging. For the producer, an entrepreneur by nature, this is a fun project with good potential and modest risk. For the pizza shop owner, it's a shot at the American Dream. He has always dreamed of catering to the rich and famous and a home in Malibu.

What has just been described is what Bill Gates, co-founder and chairman of Microsoft Corporation, likes to do when he negotiates. He goes beyond price to a higher strategic level. He and those with whom he negotiates look for opportunities they can create by mixing their strengths, weaknesses and needs into new values and opportunities that were unrecognized or untapped earlier.

Let us now explore another negotiation. This one is between marketing and accounting executives concerning something always important to salespeople; that is, getting their expense reimbursements approved in a timely fashion.

THE EXPENSE REIMBURSEMENT NEGOTIATION – RESOLVING A RULES AND RESPONSIBILITY DISAGREEMENT

You are a busy sales representative at a drug company with two major responsibilities. One is to meet with physicians in your area to provide samples and explain the effectiveness of your products, and the other is to sell these products to local distributors and drug stores. You incur considerable business expenses by having lunch or dinner with customers, inviting them to the theater or ballgame and, twice monthly or so, supplying lunch to the doctors' office staff.

Sales department procedures stipulate that expenses be submitted for approval weekly and reimbursed by accounting every two weeks. Salespeople must, of course, maintain proper records and receipts for income tax purposes. For a busy salesperson keeping track of these myriad pieces of paper is a nightmare. Most are temperamentally unsuited to such detail work.

Also included in the reimbursement sales procedures are expenditure limits for lunch, dinner, theater tickets and doctor office lunches. Each salesperson handles the records and receipts in their own way but all are expected to submit them weekly accompanied by a standard company expense form. Unfortunately, almost every submission for approval shows that some expense receipts have been lost, other receipts are barely readable and still others show expenses in excess of acceptable limits but do list good reasons for doing so. Salespeople in the field sometimes submit their summaries on the back of envelopes because they run out of company forms while traveling.

The result is weekly chaos, late reimbursement, constant negotiation and renegotiation between those that sell and their managers and between accounting and sales personnel. Sales morale suffers, people get angry, some get even by fabricating or loading expenses and a few give up keeping good records in hopes that the Internal Revenue Service won't audit them and that accounting will let it slip through.

The head of accounting and the sales manager are peers. They have been told to straighten the mess out by the Chief Executive Officer, a former salesperson. The negotiation between the controller and sales manager opened with screaming at one another. Past mistakes by each quickly surfaced. Both then began to search for some common ground by finding a common enemy, namely, the incompetent recordkeeping of people in sales. This did not help much but released some tension. They then got down to the business of finding a way out of the weekly chaos.

Together they assembled a team consisting of themselves and three others in the company: a representative from IT, one from systems and procedures and another well-experienced salesperson. Each member was assigned to study parts of the problem. Systems looked into the detailed work involved in maintaining records and receipts by the sales and the accounting department. They found some unnecessary elements in the existing system. They determined that some expense limits had to be raised to reflect inflation and others eliminated by combining them into acceptable lump sum allowances.

The IT representative advised that a new application is available for the Blackberry devices. All salespeople would have to be supplied with the new Blackberry application fully integrated with company computers to track their expenditures daily. This would enable management to highlight any divergence from acceptable limits or procedures and allow them to request prompt justification or correction.

A new procedure was then created by the team that reduced work for both the sales and accounting departments. Report quality was improved and simplified. The IRS was asked to render an opinion on the new system and approved it for tax purposes. The team requested funding from corporate to purchase new Blackberry applications for every salesperson and to train them properly. Four months later the system was implemented, bugs were removed and the expense reimbursement problem was substantially reduced.

When people put their minds together to find a better way they find it. With that they gain respect and kinship for each other even if they had been at odds before. Conflicts and disagreements still occurred later from time to time, but these were resolved more easily and less acrimoniously than in the past.

HOW TO MOVE A COMPETITIVE NEGOTIATION OR ONE ABOUT TO DEADLOCK INTO A COLLABORATIVE MODE

Two people get together to iron out differences they wish to reconcile. Before long they inadvertently say or do something that adds distance to the gap separating them. Compromise generally serves to bring them closer to agreement but often fails if the gap is large or one of the two has not been tactful in expressing him- or herself.

Settling differences in an oncoming impasse like this can best be accomplished if the parties change their mode of dealing with one another. Each by now is exhausted; they have said all they can about the remaining difference and moved as much as deemed responsible or wise. Further jousting for concessions seems futile. A change in strategy is called for.

Collaborative Both-Win® negotiating is the way. The magic of this approach is that it transforms their bargaining attitude from competitiveness to cooperation, from self-centeredness to mutual gain. The nine Both-Win® segues that follow work well in moving a competitive negotiation to one in which joint effort between parties takes center stage.

• The "Let's find a better way for both of us" approach. This approach is simple and direct. Just suggest to the other party that a better way for both is available if we look for it together. It's wise at this point to have one or two possible ideas to suggest as 'trial balloons.'

• The "Ask for something in return" segue. The hidden power of asking for something in return when you make a concession is that it provides negotiating space for further talk and opens previously unexplored avenues for agreement.

For example, in a negotiation between a sales representative and accounting, the salesperson has requested that his prospective customer be provided a 3%-10 days discount for prompt payment. Accounting is appalled enough to "flinch." Their policy has always been net 30 or at most 1%-10 days for customers large and small. They offer 1%-10 days because the order is large and the customer reliable.

The salesperson makes a counteroffer: "Allow me to give the customer 2%-10 days provided they assure us that they guarantee to purchase from us all their needs for this specific component for one year." As you readily see, this counteroffer cannot be answered in the negative too easily by accounting. It opens talking doors in a variety of directions, some of which can result in innovative Both-Win® solutions. Why not an even larger order, or one involving advance payments; maybe more items in our product line or help in getting new business from another subdivision under the customer's control?

• The "Ask the other side for help" segue. When in doubt about what to do next or how to bridge the gap or difference, ask the other party to suggest ideas. You'll be pleasantly surprised at how pleased they will be to help in most cases. The existing difference may be as unpleasant to them as it is to you. Besides, they may know about avenues for potential mutual gain that you are not aware of. You have little to lose. It's always uplifting to be asked to help.

• The "Ask higher authority on their side for help." This is a variation on the previous segue but an important one. Experiments confirm that people in authority like to help others when requested to do so in a courteous manner. Often they know more about solving a problem than those at lower levels because they have had experience with such matters already. Their advice may well become a point for further modification and collaboration with the other side because someone at a higher level in the organization had a role in suggesting it.

• The "Krunch" segue is appropriate when you make an offer or concession to the other that they reject with the remark, "You'll have to do better than that." This objection, which I call the "Krunch," is hard to handle, both because it is so general and because it always appears so firm.

The best way to respond is to move the discussion from the general to the specific. "What do I have to do better than?" is a "help me" question that sometimes elicits information useful to further collaboration, especially when the relationship between parties is good.

If the other hesitates or refuses to give more information, persistence on your part helps. Those who say, "You've gotta do better than that," tend to say more if pressed to do so in a courteous way.

The "Krunch," and your response to it, is an opportunity to move the negotiation from a competitive to a collaborative mode. It allows you to offer "what if" and "would you consider" alternatives in striving to improve your initial concession or offer. These open the talks to mutual gain opportunities.

• The "Consultant or Third Party Advisor" segue. Moving from a conventional competitive or transactional arms-length mode of bargaining to one that is collaborative and we-centered is rarely easy. Both parties are, after unresolved frustration and talk, encumbered with positions and statements that make cooperation difficult. It is at that point that consultants or third party advisors or staff can help move stalled talks to a Both-Win® path.

A third party advisor can be anybody in either organization who is recognized as knowledgeable about the matter under consideration and reasonably trusted by both sides. The advisor may be an in-house engineer, a staff member, a technical specialist or an outside consultant whose role is to suggest ways in which they can integrate their needs and resources for mutual gain.

• The "Planning Purpose" segue. Engineering often requests purchasing to provide cost estimates of designs and assemblies they may wish to purchase sometime in the future. These designs are generally not set in concrete nor are the estimated quantities or requirement dates established. All that is desired by engineering is a rough planning purpose estimate.

For purchasing, such estimates are a splendid opportunity to incorporate a potential supplier's knowledge and experience into the planning information requested by engineering. Purchasing is in a position to guide the future procurement along lines that will lead to a better agreement for the company and the outside supplier. Purchasing is also in a very good position to incorporate mutual gain ideas into the design, production and procurement process at an early stage of development. Partnering between suppliers and customers serves a similar role by fostering creative collaboration to reduce costs and increase efficiency.

• The "Listening with the third ear" segue. Listening with the third ear means listening with all your senses and all your attention. Even non-task talk is full of content. Nothing that is said or displayed is extraneous to the matter or issue involved.

What is unsaid or skipped over lightly may be important. Body language, voice and gestures tell a story if observed closely. The reaction of others at the table may reveal as much or more of what is essential than words themselves. Observant and involved listening that picks up subtle clues about hidden interests leads to opportunities for further talk and collaboration.

• The "What If" and "Would You Consider" segue. This approach allows you to try out different ideas and get the other person's reaction to them. Such knowledge is useful in any negotiation. The examples that follow illustrate how these segues create negotiating space and open the door for Both-Win® ideas.

A key scientist has announced to her project manager that she is leaving the institute to care for her sick father. The manager of human resources has been asked by the project head to find a way to reverse or alter her decision.

The manager after some introductory talk asks the scientist, "Would you consider staying with us if we change your workweek hours to less time in the laboratory and more at home, or otherwise alter your workweek to better fit your needs?" This segue could lead to possibilities not considered earlier by the person leaving. If that approach did not help, the manager might suggest, "What if we were to give you a six-month leave of absence including health benefits? As you can see, we value your services and want you to stay."

In another company, the manager of marketing and sales has just ordered 2,000 brochures from the supervisor of the company's in-house reproductive services. Sales must have the brochures by June 1 for a mailing campaign. The supervisor is reluctant to commit to the required delivery date but quotes a price for the 2,000 brochures. The marketing manager, anxious to proceed, asks, "If we increased the brochure quantity from 2,000 to 5,000 is there any way you could meet our date and fill our needs? What if we could help you get the capital funds to purchase larger and more up-to-date equipment—would it be possible to lower our unit cost? We anticipate a steady requirement for 10,000 brochures a month by next year."

"What if" and "Would you consider" are questions a negotiator should always think about asking when there is a need to get more information about exploring alternatives that might lead to Both-Win® opportunities.

THE NFL AND NBC NEGOTIATION FOR FOOTBALL BROADCAST RIGHTS

Most of us only watched the 2007 Super Bowl. Here's the background on a real world collaborative negotiation that the National Broadcasting Corporation (NBC) had with the National Football League (NFL) for broadcast rights to NFL football.

It all started with NBC wanting to raise their ratings and deciding that NFL football was the way to go. The negotiation began as most negotiations do with NBC making an offer for NFL broadcast rights, which the football league rejected as inadequate. Talks continued for a considerable time with insufficient give and take on both sides to reach settlement. Both sides remained determined to hold out for an agreement that met their needs without leaving too much on the table. With deadlock imminent they decided that a new negotiating strategy was necessary to reach agreement.

The new strategy was to move talks into a collaborative Both-Win® mode rather than remain centered on conventional competitive bargaining. The scope of issues was enlarged from simply broadcast rights and price to issues of higher value; that is, those issues that created new opportunities and benefits for both sides not previously explored. Suddenly the negotiation involved not only the NFL and NBC, but also General Electric, the huge corporation that owned NBC.

After being shut out of NFL broadcasting for nine years, NBC successfully negotiated a six-year deal with the NFL for what was then a huge amount of money and mutual benefits that will go on for years, benefits that accrued not only to the NFL and NBC, but to General Electric as well. This was all the result of a we-centered collaborative Both-Win® negotiation that opened the door to new opportunities and entrepreneurial innovation.

HOW DID NBC GAIN FROM THE DEAL?

- Four hours of potential top-ten prime-time programming every week.
- Two Super Bowls (2009 and 2012) with their large advertising dollars.
- The annual Thursday night opening game.
- Two wild-card games each season.
- A platform to promote NBC's prime-time lineup of shows.
- And the right to choose the late season games it will broadcast so fans can see the most competitive games at the end of the season (a right the NFL would not provide before).

HOW DID THE NFL GAIN?

- GE Finance will play an increased role in the NFL loan pool financing program that helps NFL owners finance new stadium construction.
- GE's new Security Services Unit will promote and provide enhanced stadium security to NFL owners.

- Fans and players will have the advantage of on-site medical technology provided and promoted by GE Medical Products.
- And, it costs a lot to illuminate these football stadiums. GE is the leader in energy efficient lighting technology and manufactures a lot of light bulbs.

WHAT GENERAL ELECTRIC GOT?

- Access to the NFL as a customer of its financial services and capital.
- The sales of its security services to NFL stadiums and owners.
- The sales of its on-site high technology medical equipment at each NFL stadium.
- The sales of new lighting technologies at all the NFL stadiums.

Outside financial concerns estimated that the value of these GE add-ons could be worth as much as $500 million in profits to GE. This is an example of how a collaborative Both-Win® negotiation can be brought to bear in any negotiation to create a better deal for both parties than either thought possible or likely at the start of negotiation.

TWENTY-ONE COLLABORATIVE BOTH-WIN® TRADEOFF AREAS THAT GENERATE COST OR WORK SAVINGS AND ENLARGE VALUE

Collaborative Both-Win® negotiating rests on the premise that there is a better way to design, change or do anything if the parties bring their ideas, needs and talents together to search for it. When two people are engaged with one another to resolve a problem or settle some disagreement or difference between them, they have a new and accessible tool to guide them to a mutually beneficial agreement—the collaborative Both-Win® negotiating process.

Negotiators can now approach the other side with a number of positive suggestions that will potentially lead both to lower cost and less work. The trade-off areas that follow offer opportunities for mutual reward. The search for a better way rarely involves genius. What it does require is a step-by-step look at what is presently being done and an open discussion of how it can be done more effectively. Innovative solutions usually follow.

1. Scope of work (SOW) tradeoffs. Not everything in any SOW is necessary. Some work can be cut back, some enlarged. Some left for next year with new budget funds. Other work may be done later when changes in scope are renegotiated. Study the Statement of Work carefully. Cost/benefit savings exist there.

2. Specification tradeoffs. Specifications describe the essential attributes of the product or service being provided. These can be changed to reduce cost or effort and still serve their desired purpose. Parts of the specification can be combined, others left out, still others made smaller, lighter or more durable by new materials or technology.

3. Division of labor, classification and talent tradeoffs. Look at who does what for whom. Can others do it better with more focus and perhaps less talent? How much does each class of labor earn and how many hours are involved? Can high-priced talent be assisted by those less skilled to provide cost reduction or benefit?

4. Quality control tradeoffs. Everything done requires some level of checking and quality control. Savings can be found in how checking is done, who does it, where, when and the standards to be tested and controlled. Often statistical controls are as effective and less costly than tedious item-by-item inspection.

5. Technology tradeoffs. Technology is changing at an explosive rate. Every few days we read about some new process, equipment or technique available to do almost any job or task. Whatever you are presently doing, there exists at this very moment a better way to do it, and if not now, tomorrow. The vast resources of the internet provide a tool to keep track of these worldwide developments.

6. Reports tradeoffs. There are too many reports, all too frequently issued to people who do not read, need or want them. Some are too elegant for their purpose. Others simply miss the reader's purpose completely. Some reports are so large and complex that nobody really understands them or has the time to seek understanding. The flow of reports seems never to diminish in quantity and length, but it should.

7. Meeting tradeoffs. Meetings are even worse than reports. Most are attended by too many highly paid people and helpful to few. Meetings are held too often for purposes that are not quite clear and that fail to cover what they hoped they would. Meetings suffer from a leadership gap, an agenda gap and a rules gap. Time and money savings are always possible here.

8. Structural factor tradeoffs. Where work is done and when affects how well it will be done. So also do the rules surrounding what is to be done and how. These matters make a lot of difference in terms of cost and quality. For example, union rules in the movie business impose substantial charges on start and stop delays. Shooting one minute more than the union day or failing to break at designated times creates endless production continuity problems.

Structural impediments to efficiency exist, often unseen, in systems and procedures, in computer programs designed to make work easier and in rules and regulations formulated by politicians in every city and state. Those who take the time to understand these structural factors governing work will be in a better position to make better use of resources and to lobby for productive change.

9. Space and location tradeoffs. Efficiencies can be realized if analysis is addressed early enough to such matters as where offices are located, the interaction of executives for communication purposes, the space they need to do efficient work, their proximity to services and the level of talent required. A brilliant scientist located in a beautiful office a tenth of a mile from her hundred person laboratory affects the real cost and efficiency of the laboratory as well as the scientist in ways that should be clearly understood.

10. Facilities tradeoffs. Friendly stress-free facilities help people work efficiently. Reasonably well-appointed dining rooms, healthy foods, conference rooms, quiet areas, nearby parking and special services for employees with children should be more common. Where people sit, where they make copies and where they get a cup of good coffee says something of the sociology of the organization. On the other hand, some facilities I've seen, like executive dining rooms, are too elegant for their purpose. They get in the way of collaborative innovation rather than enhancing it.

11. Equipment tradeoffs. You can buy a washing machine with bells and whistles that you will never use or buy the basic model.

Somewhere in between is the one for you, even if you are Bill Gates. Almost every piece of equipment purchased, be it for the machine shop or for an advanced laboratory devoted to precision testing and quality control, can do more than you will usually need and less than you will occasionally demand. Find a middle road. Let outsourcing fill in the capability gaps you decide not to cover. It will probably be less costly in the long run.

12. Service allocation tradeoffs. Not everyone needs the same level of service or the same level of maintenance. Much depends on the volume of usage, the proximity to the user, the time of day the service is needed, the number of repairs required, whether outsourcing is readily available and the salaries and talents of those using and providing the services. Good tradeoffs are possible here.

13. Communication and information flow tradeoffs. A large accounting firm did a study on its internet use. Not really to its amazement, it found that most employees used the Web almost as much for personal purposes as for business. A fortune was being spent on the maintenance and repair of computers used in ways contributing little to productivity. We cannot work without the new devices but we need better control of their use. The accounting firm had the courage to institute strong internet controls governing personal affairs. After some initial complaints, the new work rules were universally accepted at savings that surprised everyone involved.

14. Partnering for Both-Win® synergy. Partnering of suppliers with their customers has proved enormously successful. When suppliers integrate their resources, needs, information and relationships with those of the buyer, they create efficiencies that lower cost and benefit both in many ways.

Partnering is as applicable inside the organization as it is between buyers and suppliers. Two interacting departments can within a company constitute a workable partnership. So also can two individuals dealing with one another on a daily basis. The principle is the same.

The two parties, united together as partners, work collaboratively to create new approaches to doing their jobs. They will succeed because they can then combine their assets, ideas and talents to better fit and meet their mutual and individual needs and problems.

15. Systems, procedure or process flow tradeoffs. Every system, process or way of doing something is to some extent obsolete or not serving the original purpose it was designed to do. Savings in unnecessary work or material can always be found if we study the process or procedure carefully and modify it to serve current conditions and needs.

16. Worldwide outsourcing tradeoffs. Outsourcing, even on a global scale, is now feasible for a wide variety of needs and services at little risk. When faced with what appears to be an intractable difference in cost or delivery, both sides would be wise to consider outsourcing part of the work they do for others.

17. Transport and shipping tradeoffs. Moving and handling costs constitute a surprisingly large part of total cost even in day-to-day workplace interactions. In every office people move from place to place as they transport product or information to one another. Technology with its flood of new devices is changing how we interact to get work done. Opportunities for mutual gain reside in looking closely at how things and people in the office move about.

On a worldwide stage, transportation and shipping costs are an enormous part of total product cost. Fierce competition between air, rail, surface and ship is exacerbated by volatility of oil prices and carrier supply; these costs demand considerations.

The best assumption on the part of those involved in the movement or cost of products, people or information is to assume that what is being done today can be improved. New means of teleconferencing, twittering and email as well as smart phones and hand-held computer tracking devices are being developed daily. Moment-to-moment and eye-to-eye contact between associates separated by thousands of miles is better and less costly than ever. We in the workplace have no choice but to embrace the tools of our new age or fail. The high cost of transportation and shipping and the impact of new technology make this a prime target for creative Both-Win® success.

18. "Just-in-time" tradeoffs. When we think of "just-in-time" it is usually in regard to inventory matters. We want to assure that what we need to produce or sell is ready on time without risk of excessive inventory or of shortage.

The "just-in-time" principle applies as well to the efficient use of human resources. Both-Win® savings can be achieved if we balance our workload and talent mix with pools of people from other departments and a better mix of full time employees with part-timers or contract personnel.

The principle can also be put to work in support and service activities. Needs vary from time to time and place to place. "Just-in-time" tradeoffs may serve to narrow intractable budget or resource shortages by better balancing needs for service with availability.

19. Cash management tradeoffs. Most individuals and companies handle their cash flow needs poorly. They leave too little in reserve and suffer credit problems or leave too much in checking accounts that earn nothing. Some compound their cash problems by borrowing at terribly high rates and failing to pay off balances on time.

Cash management tradeoffs balancing revenue and outgo deserve a higher place in the budgeting process than smaller organizations give it. Most of us, not trained in finance, fail to understand the price of money. I am acquainted with a consultant who prides himself on one thing he did for a client. He changed the way the company billed the government on time and material contracts. By moving the billing period up one day the company earned an extra three million dollars a year.

20. Insurance tradeoffs. There are good reasons why the insurance industry is so successful. Corporations and individuals pay in advance for possible untoward events that often have a small or modest probability of happening. Worse yet, they rarely review their policies to adjust for changes in competition or objective reality. The ratio of what we pay for security and how much risk we should be willing to take is amenable to constant analysis.

21. Visibility and transparency tradeoffs. Politicians and businesspeople speak passionately about the importance of transparency in seeing how funds are spent and results achieved. The trouble is that visibility is harder to achieve than talk about. There is, however, something we can all do to gain visibility in any workplace negotiation. We can pay attention to how performance will be measured and determine how to establish milestones against which to audit progress. An annual budget or performance review that neglects these matters will not provide the transparency necessary to manage prudently.

Collaborative Both-Win® negotiation is the most powerful strategy in a negotiator's arsenal. It has the potential to create and enlarge value rather than merely share or distribute it as conventional competitive bargaining does. Collaborative negotiating binds the parties together and makes it easier to reach mutual gain agreements.

The case for collaborative negotiating is a strong one, especially in the workplace where we depend on each other to get the work done despite differences and disagreements. In the demanding, competitive world now emerging, collaborative negotiation of workplace differences between talented and well-educated associates will better resolve these disagreements productively than commands from superiors.

14

How Your Three Silent Partners Lead to Prudent Longer-Lasting Outcomes

Whenever we negotiate a new agreement at work it is likely that somebody's job will change or that an existing administrative control will be altered. Such changes often create new problems and upset the desired agreement. Unless these potential impediments are taken into account and resolved prior to reaching agreement, the deal bargained for will not work out.

One way to look at these future problems and avoid them is to imagine that there are three unseen but demanding negotiating partners sitting at your side who seek satisfaction before they sign on to the agreement you are ready to close. Your three partners are what I call the "Past Partner," the "Transition Partner" and the "Far Future Partner." Each is there to protect their interests in the agreement and to assure that you pay attention to their point of view and concerns.

This negotiating analogy struck me with practical impact some years ago when I bought a new 35-foot Ranger sailboat. It was a good time to buy; the economy was soft, inventories were mounting, dealers were in trouble. I negotiated a better discount than expected, wrote a check and immediately listed my old boat for sale.

Soon my mistakes became apparent. When I requested that the dealer provide a slip for the boat he was selling for me, he said he had no room because several new sailboats were coming in. Suddenly I was stuck with two slip fees at my yacht club. I now had two boats to hose and clean instead of one.

That's when it occurred to me that I could easily have nibbled for a concession from the dealer prior to closure to provide a slip, and display the used boat at no charge on his premises. Not only that, but there were two handsome maritime lanterns I had myself painstakingly installed in the old boat that I thought would look even better in the new one. Had I asked the dealer to transfer these to the new Ranger before settlement I believe he might have done so at little cost. Now he wanted $80 an hour to do this estimated three or four hour job.

Then my "Transition Partner" began to complain. It's true the dealer had provided two hours of training on the Ranger. It was a fun sail on a breezy, sunny day. The trouble was that the new boat had equipment on it I could not manage with so little training. I had to learn how to operate a complex radio, a guidance position system and some kitchen and toilet tricks. When, after signing the contract, I asked for four additional hours of lessons he priced them also at $80 an hour but reduced it to $60 an hour when I flinched. I grudgingly purchased three hours, once again blaming myself for paying something that might well have been included as part of the original settlement.

On a third magnificent sail about two weeks later I learned that the standard winch in the Ranger was smaller than I thought it should be for so large a sail area. "I'll buy a larger one," I thought. "That will be $1,000," he said after looking at his catalog and showing it to me for confirmation. I gasped for air, flinched again. "What, no discount, after all I've bought from you," I pleaded. His responses: "No," "I can't," "They won't let me." Had I negotiated an option in the original contract for additional equipment before buying the boat, I surely would have achieved a 15 to 25 percent discount for the winch. My "Transition Partner" now tells me, "Transitions are always full of problems."

As for the far future, it is not yet here but the signs already are. My guidance position system is too large and slow. It's been superseded by a better one that is far more user friendly. I'd like that as well as a new radio and an improved sound system. Had my "Far Future" Partner been at my side before closing my purchase, that partner would have insisted that I bargain for options on upgrades as they became available. My leverage was at its best then, not two years later.

The same will be true when I decide to sell the Ranger a few years from now. Perhaps I could have won some trade-in option or concession tied to a new and larger sailboat or powerboat carried by the dealer.

What I can now do is clear. Whenever I negotiate for anything, at work or elsewhere, I ask my "Three Partners" to accompany me. They help me negotiate more prudent, intelligent agreements. Agreements that withstand the passage and pressures of time and take into account past and future needs and technologies.

There is an interesting postscript to the "Three Partners" story, one that took me by complete surprise. About a year after purchasing the Ranger I visited the National Gallery in London, a marvelous place to spend time surrounded by magnificent paintings. One painting struck me for its beauty and theme. The painting is called "An Allegory of Prudence" and was painted in 1565-1570 by the Italian Renaissance master, TITIAN.

Figure 10

An Allegory of Prudence
Titian 1565-1570

On its face, in Latin, are the words:

> Prudence – The Ruler of Time
> "On the basis of the past, acts prudently in the present, so that the future does not ruin his actions."

Every agreement we make involves the past, the near future (transition period), and the far future. People, systems, designs, equities, costs, quality, production and relationships are affected by new agreements. Those on the job for years may suddenly find themselves having to do their work in changed ways. Even their physical or mental capacity to do the job may be altered or threatened. The partner in charge of the past will probably suggest that I negotiate a budget for training affected employees to meet their new requirements or perhaps demand an acceptable severance package for those unable to change. Almost every negotiating agreement between two parties in the workplace affects others and their work.

What makes this so important is something we have said earlier, that internal agreements, lacking enforcement by legal contract, are fragile. They will break if not accepted by those whose lives and methods change. You need co-workers on your side if you want the settlement to stand up over time. Titian saw this when he painted "An Allegory of Prudence" over four hundred years ago.

When next you deal with others in the workplace pay close attention to what your "Three Partners" have to say and help the other party also to do so. What follows are some issues your three partners will bring up that cannot be papered over or ignored without risk.

Moving from the past to the future is always harder than it appears to be. The suggestions that follow can make the path less difficult in workplace negotiations.

A. The "Past Partner" says, "This agreement must specify what we must do as we change from past to new arrangements." Our work, our costs and our procedures will change in real and psychological ways.

1. Old friends must be reassured and introduced to new ones who join us.

2. Old ways and controls must be brought in harmony with new ways.

3. Conflicts will arise between the old and new that will require early planning and resolution.

4. Computer, phone and other communication systems must be replaced or upgraded in whole or in part.

5. The design change now negotiated may profoundly affect production, cost and end-user satisfaction and habits.

6. Old inventories have to be disposed of or used in different ways. New purchases may be required to meet the changed design.

7. Old equipment must be utilized elsewhere or replaced, perhaps entirely. Like old furniture in a new home, it won't look or fit or do the job right.

8. Space requirements that were adequate before will no longer be appropriate.

B. The "Transition Partner" says, "On the day and for a short period after we incorporate the new agreement, problems will arise that must be addressed. Chaos will ensue if we don't take care of these matters now."

1. People will not know what to do or how. Training will be needed before the new arrangement goes into effect and immediately after it starts.

2. No one will know where anything is or how to find it. Old and new ways of doing things will be mixed together in a mess.

3. Records and recordkeeping will change. Valuable history and necessary tax records may be lost.

4. Electrical, physical or computer connections will continue to need changing. We will experience downtime expenses and delays during the transition. Physical reconfigurations will be needed to get the new equipment or arrangements working right. Skilled people must be readily available to manage the confusion.

5. Old and new relationships must be blended and brought in harmony during the transition phase. Complaints will dominate the discourse and demand immediate correction, no matter how good the new system is.

6. If it were a hospital system change, patients might die. In the workplace someone will be held responsible for the transition turmoil.

7. Can we negotiate options or safeguards now that will make the transition from old to new easier?

8. Transition turmoil always upsets those from the past more than those newly hired. Soften the impact for them. They have the power to make the best idea or agreement fail.

The "Future Partner" says, "As we get into the new agreement and live with it for a while things are sure to change. Future needs, upgrades and alternatives will arise. Anticipate these needs now."

1. Upgrades will be demanded of the new systems or design. Can we get favorable deals now to procure these upgrade options later?

2. As time passes, the benefits and contributions of all parties to the agreement will change. New equipment and tools will become available to do the work required. Can accommodations be negotiated and incorporated now to offer our people a fair distribution of such future benefits like less work or lower costs later.

3. Things break down over time. Can we assure that the same or better services we will need later will be available? Can warranties be lengthened? Are additional in-house facilities and reserves required?

4. At some point in the future the arrangement we are now negotiating will be obsolete. How can we move from this to a future agreement? What trade-ins can we arrange now that will help both parties later? What will our people do then?

5. How can we get the organization to welcome future changes

and be part of them when they come?

6. Copyright, proprietary and trademark protections must be implemented quickly or we will lose future control. Are our lawyers fit and ready to meet the new proprietary needs?

7. What improvements or options do we want now that will help in the far future? Can we free ourselves now to make the necessary changes later or lessen costs or penalties for doing so?

As Titian wrote in 1565, "Prudence is the ruler of time." All of us are aware that we live in an age of change and discontinuity. It is for that reason that we are wise to employ our three partners when negotiating: the "Past Partner" to assure that we learn from the past and care for its needs, the "Transition Partner" to assure that the transition from old ways of doing things to new goes smoothly and the "Far Future Partner" to foresee and ameliorate future pressures on our fragile agreement. Associated with our "Three Partners" we can together negotiate a more prudent and intelligent agreement. Without these partners we cannot attain long-lasting consensus and agreement.

15

Closing with Commitment, Agreement and Promised Performance

Closing an internal agreement is not easy. Assuring that it will work as agreed is even more difficult. It requires that both sides abide by their commitments despite the many changes that may occur over time, some of which they will have little control over. Most people go into workplace negotiations with good intentions. They generally wish to reach an outcome satisfactory to both parties but, of course, favor their own position or viewpoint over the other. Neither side is there to waste time or amuse themselves. Negotiation is too serious a business for that as Jules Feiffer's cartoon (Figure 11) clearly indicates.

Jules Feiffer, one of America's most brilliant cartoonists, gets to the heart of the psychological conflicts facing negotiators everywhere. In this cartoon, as you study the faces and gestures of the protagonists, you better understand the ebb and flow of emotions associated with bargaining and deadlock. It is, in my opinion, the best cartoon on negotiation ever originated.

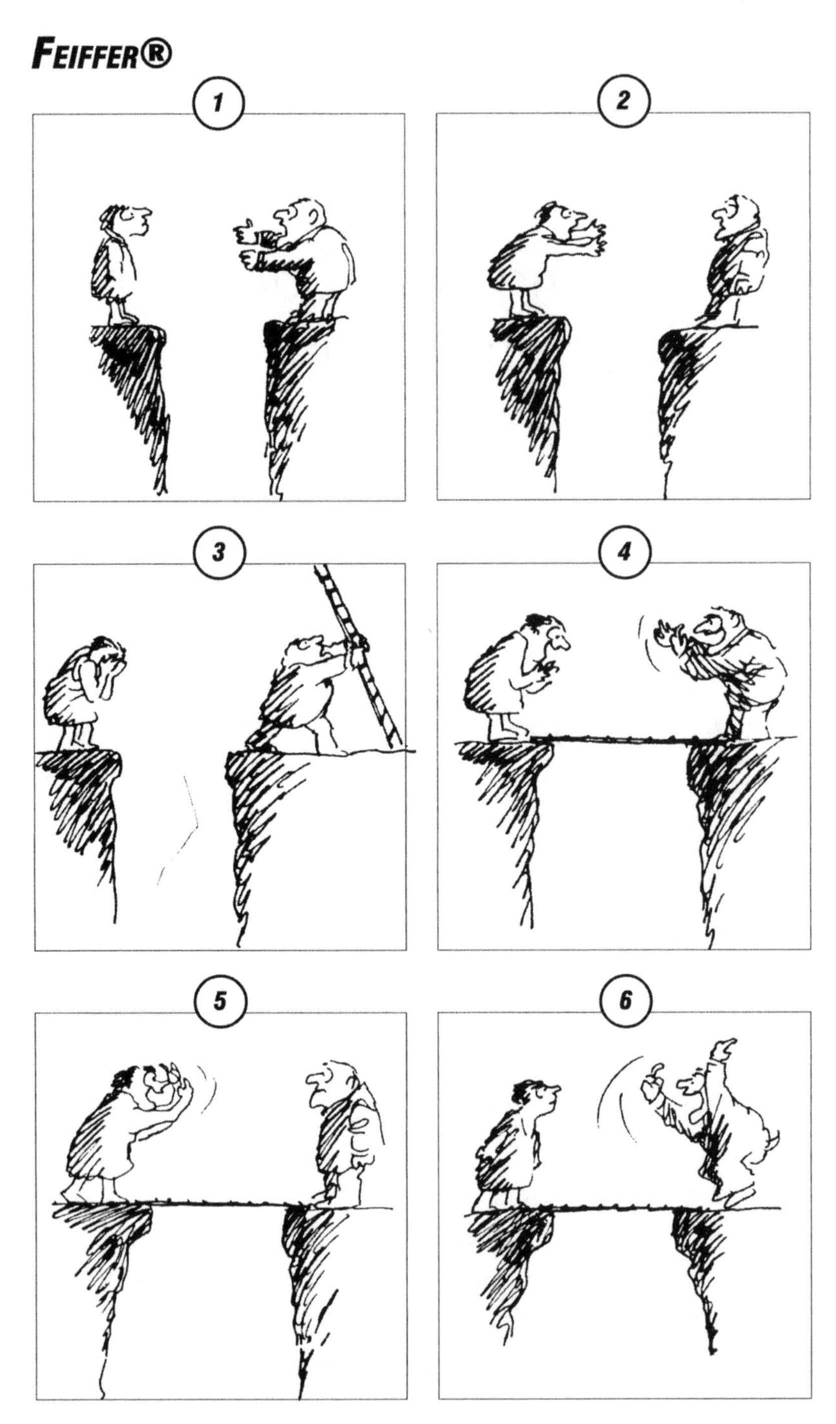

Figure 11

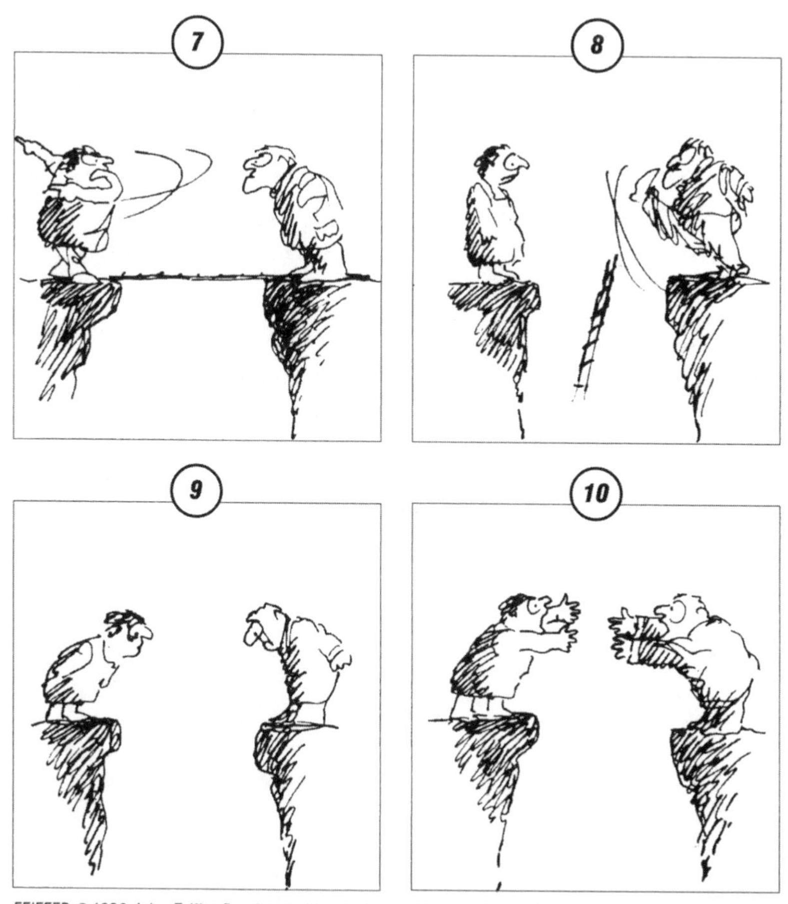
7
8
9
10

As you follow Mr. Feiffer's flow of events, you see how urgently they desire to reach agreement. You then see the joys of collaboration as they find ways to bridge the gap between them. Then, as in most bargaining situations, last minute hitches or problems occur. These hitches threaten the impending agreement and bring the process of reconciliation to a halt. The negotiators are left longing once more for the agreement that was so close at hand.

I have conducted a number of experiments in which deadlock and its effects were factors. Jules Feiffer's insights are correct. People who have a strong equity in reaching agreement are seriously disturbed by failing to settle. They welcome any new opportunity to reach agreement if it is offered without loss of face and in good faith.

ELEVEN APPROACHES TO CONSIDER AS CLOSURE DRAWS NEAR

Closure, even after considerable give and take, is often difficult to attain. There are always some issues not adequately discussed and matters not quite settled. Yet, after a period of time, most of what can be said has been said over and over again by both parties and a general understanding exists. Both know that it would be better if every point were nailed down but are apprehensive that by doing so they might undo the settlement that is so close at hand. As closure draws near the eleven techniques listed below are designed to help negotiators nudge talks to agreement.

ELEVEN APPROACHES TO CLOSURE

1. Physical Actions That Nudge Talks to Agreement
2. Psychological Approaches That Lead to Closure
3. A Walk in the Woods
4. Good Nibbles and Bad
5. Creative Ways to Split the Difference
6. Delight Factors
7. Last Minute Hitches
8. The E-Mail Summary of Agreement
9. The Urgency of Follow-Up and Audit
10. Performance Must Be Measured.
11. Forestalling a Breakdown in Talks

Exhibit 15

ONE: PHYSICAL ACTIONS THAT NUDGE TALKS TO AGREEMENT

At the moment of closure, a negotiator has to make a difficult decision. Unless what has been offered is very attractive, he or she is left to choose "the bird at hand or the two that may be in the bush." There comes a time in the bargaining process where little can be gained by further talk. Everything that can be said has been said more than once. Both have made it as clear as they can that further concessions are not possible or probable. Collaboration has been tried and found wanting. It seems useless to spend more time on reaching agreement. The agreement reached is good enough or all that can be achieved. Yet talks drone on. What can be done?

Some actions can be taken to move the indecisive party toward decision. I've seen people take a bottle of Johnny Walker Blue from their desk and propose a toast to the not-quite-hatched agreement. A good Cuban cigar serves the same purpose and is a favorite of former Governor Arnold Schwarzenegger of California. Taking the initiative by summarizing the agreement on a laptop computer or even the act of borrowing a sheet of paper and jotting a draft of points in common can move both parties toward "Yes." Sometimes it's best to say, "Let's celebrate by going to a really good restaurant for lunch. All this talk has me starving."

When further talk seems likely to be unproductive, a pleasant physical action can facilitate a cordial close.

TWO: PSYCHOLOGICAL APPROACHES THAT HELP MOVE TALKS TO CLOSURE

Negotiators settle when each believes the other side has conceded most of what it will and further efforts are not likely to be very productive. At this point, the desire to close outweighs the desire for more concessions and the parties move toward closure. Reaching this point sooner is often preferable to letting the almost closed negotiation go on and on because already-settled issues sometimes fall apart with too much talk.

The nine psychological approaches suggested can gently move the bargaining process from indecision to agreement.

One: Assure the other person that she is wise to reach agreement. Give her good reason to support a closing decision now. Good references from pleased associates help. Tell the other why they will be pleased and satisfied. Don't belabor the reasons or it may create doubts instead of reassurance.

Two: Act as though agreement has been reached on the main issues. Start talking about details like when the new agreement will begin, the wording of a procedure or whether they or you will let others in the organization know of the new arrangement.

Three: Make repeated requests for agreement and closure. Don't be afraid to say, "We know everything we need to know to agree, don't we?" Say it again as you go along.

Four: If you get a "No" answer to the above, ask why. The other party will probably tell you. You will then have something specific to overcome or improve on. Do it again if closure doesn't follow.

Five: Make the benefits of agreement as tangible and real as possible in terms of the other party's needs, not yours.

Six: Fear of loss can be a stronger motivator for settlement than desire for gain. Experiments show that people offered a three out of four chance to win $100,000 and a one in four chance to lose their own savings will not take this favorable wager. One hundred thousand dollars for most is a very serious loss. On the other hand, when offered the same bet as part of a large ten-person syndicate they readily accepted the risk.

Many negotiators are more strongly motivated to avert loss than to gain something by prolonging bargaining. Talks can be moved to closure by laying out for the other side the negative consequences that may naturally follow if agreement is not reached at this time. In doing so be careful not to threaten or otherwise jeopardize the relationship you now share.

Seven: Offer the other party a choice between acceptable choice A and acceptable choice B. It shifts the other party's decision from choosing to agree or not to choosing between two satisfactory alternatives. Research shows that when people have too many choices, even good ones, they find it hard to make a decision.

Eight: Make the final deal a little sweeter than the other thought it would be. An unexpected kindness or treat carries a special value as talks close.

Nine: Tell a story that supports closing the deal now. An appropriate non-threatening story can make closure more persuasive than a wealth of rational arguments.

Roy, the Associate Engineering Manager of Power Supply, Inc., is in the midst of an annual budget negotiation with Mel, the Engineering Manager. Roy has requested funds to hire a full-time Design Engineer with extensive experience in human engineering to design the outside configurations of the firm's various power supply units in a more aesthetic and user-friendly fashion.

The Engineering Manager is very reluctant to grant this large and unprecedented request because he considers it unnecessary, especially in the face of declining sales and a recessionary economy. Power supply units have always been designed as black boxes with little attention given to outside configuration matters except for weight, length, width and height specifications. While there are a multitude of control knobs, switches, dials and buttons on the front panel, little direct attention has been paid to what has to be done by end-users in working with the unit. End-users are assumed to be sufficiently competent to read the company's well-written technical manual and follow its instructions.

Roy believes that a human engineering design approach for power supplies is now sorely needed. The Engineering Manager believes it to be a waste of time. They have reached accord on all important budget issues except this one. Roy, an avid user of Apple computers and phones, has brought his iPhone and iPad to the meeting. He shows these two beautifully designed devices to Mel and tells him how Apple sales have soared as a result of their attention to product design and end-user hospitality. He hands the phone and pad to Mel who plays with them for a few minutes, then says, "How do we get a person that can do that for us?"

People act in their self-interest. These nine approaches lead the other person toward closure because they take into account their needs and help them relieve some of the tensions inherent in making a "Yes" decision.

THREE: A WALK IN THE WOODS

Some things are best not settled in the light of publicity or under the scrutiny of those at the table. Much of what is said in the negotiating room is said not to reach agreement but to prove to others that their views are being expressed and fought for. Off-the-record talks permit the opposing parties to tell the other what the real impediments to agreement are and why some issues are more important than others.

Off-the-record discussions also set the stage for later accommodation at the bargaining table. In her ten-year research study of labor negotiations, Ann Douglas found that private talks between principal negotiators frequently preceded settlement. I had the same experience in customer-supplier negotiations. What we learned from each other during private meetings could not have been said in front of others. Yet it was what we learned 'off-the-record' that closed the deal.

Off-the-record talks foster movement toward settlement because the negotiators can talk about their personal feelings as well as their organizational constraints on a person-to-person basis. They can privately indicate a willingness to compromise or to exchange one issue for another. These informal moves toward reconciliation might be politically unwise if discussed at the table in front of others.

There is a downside to off-the-record talks. Good negotiators know that not everything can or should be said off the record. They also know that some people, especially those with a strong need to be liked, talk too much in the privacy of a comfortable restaurant or under the gentle influence of good wine. Therein lies the danger inherent in a walk and talk in the woods.

FOUR: GOOD NIBBLES AND BAD

Nibbles granted the other side may help them decide to close. There is nothing wrong with the salesperson selling an expensive suit to offer a free shirt or tie to move an undecided buyer toward settlement. If the nibble offered is reasonable, it helps seal the talks and encourages future business. So also does a free sample of your work or an offer to expedite completion at no extra cost. These are what I call good nibbles.

Not all nibbles pass that test, especially those that take place below the surface after agreement has been sealed. Such nibbles erode the spirit of the deal and, in time, undermine the agreement. The settlement, previously accepted as satisfactory by both parties, now tips the scale in favor of the nibbler. Enough such tips and the eroded deal is history.

People at work usually try to show they are nice, sometimes too nice for their own good. They give away "stuff" they shouldn't. What is "stuff" in today's workplace? Stuff, if you are an accounting supervisor, is a report your staff was asked to provide that you agreed would be put together not by your people but by the department serviced by you. By the time you learn about it months later, the report had been done not by the other department as was intended, but by your staff. "Stuff," if you are an information technology manager, is the extra programming given away by your people that was not included in the original scope of work promised and agreed to. It is the special effort by your group for which there was no budget provided.

If you, the purchasing person, agreed with the material receiving manager that receiving would be open to accept goods from vendors from 9 to 6 P.M. on Monday through Friday, then closing the receiving door at five is a nibble by material receiving you cannot abide. It forces suppliers to make an extra trip the next morning to deliver what may be a badly needed component or piece of equipment. All this is "stuff" or nibbles never bargained for, or authorized at the negotiating table, are examples of bad nibbles that slip into the deal and erode your expected satisfaction from it.

The best approach to unwarranted nibbles is to recognize them early and to politely cut them off as soon as possible. Nibbles will grow if unaddressed. On the other hand, if your business judgment says that a nibble must be stopped, or is too expensive to live with, ask the nibbler for something in return. That may stop the nibble or make it beneficial to both sides. There is an infinite demand for free nibbles. It's amazing how placing a price on a nibble, even a very small price, can reduce the demand for nibbles significantly.

FIVE: CREATIVE WAYS TO SPLIT THE DIFFERENCE

There are many ways to split the difference when the gap between negotiators is not too large. The most simple splits consist of dividing the difference in some way that cries out, "If not here, where?" A split in half where there are two parties involved, or in quarters where there are four, makes for an uncontested arrangement most times. Splitting the bonus pool by revenue produced, or by the number of A-, B- and C-level executives, or in proportion to earned annual income, can help lead a bonus committee to consensus and closure. I have been in negotiations where flipping a coin determined final distribution and outcome. Simple solutions facilitate agreement.

Splitting the difference even in a simple way does have a danger built in. The next time someone on the other side says, "Let's split the difference," watch out. Before you are tempted to say "Yes," calculate how much of the difference you will give away by signifying agreement. It may be, as Shakespeare once said, "by much too much."

Sometimes, on the other hand, complexity is called for. As we said earlier, satisfaction is what we negotiate about, not dollars, goods or services. What is interesting about satisfaction is that it has a time dimension. Some prefer their satisfaction early or in advance while others prefer it to occur far in the future. Changing the time shape of satisfaction has the power to bridge bargaining gaps. When indecision or impasse looms, one way to avert it is to customize the shape of satisfaction and dissatisfaction to fit the specific time needs of each side. The calculus of satisfaction differs from person to person and from one time period to another.

Negotiated benefits, rewards and work contributions can be provided all at once immediately, later or at the end of performance depending on a person's preference, age and lifestyle. Some now, more later and the balance at the end may suit some negotiators more than others. Benefits may also be offered over a period of time, then triggered to increase or decrease by some event, index or performance milestone later.

If these creative approaches fail and a gap remains, it can prove useful to establish a joint committee to study the matter and make a recommendation. Committee decisions often serve as the catalyst that bring the disputed sharing formula to rest.

SIX: DELIGHT FACTORS

Few concessions give as much satisfaction as a surprise treat provided near closing with no strings attached. In my book, The Negotiating Game, I described how much goodwill an arctic fur trader gained when he gratuitously gave an Eskimo hunter returning to the cold north some sweets and goodies for his family. Without a word the Eskimo discovered hidden in his sleigh a special skin he had previously "overlooked" and left it for the trader. These delight factors made subsequent negotiations between the two easier and more fun.

SEVEN: LAST MINUTE HITCHES

If there is one thing you can count on in negotiation it is that last-minute hitches will arise. The negotiation so close to closure will show signs of unraveling before it is signed.

Why are last minute hitches and how you handle them so important to those who negotiate in the workplace? It is because such hitches add enormous stress to the negotiating process as closing approaches. People respond to stress at the bargaining table by making mistakes, missing nuances and omitting important details. Experiments confirm that even experienced negotiators make larger concessions than usual as talks move to conclusion.

Negotiators who anticipate last-minute hitches are less likely to be stressed by them or fearful that the desired agreement will drift away. They recognize that as final agreement gets closer, words and phrases take on different meanings. They define duties, obligations and performance standards in specific rather than general ways. Suddenly, both parties at the table know that the words they choose define exactly who does what, and when, and how actual performance will be measured. Potential problems become visible as details are discussed and settled. These last-minute hitches and their resolution determine whether the final agreement will work or fall apart.

Last-minute hitches, in my view, are natural and beneficial to reaching lasting and prudent agreements. They should be accepted by both sides as a necessary and positive part of the negotiating process; they should not, as is often done, be a reason for accusing the other side for going back on their word.

EIGHT: THE E-MAIL SUMMARY OF AGREEMENT

Many workplace agreements abort within days. After people spend long and difficult hours discussing issues such as budgets, schedules, costs to complete or personal matters they finally reach agreement. Both sides are pleased to have the talks behind them. All that remains is for each to do as agreed; at least, that is what they hope will happen.

The trouble is that in most internal negotiations, it is likely that both sides will walk away from the table with different pictures in their head of what was agreed to. The reason is that it is virtually impossible, except in the simplest negotiations, to remember all that was said in the course of give and take. Some parts of the discussion occurred early in the talks, others later, and still others at the last moment. Some points or concessions when made were tentative, others in jest, some firm. Task and non-task talk were mixed. In such a disparate flow of communication and information, it's not surprising that even important matters may be difficult to recall or be misinterpreted.

For this reason, it is essential to recapitulate the agreement and its details at closure. To do so accurately, good notes taken during the talks are called for. In external buy-sell or contract negotiations between companies, a written memorandum of agreement by both sides is common. A formal contract always follows. Even with that, serious misunderstandings still take place.

Unfortunately, a written memorandum of agreement is rare for most internal workplace negotiations. Formal summaries of agreement are not documented and signed unless stipulated by company policy, government regulation or unhappy past experience involving civil rights disputes or lawsuits. Is it any wonder that internal negotiations are fraught with post-negotiation arguments?

All of us have been involved in "You said-I said" disputes. The way to reduce these arguments is to summarize in writing exactly what both sides agreed to as talks end, not later. If a written agreement seems too awkward at that time, then repeated verbal summarization is useful. Saying something like, "This is my interpretation of what we have agreed on. Do you agree?" Words like, "Is there something you would prefer to add or change?" helps. Going over every point in detail takes time but reduces aggravation later.

Better yet is what one good manager I know does regularly. He ends every meeting or negotiation, be it with superiors, peers or subordinates, by not only reiterating what was settled but also doing one more thing. He sends all parties at the meeting an e-mail representing his summary of the outcome and solicits their response. Everyone he deals with has grown accustomed to his way of documenting agreements and filing them for easy recall later. "You said-I said" arguments with him are rare. His e-mail summaries carry the "power of legitimacy" and limit the range of disagreement.

NINE: THE URGENCY OF FOLLOW-UP AND AUDIT

Follow-up and audit are the neglected stepchildren of negotiation. People with differences and disputes spend long hours discussing their grievances and working out a new plan of action. They then make a glaring mistake. Instead of meticulously following-up and auditing to see that all they bargained for is being done, they choose to hope for the best.

There are many reasons why internal agreements break down. One is that the people who actually make the deal are rarely the people executing it. A company controller negotiates with the manager of sales. They work out a system for handling sales reports and reimbursing expenses in a timely way. The agreement is implemented and welcomed by all concerned. Busy salespeople in the field soon take shortcuts and push the rules a bit for reasons of self-interest or efficiency. The clerks in accounting do not know exactly what to do with the now somewhat questionable expense reports so they pile them up waiting for clear direction. The controller and sales manager who negotiated the deal get wind of the problems only weeks or even months later when complaints about late reimbursement have mounted. A good system now stands in danger that could easily have been rescued with early follow-up.

Another problem that often arises is that the people involved in the original negotiation change jobs. Some leave the company, others are promoted, still others move to other departments as functions expand and contract. Those left to mind the store may have other, more serious problems to cope with. Priorities change as people change. Earlier agreements, though sound, may falter from lack of care or constituency to make them work.

Hands on follow-up and audit are called for if you want the performance you bargained for to be realized. Hoping for the best won't work even when both parties have the best of intentions. Audit of the agreement is essential and audit just doesn't mean looking at what is easily seen. It means looking carefully even where transparency is bad or obscure.

This point is illustrated by a Hungarian folk tale about Moritzka, a simple but well-liked peasant in a small village. One warm evening, the villagers are on their way to Mass. They see Moritzka on his hands and knees looking for something under a lamppost. They ask what he is looking for. Moritzka replies, "I'm looking for my crucifix. I dropped it."

The villagers, eager to help the simple man, ask him where he lost it. Moritzka points in the direction of the river about 100 feet away and says, "I lost it there by the river."

Surprised, the villagers ask, "Moritzka, why are you looking here, if you lost it there?"

Moritzka replies, "Because the light is better here."

The late humorist, Art Buchwald, put it another way in a piece I read in the Times. It was a funny but true story about a 28-year-old investment banker who bet a billion dollars of his bank's money on derivative bonds and lost it all. The 230-year-old British institution went bankrupt.

Buchwald asked jokingly, "How can anyone lose a billion dollars in a vault without someone knowing about it?" His answer: "As I understand it, the bank was watching the man's expense account closely, but overlooked what he was doing with the bank's funds. This happens all the time. We always focus on the petty cash but ignore anything with more than three zeros attached to it."

Negotiators tend to assume that what they bargain for and agree to will be done. Then they leave the job of follow-up and audit to others. The trouble is that nobody ends up doing a very good job checking performance. The reason is that we are all a lot like our Hungarian peasant; we check for discrepancies or problems under the lamppost, where the light is good. Where it is dark and hard to see, we don't audit or look. That's one big reason we do not get the performance we bargained for.

TEN: PERFORMANCE MUST BE MEASURED

It is not enough for two department heads to agree on a budget allocation or a new procedure for alleviating a problem. Another matter that often arises to impact relationships is the parties' unwillingness or inability to define and settle how performance will be measured. When two negotiators fail to agree on this issue at the table, resolution later will be far more difficult.

In that respect I recall a negotiation that took place years ago. The 300-person purchasing department of a large corporation was moving from one building to another two miles away. Bids for moving were obtained from outside sources and the company's own moving operation. The company's own moving department's proposal was lower than the outside sources. Negotiations between the purchasing manager and manager of the in-company moving operation went smoothly and an agreement was reached regarding the final price, what was to be moved and the timing of the project. All moving was to take place over the weekend and be done by 5 A.M. Monday morning.

On that Monday morning when the purchasing staff reported for work in the new building they found their offices a mess. Litter was everywhere: empty paint cans and brushes on the floors, wall construction materials in piles, heavy layers of dust on everything, and corrugated boxes, full and empty, strewn about.

A hasty conference was called between the purchasing manager and the in-company moving manager. Purchasing soon learned that in the moving business the word "done" with respect to performance means moving what is to be moved, when and where it is directed to go by the customer. "Done" does not necessarily include cleanup unless clearly stipulated in the contract and defined precisely in terms of what, when and who will do the work. It took purchasing days of delay, painful effort and added cost to do what they assumed would be done for them.

The cleaning disaster taught the purchasing manager a lesson he should already have known. When dealing with others in your own organization, or elsewhere, the rule is clear: always define the scope of work to be performed, who will do it and how it is to be measured. Precision in the use of words is crucial. In that light, a few words from Confucius on the importance of precision are warranted.

There is a parable from Confucius dating back 2500 years that tells us a great deal about the Chinese approach to the need for exactness in negotiation.

> A disciple said to Confucius when the reigning prince was negotiating with Confucius to enter his service: "The prince is waiting, sir, to entrust the government of the country to you. Now what do you consider the first thing to be done?"
>
> "If I must begin," answered Confucius, "I would begin by defining the names of things."
>
> "Oh! Really," replied the disciple, "but you are too impractical. What has definition of names to do here?"
>
> Confucius replied, "Now, if names of things are not properly defined, words will not correspond to facts. When words do not correspond to facts, it is impossible to perfect anything.

When we cannot perfect anything, law and justice cannot attain their ends; and when law and justice do not attain their ends, people will be at a loss to know what to do."

"Therefore, a wise and good man can always specify whatever he names; whatever he can specify, he can carry out. A wise and good man makes it a point to always be exact in the words he uses."

ELEVEN: FORESTALLING A BEAKDOWN IN TALKS

In this section we will consider ways to forestall breakdowns before they harden into long-term bickering or wars. The suggestions that follow will help get stalled talks back on track. They allow a negotiator to rebuild negotiating space for talk without loss of face or bargaining power for either side.

- Change the time shape of performance. Not everything need be done now, next month or next year.

- Get the help of someone both sides can trust and respect to mediate the difference. That's what the Chinese and Japanese do so effectively.

- Alter the risk factors that make it hard for one side or both to say "Yes."

- Change the scope of work. There is always some room for give and take in the work to be done or the way it is done. Getting into the details serves to enlarge negotiating space and point the way to economies of effort.

- In most negotiations, as the end approaches, the sum of

settled issues generally outstrips those that are not. Nobody at the table relishes the idea of walking out after so much has been accomplished. It pays to recapitulate all matters already settled and those still open. The balance usually favors moving on to closure.

• Determine if the gap that separates you can be bridged gradually: a little now, more later and completely next year.

• The best way, by far, to break an impasse is to collaborate with the other person to search for and discover a better arrangement for both sides. Change the mode of negotiating from the conventional competitive mode to one that is collaborative and Both-Win®; that is, coming from an essentially self-centered mode to one that fosters mutual gain.

The magic of collaborative negotiation as a tool for breaking deadlock is that it enlarges and creates new value for both sides to share. In doing so it synergizes the resources, needs and interests of both parties into a working partnership.

Don't give up easily when talks look like they are falling apart. Persist. Both sides, not you alone, are troubled by the impasse. Both are desperate to agree because they have already invested a great deal of emotional equity and work in closing. Try one or more of the suggestions for forestalling a breakdown. They will work for you as they have for others over the centuries.

* * * *

Not a day goes by in this still-new century that we are not reminded that our economic world is indeed flat. Competition in the global marketplace is more fierce than ever. The battle for market share, control of resources and technological dominance will continue for the balance of our lives. On a personal level there is little doubt that our jobs, our salaries and our standard of living will be increasingly affected. We see evidence of these changes everywhere.

The workplace itself is changing under our feet and we must move with it. Disputes and disagreements between superiors, peers and subordinates are likely to increase as more of us become knowledge, information and service professionals rather than production or manufacturing executives. Top-down decision-making and management, while still dominant, will gradually give way more and more to team and project organization.

We can safely project that members of these teams will be better educated than those of earlier generations. Each will have developed technically and professionally along paths of specialization previously unheard of. These "idea" people will feel strongly about their viewpoints and concerns. They will defend their ideas vigorously and have a lower tendency to be passive when confronted with conflicting views or values.

The same factors will come to play on the factory floor and service sectors not at so fast a rate as in the professional classes. They will also demand a greater voice in how things are done and managed. They will want to negotiate a greater range of workplace issues.

We are in the age of collaboration and negotiation as far as ideas and viewpoints are concerned. How we handle and resolve the rising tide of conflict is crucial. We can continue to deal with each other as we have in the past and accept an increasing level of dysfunction, or we can embrace a new approach that fosters the open exchange of ideas and increased innovation.

What we propose in this book is a new approach or model for working together and resolving differences harmoniously and productively in an economic world centered on ideas, constant innovation, individual choice and intense competition. That model, "The Effective Negotiating® Virtuous Cycle," with its emphasis on Collaborative Negotiating, Being Heard and Listened To, and Building Positive Relationships, when applied by each of us in the workplace, has the power to help us work together more effectively and lift our level of creativity to greater heights. With that our success in the global marketplace will grow.

Index

Y